The Manager's Mentor

A Practical Companion and Guide to Managing Yourself and Others in the Human Services

Owen Booker

Russell House Publishing

First published in 2008 by:
Russell House Publishing Ltd.
4 St. George's House
Uplyme Road
Lyme Regis
Dorset DT7 3LS

Tel: 01297-443948
Fax: 01297-442722
e-mail: help@russellhouse.co.uk
www.russellhouse.co.uk

British Library Cataloguing-in-publication Data:
A catalogue record for this book is available from the British Library.

ISBN: 978-1-905541-24-9

Typeset by TW Typesetting, Plymouth, Devon

Printed by Alden Press, Witney

Russell House Publishing

Russell House Publishing aims to publish innovative and valuable materials to help managers, practitioners, trainers, educators and students.

Our full catalogue covers: social policy, working with young people, helping children and families, care of older people, social care, combating social exclusion, revitalising communities and working with offenders.

Full details can be found at www.russellhouse.co.uk and we are pleased to send out information to you by post. Our contact details are on this page.

We are always keen to receive feedback on publications and new ideas for future projects.

Contents

About the Author

Owen Booker has experience of the voluntary, independent, and statutory sectors, locally and nationally. He has been teacher, trainer, advocate, care worker, manager, lay inspector, and director; and worked within residential care, social work, education, and therapeutic community settings. Those settings have included some of the most significantly damaged and disturbing children and young people.

Over the past ten years he has specialised in conflict reduction and resolution in human services through freelance consultancy, training, and as expert witness. He has also retained part-time work within local authority Education Support Services. His direct clients have included local and national child care organisations and education providers from nursery to university level. He has been associated with Voice as a children's advocate. He contributes to professional discourse with occasional journal articles and other published work. He is the author of *Averting Aggression* (RHP 1999, 2004 2nd edition).

Contact via
www.pptc.fsnet.co.uk
or directly to
ob@pptc.co.uk

Introduction

This book aims to take the *mystery* out of management and put *mastery* in by providing a plain-speaking companion for managers to consult. It is a 'how to' book and offers ideas against which they can compare their practice and understanding.

What does a manager do?

Most people would claim to have a clear enough idea about the majority of work done by others because it is observable – as it is in the case of people who impact routinely on us. We would all probably agree what is the work of others such as a doctor, a tyre fitter, a bank teller, a shop assistant, or an estate agent. And we think we know when that work is done well or badly.

Ask *most people* what a manager does, and suggestions turn to ideas of accountability – the person responsible for, the person to complain to, or the person who sits remotely making decisions. When services or a commercial enterprise or our employer fails us in some way we usually finish up seeing our letdown as a consequence of poor management. The manager tends to be a shadowy figure, and when we do see one – possibly put on the spot by an investigative TV reporter – we remark perhaps how ordinary they appear. But it's where the buck stops and the blame begins. The public bay for blood; authorities topple the culpable. Not surprisingly, the conventional view on management is all about end results – 'delivering the goods'.

Ask *managers* what they do and descriptions tend to focus on juggling time, and people, and resources, and demands. They describe stresses and strains and compromises, and being caught between opposing pressures from above and below and over which they have little control. The conventional view of many managers about their work is that no one loves them: when they get it right it's forgotten about ten minutes later; and when they do well, the results get hi-jacked and become set as new targets.

Ask *an academic* about management and out pour high-minded theories. These deconstruct the role to focus on its parts: with notions about the nature of leadership, organisational cultures, management style models, and the way different psychologies can light up different views of the role. The convention of theories is that all phenomena are explicable. The science of management provides blueprints against which real management can be compared.

Ask *yourself* what management tasks you personally have or what management skills you use (just in your private life) and no one who asks that question will be without any. Simply doing that task is a self-appraisal skill – and how well you recognise your own skills will depend on cool honesty. How well you recognise your practical attributes and personal traits is valuable because self-knowledge is the means to an organised, effective, and satisfying life.

The fact is, everyone has management tasks and, to a greater or lesser extent, the skill to do them – ask any busy mother! For example, getting a young child to school, on time, in the right frame of mind and with all necessary equipment, requires:

- Talk and preparation with the child.
- Some prior organisation with a mental or paper checklist to ensure proper dress, PE kit, lunch money etc.
- Arranging transport, after-school supervision if needed.
- And some failsafe backup arrangements.

Similarly, getting a dependent client to attend a court on time requires:

- Preparation and liaison with the client.
- Some prior counselling or other work to do with the hearing.
- A mental or paper checklist to ensure appropriate dress, necessary documents, provision for refreshment if necessary.
- Arranging appropriate transport and supervision.
- And some failsafe backup arrangements.

A similar range of actions would be necessary for yourself if you had an important presentation to deliver. Some people 'manage' such tasks well, others hash them up. The skills of management are mostly quite generic – the components are commonplace requirements of all sorts of managers, but how they hang together when vested on one person can make them into a fool, or a king. Managers differ in ability one person from another in as variable ways as people are each unique.

I don't claim to be an expert manager, but I've had to deal with the mundane as well as some tough matters and sensitive issues in all about as extreme as they can get. The way I view managing is a result of providing consultancy to and having close contact with a number of different organisations as well as working as a manager myself at different levels in education and care; and I've been on the 'receiving end' of other managers at different professional points within groups of people who have been managed well, indifferently, and badly.

Mary Parker Follett (1868–1933) who wrote on the topic in the early twentieth century, defined management as 'the art of getting things done through people'. I'm happy with that, as it fits my experience.

Who is this book for?

This book is intended for people whose careers have led them to the point where they manage colleagues more than they do any other direct work. They may be a team leader or section manager among other managers, or be the more independent manager of a separate unit or facility. The organisations I have in mind that the manager might work in are not specific but they will be providing people in groups or individually with a person-based service of some kind, and this may be a public, private, or commercial service business.

Most of all, I address the book to people who are passionate, committed and determined. If you have those qualities you will be successful, because those are the qualities that get things done more than any careful planning, bean counting, or even always doing as you might be advised.

What do I want you to gain from this book?

After reading this book I hope you will be more successful and achieve your hopes more readily. Your decisions are more considered when you review necessary issues first, and when that review is assisted by good advice your confidence grows – that's what mentoring is about. This book has advice on all the common issues of management, provides contextual or background knowledge, and will make you think, so that you develop your management ability.

If through this book I help you to manage with pleasure and excellence that's a privilege. Thank you.

How should you use this book?

This book can be read through from beginning to end or dipped into by choosing the part that seems to best relate to what you want to think about. How it offers help is directly reflected in the chapter titles and the content organisation. It is not heavily referenced or peppered through with sources to bolster credibility, but it does contain a lot of ideas and some tools and participation tasks (*Activities*) to use and engage with. A lot of ideas are only touched on or at best a potted version is presented; a few points are revisited because they are relevant to more than one context. Most ideas of value are each quite extensive and I can't cover everything about them in this book, but I hope you might do your own further research and reading according to your needs – more on this in *References*, at the end.

All the words in *italics* within the text that are clearly 'idea' words can be sourced within wikipedia (though some of course are just italic as a means to highlight a point). If you read the first chapter and some comment in Chapter 6 you will understand why this is my main reference. Go to www.wikipedia.org and type the bit in italics into their search engine window and follow the links of your choice.

I don't shirk that you should understand the processes you are part of – to have some ease and familiarity with concepts associated with 'the art' of management; but I will try not to bamboozle you with to much 'management speak'. I give my honest and immediate best advice.

And finally . . .

The words I use are interchangeable, unless the context is clearly otherwise, whether you are called a manager, supervisor, or team leader, and others may be colleague, worker, employee, member, or volunteer. I also refer to the manager and others with the masculine pronoun, but that is just a writer's convention – whereas in true fact I admit the best ease I have personally found in my work relationships has been with women colleagues.

CHAPTER 1

What You Need to Know About Managing: Some Theory

1. Understand leadership

The leader has the notion. The hordes get into motion. To take elephants over the Alps; that was Hannibal's brave and brilliant idea and his whole army followed him. But whoever it was who saw to food and fodder were the competent 'doers' that made the journey possible; they managed the impossible.

Great leaders understand that their power stems from keeping the hordes motivated. Leaders can only be leaders if they have followers. This implies a relationship deal: that the leader appeals to the hearts and minds of sufficient people because the followers believe the leader will bring about something desirable. This is a truth whatever the situation, whether leading concerns the matter of only two or three colleagues who work together or means taking forward a huge organisation with hundreds of employees.

'Savvy' leaders concern themselves with *Vision* and *Articles of Faith* to appeal to the hearts and emotions of their followers, and they offer bold or clear strategies that appeal to keen minds and rational opinion. Leaders understand the WIIFM principle (*what's in it for me*) by promising outcomes that have mass appeal and dispel the doubts of dissenters. Leaders must then ensure some early gains. Successful leaders surround themselves with highly capable people that they have chosen who can manage the minutiae of getting things done in the right place at the right time.

On the bridge of the Starship Enterprise when Captain Picard says 'make it so!' this is his direction. It is Picard's lieutenants, Warf or Ryker who get on with doing it. Managers keep the ship powered up and purposeful.

Leaders usually judge the character and mood of the time accurately and have a big nose or a heightened view that allows them to sniff out the developments or foresee the movements that others don't, and their managers may well not because they are too busy with other details. And in choosing their lieutenants, leaders may pick people that others initially question but later find

are valuable (they have blossomed, or have unusual talents).

Leaders' personalities tend to veer between the extremes of gruff and grandiose but they nearly all use their elevated position to keep aloof from common scrutiny – and they dislike being too closely questioned, because they are good on big pictures not detail. Leaders when most trusted can take people along windy tracks that cause much grumbling or puzzlement until the view is revealed and belief in the leader renewed. Most leaders rely on trust, and faith, and their past successes to sustain direction, but all fire up the energy of others with persuasive and powerful oratory when necessary.

To stay in power by popular mandate and not by oppression leaders must be sufficiently likeable and trustworthy. We want to like them, and we want them to like us and look out for us. That's the deal. We like them and we know them by their actions and mostly we want these to be beyond reproach. They must be more perfect than us and show a near ideal range of attributes all the time. A test of their overall creditworthiness is how readily or not we do forgive any indiscretions or errors.

Some leaders become loved, and some of the greatest certainly so. This is true at the time even if as years go by common sentiment and culture becomes altered. Interestingly the foremost such leaders are particularly well represented in a contrasting way for either humanitarian or military standing rather than direct political achievement. Such people are exemplified by Gordon of Khartoum, Horatio Nelson, Nelson Mandela, Mother Teresa, Mahatma Ghandi, Churchill, and Martin Luther King.

Great leaders are pretty much loved universally among their followers; less great leaders will produce some dissent of view and are only liked. Even lesser leaders produce more variable viewpoints and are put up with and accepted as competent at best in the absence of someone more desirable. We are more willing to follow and find most credible persons we can like and respect because they are most like ourselves as we would best imagine we might be.

The more complex or democratic the society, the less there is strong correlation between the quality of leadership and the quality of their managers, or with team or corporate competence. Historically the event in which we might recognise that fact most dramatically is the example of British and Commonwealth losses on WW1 battlefields ('lions led by donkeys') when battle leadership was strategically very flawed despite a well organised and efficient military structure.

Contemporarily we have come to accept the constant replay of political purchase by vote-winning promises. The promises are a declaration of priorities. Invariably the relationship that the leader has with the body of voters is tested sooner or later, as priorities get re-ordered and promises become compromised. All political leaders – even the despotic ones – are initially dependent on civil servants and the pervading civil structures. How things are done, whatever is prioritised, depends more on maintaining effective and strong civil services (managers of things to get done) than on cabinet ministers – who are mere figure heads, usually ignorant about the service they head but who accept being the patsy when reason arises for applaud or sacrifice.

We see this most to national cost when ministers branch out from being a figure head. When ministers, through political interference, cause the managers and their arrangements to be under-funded (as some would say of British Rail, formerly the UK's integrated rail system) disassembled (Britain's National Health Service) or over-stretched (currently, the Home Office) then the efficiency and condition of those services deteriorates and weakens.

Once the Enterprise has a direction (however controversial) the lieutenants get all under-way. They have the skills to get things done. The work is done by their team, be they medics, engineers, social workers, or sales force. In turn, the managers must motivate their people and instruct team leaders (middle and other 'down-the-line managers'). The manager who leads a team at any point in a management structure usually has a main skill and a mix of other skills such as technical, administration, judgement, knowledge, lore, or imagination etc. But as well as knowing 'how to get things done' at whatever level they work, all managers have to lead by motivating and inspiring their team so that they enthusiastically share one accord and common purpose. **All managers are leaders.**

Even the simplest societies and the least complex co-operative human tasks are structured with some form of cascading leadership. When the undertaking is the size of a Babylon, such towers of whatever form will have terraces dappled with the colours of leadership in bud and blossom. We nearly all in some degree show and use leadership in our daily endeavours. Two men may go and load a barrow of bricks but only one can push the load along. Which one leads?

You are a wannabe leader even if your team only comprises the few people that help you manage your small setup. Maybe you aspire to be a greater leader; maybe you admire Richard Branson, or Jonathan Porritt? You may wonder how you might measure up against the leaders you admire; do the leadership attributes questionnaire.

In the real world leadership is not straightforward, however good the personal attributes. To illustrate here is an (unreal world?) example:

Let's say, generally, it would be good for the nation if it were possible for everyone to have nice red noses. A lot of people haven't got good red noses, but then someone discovers a paint that is just the job. Politicians eager to keep people pleased decide there should be a Red Nose Service and appoint a Service Supremo. They take their responsibilities very seriously.

The Supremo gets experts to investigate nose painting and they tell him exactly how much paint is needed per person, and how many people will need their noses done. They organise sufficient local managers in each area and calculate, order, and distribute the amount of paint needed for a first wave of painting. They know that some people for personal reasons will decide against a red nose, but others not yet counted will come forward. There will be bigger noses and smaller noses which will average out, so no margins are built in and their bean counter experts approve this.

The Supremo instructs their local managers to train and keep employed an appropriate number of nose painters, and to get on with the job. Managers measure the paint quantities used, tally the numbers of noses painted, and occasionally check the painting quality. They report back to the Supremo, and so it continues. The Supremo and the politicians bask in the glow of so many red noses painted (although for obtuse reasons they talk about them as having been delivered). The managers get a pay rise and it all works well.

Your leadership attributes	Always (3)	Invariably (2)	Usually (1)	Depends on (0)
1	Not afraid to voice uncertainties				
2	Acknowledge own vulnerabilities				
3	Respect confidences				
4	Trustworthy, as in conscientious				
5	Honest, as in straight and plain speaking				
6	Fulfil commitments				
7	Listen more than speak				
8	Considerate to individuals				
9	Considerate to team/group				
10	Positive and optimistic outlook				
11	Respect doubters as well as yes-men				
12	Others find you approachable				
13	Others describe you as a good leader				
14	Spoken views never vary from written				
15	Never take contentious advantage				
16	Even tempered				
17	Assume blame quicker than ascribe it				
18	Value candour				
19	See problems as worthy challenges				
20	Value self but never at cost to others				
Totals					
Final score					

Do the questionnaire honestly – do I need to say that? If you really want useful independent judgement arrange secretly that a number of other people rate you as well and average up and compare the results. To assist you interpret your results there is a guide separated away in the *Bibliography* at the end (do not read it first!).

Oh! No it doesn't!

A couple of years or so later, people in Pernikittyshire have found that Pillar Box Red is shinier than the Robin Red supplied and have started a clamour for this that is moving across the country.

In Leftyland red nose inspectors report that too much paint has been ordered and there are not enough painting rooms despite there seeming to be an excess of painters not doing much and angry people waiting for their red nose. The Supremo sacks that manager.

In Slow Borough the managers woke up late, and in panic they paid a gang master a lot of money to get in hundreds of painters from Somewhere and Abroad. They don't speak English and the quality of painting is very variable, but all is going at great speed now.

In Trendy Town a lot of tall, snooty and self-important people, who have very nice red noses already thank you, begin to question how necessary it is to have a painted red nose. They think it is a waste of public money as it doesn't sufficiently guarantee happiness; cutting dull noses off is cheaper. Any one who needs a red nose should pay for it themselves. They point to the savings in paint made in their area and claim they should have its worth in varnish so they can all have their nails done. All the politicians live in Trendy Town and get invites to parties; Trendy Town people have big say.

The politicians get into a spin and call the Supremo to account. The Supremo points out what a difficult job they have had, but they were only doing what they were asked to do. The politicians give the Supremo a knighthood and then pay him a lot of money to pack up and go Somewhere or Abroad.

The politicians wipe their hands of red noses and tell everyone any painting necessary must be sorted out locally. Each year they put ever smaller amounts of money for red nose painting in a tin and say the local worthies must ask for it. The local worthies fight and argue a lot among and between themselves. Everyone starts to get an opinion about the infighting as it's on the news a lot and for the local worthies it's a big deal, and the old folk remind each other about when red noses were free and cheerful.

2. Master management lore

Over the years different ideas about management come to the fore and at times these can seem like fashions that come and go. That does not mean that they may not endure in some form and most do contribute in some way to understanding how organisations work. *Management* concerns getting things done, whatever the in-vogue views. *Management* measures quantities on a regular basis and regularly adjusts the steps to reach a goal. This is the case even where there is no grand plan.

To master management a manager must be aware of developments, where they come from, why they appear and how they will impact on getting things done. To hold a steady course a manager must know how the wind will blow and how to keep steady through any squall; this means they must have some idea of the bigger system of climate pressures and weather trends that impact on the waters in which they are sailing.

Ideas about management either explain or measure how things get done. Mostly the ideas impact when they pressure managers to demonstrate practice in new ways. Your work gets examined through glass of a particular colour. Classic examples of new ways to measure have been the introductions in public services of 'best value' 'accountability' and 'performance monitoring' comparisons.

All managers will benefit from some understanding of the historical developments in management practice and lore over the past couple of decades and be to some extent conversant with the details. How much so, will depend on the level at which you manage or wish to, and the degree the work has a strong political interest. Responses to pressures whether embraced or resisted are most effective when the context of those pressures is understood.

Early views and awareness about management arose in industry and commerce, and focused on five functions:

- planning
- organising
- leading
- coordinating, and
- controlling.

Today this list is seen as too narrow. 'Management' is now practiced in public administration of all kinds and in very much more complex forms than within trade and manufacturing.

The expression 'management is what managers do' occurs often. This suggests difficulty in defining management because of the shifting nature of definitions, but also that the managerial elite have garnered up sufficient professional control to mystify what they do, and this is protected by entry qualifications such as MBA degrees. Whatever the sector a manager might come to work in, university departments that teach management are usually called 'business schools' and in these the key common ideas are gathered up and structured into a body of knowledge.

In fact, most ideas are still generated within private sector industries or by academics who have links to commerce, and they are then transferred to the public sector or become seen as relevant in new applications. Here are the foremost ideas.

Total Quality Management (TQM)

TQM emerged in the 1960s. TQM is a systems approach that seeks to make every stage in the production process of such enduring quality that the end product is quality assured. Interestingly TQM as an explanation for a rigorous approach to each step along a manufacturing process was a Japanese academic idea; but it was first appropriated by the US Navy! An idea that began life applied to manufacturing goods was taken up by naval air command to specifically improve safety and operational efficiency; later it was applied to commercial services such as tyre fitting to improve what they offered for sale; and finally application was found to public services such as care and health.

New Public Managerialism (NPM)

NPM also concerns ideas borrowed from private commerce and transferred to public services. NPM came to a peak in the mid 1990s together with its supporting notions such as TQM. The central idea of NPM is that competition is the best way to energise the market and ensure *best value* and choice for the end consumer. Government has been very keen on developments based on this idea because they reduce direct demand on the national exchequer.

NPM lay behind the upheavals of the 1990s when Local Authorities (LAs) disposed of residential care homes and public housing into trusts or similar organisations and by direct sale to the private sector. Similarly the National Health Service was broken down into independent regional trusts (hospital services)

and primary care units (doctor services). Public-private partnerships were encouraged. People working in public services had to learn the manner of business and markets. Language and viewpoint was transferred so that service users became seen as customers or consumers. Customers were given performance charters and consumer-type routes for any complaint. Ombudsmen sprouted. But expectations were raised at the same time that financial cuts were imposed. All kind of tensions increased. Closer analysis of 'best value' illustrates the issues.

Best value

This was a government 'initiative' entitled Circular 10 (DETR, 1999), that LAs were to implement, to replace competitive tendering that had hitherto been the 'buy on price' tendering criteria for purchases. It was intended to improve service quality through efficiency savings and more effective procurement and to replace the simple procedure of accepting the cheapest option when services were bought in (although some services close to government control such as education were exempted). A 2 per cent year-on-year saving target was imposed.

The imperatives were the *4 Cs*:

- challenge
- consult
- compare
- compete.

The throes of implementation and cost saving began a huge movement away from direct services and towards leasing and short term purchase of supply services. It exposed divides between regions that had different worker shortages and turnover rates, consultation raised issues concerning hidden shortfalls usually involving issues of care quality, and the outcome often meant that many incidental benefits that indirectly supported the greater arrangement and made it work became sloughed off, and there were numbers of instances where both services users and employees were angered.

Best value meant that *financial management* came into closer scrutiny. How public money is spent by each authority was examined, together with ways to compare the spending efficiency of local authorities and report the results using three levels of star rating. A lot of public sector energy goes into *Audit Commission inspections* and the

Performance Management systems of LAs. But the focus on common comparison data such as Local Authority star ratings can be at the cost of ignoring other local high-concern issues such as seasonal unemployment or high in-migration. Also, when service directors enjoy the accolades of star status, it can be that managers of first- and second-tier services feel distant and cynical, and typically they will be more stressed, they may have had to reduce levels of permanent staff, and may feel they are now providing a poorer quality of service although the figures suggest otherwise with more (work done) for less (lower costs).

Ironically of course the independent sector and staff supply agencies have profited most from public service best value developments. They have expanded and made money. The shift to agency personnel means many services can be presented as more efficient and responsive, but at user level this may mean for example that a dependent person now has a succession of different (perhaps indifferent) carers. With the loss of continuity provided by a direct service worker this service user may well have lost the trust and companionship they enjoyed that contributed in very meaningful but unmeasured ways to their well-being.

Performance management

Performance management now runs throughout all public services. The strength and thickness of the thread varies from service to service and across local authority and other public services such as National Health. Whatever is monitored the process is much the same. A number of key indicators across all services are chosen, evaluated, and compared to past performance (seen as more valid once the process is underway), and compared with comparable situations or services elsewhere. This is how LAs are awarded their star rating; and is also how managers (and most workers to a lesser extent) are deemed competent or not by a similar internal process – the annual *performance appraisal*. Currently the Department for Communities and Local Government (DCLG) is responsible for the implementation and overseeing of best value, and does so currently by setting 90 *Best Value Performance Indicators* as targets for the different services and the overall corporate management (www.bpvi.gov.uk).

This accountability process has had some useful outcomes. It has focused minds and

exposed weaknesses in middle management in many services and organisations. It has been used to winkle a few of these weaknesses – and people – out, but more usefully has pointed to the need these people have for their professional development and training to be better considered and provided for. And the different inspection regimes in general have noted the tendency for first line managers (maybe you?) to make very significant input into maintaining standards of practice and supporting their staff to keep up their individual skills and knowledge.

But not all is rosy.

Management models

The *classical model of management* is of an ordered world that is predictable. Information (assuming sufficient accuracy) is used to make predictions, and managers simply make decisions to alter different inputs within their organisation and be confident that the expected outcomes will occur (like the first year or so of painting red noses). Strict adherence to NPM principles and an 'audit culture' places emphasis simply on costs (per unit) and throughput (product) and seldom values other qualities that are important to people particularly when they are in personal need. The audit method is the same for all local councils with the same criteria particular to each type of service. NPM does not support locally democratic means to determine the service priorities in any one area.

Everyone has become increasingly aware that public services cannot be run as if they were private ventures. But stuck with change that is now entrenched but not sufficiently 'delivering' the only remaining hope is to focus on top management.

The spotlight now is on *leadership*; its importance and quality. In a way the circle has turned fully, as this is where the 'buck' historically has always stopped. People have enduring residual senses for a natural order and cultural minimalism that they perceive pervaded in a less complex past. This makes it essential that leaders have ideas that help explain why things happen in the organisations and societies they lead and how they might best interact with people and lead them. The more society is complex, then the more we need leaders who can manage the complexities. We will pay them more but expect more of them, for one very good reason. People will notice them most when things 'don't get done'. Blame is not new; it has ever been human reaction. Remember that leaders and senior managers often only get the important detail when they hear complaint. The quality of under-managers and the flow of information from all levels are critically important to leader survival.

The realities of modern management are increasingly complex, and two recent ideas show how that is. These two theories are borrowed from the sciences.

Chaos theory

Chaos in this context carries a meaning closer to its original Greek than current everyday use. The chaos is space or void (opportunity) that is full only of unformed potential. The greater the void, the greater the potential is that it will be filled with complexity. The actions and developments that come to fill voids are interlinked; therefore even small events or alterations can begin changes that lead to great consequences – this is known as the *butterfly effect* (a small disturbance in the air can begin a chain of occurrences that results in a tornado). This of course is the stuff behind much great drama as well as slapstick humour (from Shakespeare to the capers of Chaplin or Michael Crawford). Consequently innovators who introduce small changes or developments in organisations may not be able to predict what the final outcomes will be (and I guess most of us have experienced something of that). This idea completely opposes the classical model of management which is fixed and predictable, and chaos theory lies behind the idea of complexity.

Complexity theory

Matters are potentially *chaotic* unless we intervene. *Complexity theory* underpins the tension between desirable order and anarchic order and is used to explain how even when natural order prevails it does not mean there are no rules of logic (Darwinian evolution fits this model). In *chaos*, structured actions, rigid views and life systems will be abandoned or will die eventually because they do not work when conditions change or something challenges them. Their limitations will cause them to collapse, as their brittleness makes them inherently weak (i.e. dinosaurs could not cope with rapid climate change).

Instead, softer and more flexible skills survive, such as adaptability, diplomacy, and flexibility, and creatures with these forms of sentient skill progress exceptionally well when they are combined with a thirst for information and knowledge (big-brained mammals prospered in our evolutionary past as do 'learning communities' now). Information really is power, but in this structure the information and potentially the power is universal – the whole is only as good as the sum of its parts. These skills and attitudes are wedded to a view or *vision* expressed in a set of core beliefs and ideas that inform actions. This sort of organisation is organic and likely to be owned and shaped by those who are part of it. This level of cohesion and common purpose creates a stable structure at all times even although the organisation is progressing and its architecture and way of acting may well be continuously evolving.

Complexity theory partners well with a number of recent ways humanity is coming to understand itself and embrace new technology as the agent for further development. At any one time there is a foremost agent: just as once it was metallurgy, then transport engines, today it is *information technology* (*IT*). IT aligns well with new ideas about desirable human attributes such as *emotional intelligence*, and a growing recognition (sometimes from painful experience) that generic and transferable skills are more valuable that specific craftsmanship (no 'job for life').

Business Process Re-engineering (BPR)

The management process that reflects the complexity of today's world and finds central place for IT is called *Business Process Re-engineering* (*BPR*). BPR is strategy driven (leadership again). With BPR, workflow management is considered the prime means to efficiency whatever the actual or structural elements of the organisation (such as hierarchical levels and the nature of work teams or units and the distribution of work). Approaches such as TQM seek to get continuous improvement on given performance criteria – a percentage gain year on year (i.e., 10 per cent more cases seen) but BPR is more radical, it seeks a multiple level of improvement across the organisation (i.e., everyone can point to everything they do being 10 per cent better – a multifaceted gain).

IT is realising BPR ideas. The traditional application of IT supported existing business functions: it contributed to workflow management and increased organisational efficiency (think 'just in time' manufacture and delivery of parts). The application of IT and robotics is now automating all kinds of processes and creating consistencies that ensure the quality of the product or the service, rather than raw number. With a basic quality and supply assured, people can focus on the processes behind the product or service so that it can be far more individualised or bespoke – the design or product performance is enhanced. This requires that IT is itself 'freed-up' and applied imaginatively and not used solely to increase production by accelerated automation.

IT is now playing a role as an enabler of new organisational forms, and making possible new patterns of collaboration within and between organisations. Typically the emerging new patterns of organisation rely on two key technical developments.

- Shared databases make information available instantly at many places and to many people.
- Expert systems (from computer assisted design to mail merging) allow generalists to perform specialist tasks so that organisational development (and administration) does not hang on the work of a few key people.

People within organisations experience IT impacting personally most in the manner it enhances their education, training, motivation and reward systems – 'the art of getting things done through people'. It is people who drive the business processes and activities that might add value to an output – the basic underlying idea of BPR. The attributes that characterise the business processes of BPR are all related to people and include ideas about:

- *Ownership* – the work and the development of an enterprise is obtained by democratic ways so that everyone can be involved and feel considered. In some instances real ownership is realised by the structure of the organisation so that everyone is a member or a shareholder (a lobby group organised through new technology – radical examples are the 2000–01 fuel protests and the groundbreaking February 2007 email petition to the PM against road pricing).

Also commercial and public enterprises increasingly try to show strong individuality,

fronted by promotional effort (corporate colours and logo as well as direct public relations events). Think how local councils bombard you with publicity about themselves. It is thought that one effect of strong corporate identity on employees is that it encourages them to be proud and energetic.

- *Customer focus* – helps keep everyone reminded who the work is for. It is thought that one effect of customer focus is to assist quality control as it provides a thread to use to track through all processes within the organisation to see how effective and useful is any one practice towards the end objective – i.e. when the work is physical care, the mental health of the client is not overlooked.
- *Value-adding* – this supports customer focus when an additional outcome very desirable to the customer can be provided at very little or no extra cost to the organisation – i.e. workers are trained in counselling techniques so that as they chat with their clients while providing primary care they know how to recognise and support clients with depression.
- *Cross-functionality* – the ability of members and teams to be flexible, able, and willing to do more than one task. This frees up the enterprise to work fluidly and continuously and be problem solving (not go to pot one day for want of a 'saggar maker's bottom knocker').

Example: Information Technology Applied
  IT makes possible new forms of organising and collaborating, and promotes developments such as internal and external partnerships. Rather than simply supporting existing business functions IT is having effects that change thought processes and open new horizons. IT makes it possible to flatten the hierarchy in larger organisations and create flexible, more interactive, groups of people. Perhaps this is why the most well known organisations that have these new structural forms are in the IT business, such as is Micro-Soft and Dell.
  Michael Dell founded his company in 1983, and it has since been the world's fastest growing major PC Company. His idea for success was to keep the smallest inventory possible by having a direct link with the manufacturer. When a customer orders one of Dell's custom PC's, the parts needed are automatically requested to the manufacturer for shipment. This reduces the cost for

inventory tracking and warehousing. Michael Dell mentions: 'If you have a good strategy with sound economics, the real challenge is to get people excited about what you're doing. A lot of businesses get off track because they don't communicate an excitement about being part of a winning team that can achieve big goals. If a company can't motivate its people and it doesn't have a clear compass, it will drift'.

The company is now concentrating more on customer service than selling computers since the PC market price has pretty much equalised. Michael Dell notes: 'The new frontier in our industry is service, which is a much greater differentiator when price has been equalised. In our industry, there's been a pretty huge gap between what customers want in service and what they can get, so they've come to expect mediocre service. We may be the best in this area, but we can still improve quite a bit – in the quality of the product, the availability of parts, service and delivery time.' (Paraphrased from www.wikipedia.com)

Embracing complexity through ideas such as BPR allows us to not be caught up on 'cause and effect'. Instead managers can look to how processes and human responses impact on the quality and fair distribution of services. In new fluid, flexible and more responsive enterprises monitoring performance against lists of indicators loses relevance. Because of human nature and the variability of our needs and preoccupations, rigid measures will be increasingly seen as only crude comparison and without sensitivity to the other important contributory factors and qualities that we value. Sometimes advances in marketing are more rapid than common perception.

Example: Public Corporation Identity
A district council in Shropshire caused local public furore when people noticed the dustbin trucks all carried personalised number plates showing the council initials. The public view of course was that this must have been inordinately expensive and a waste of public money.

The council had to go some length to explain to its ratepayers that the fleet was actually leased from a hire company who had arrangements with the vehicle licensing authority to routinely register new fleets with chosen letters (which they could associate with their customers), and this was done at no additional cost to this or any other council.

The necessary shift in skills for managers will be away from *control* and towards *facilitating*. It is understandable that some managers may wish to keep a controlling hand because this is what they have known from the past, or the enterprise has a high proportion of transient or inexperienced staff (although one must ask why). Reserved decision-making (where only managers make decisions) impacts negatively on the levels and distribution of skill across staff teams; it causes:

- *De-skilled staff*. They become used to deferring problems up their line of management.
- *Loss of commitment*. As the range of skills diminish so will commensurate attitudes of conscientious responsibility.
- *Loss of development*. Middle managers will not be able to relate equally well to all deferred problems, and attending to deferred issues will dominate if not overburden their work at the expense of furthering development.
- *Loss of focus on service users*. Senior managers become effective at problem management and minimising damaging outcomes, but the cost of too much 'fire fighting' is time and energy diverted away from the primary responsibility to focus on the needs of users and service quality.
- *Loss of operational impact*. When most problems are normally passed up the line until a manager makes a decision (at a senior level) the time taken before a response is made is increased; there is less opportunity for junior colleagues to learn about or distinguish the gravity of individual problems; the problem may have worsened, evaporated, or been resolved by other means.

One understanding emerging strongly from BPR structures is that the optimum size for a group is not more than about a dozen people. This number can work well co-operatively and get good results, and is the ideal size of group if they need to be facilitated by one person. Organisational frameworks are responding with new internal patterns and changing towards layered structures. These feature a number of smaller cohesive teams presided over jointly by one or more senior managers. All this is placing demands on all but the lowliest of employees to develop some management skills and show leadership attributes when occasions call for them.

A complexity model requires that the widest view is taken initially and then focus is gradually narrowed as relevant elements come into view. This approach intends that nothing is overlooked or taken for granted, and when connections between different elements are seen they are fully explored (the 'butterflies' are not ignored). By looking for connections the belief is that negative feedback and dead ends are avoided, energy is channelled well; shared vision means communication is not wasted on argument but directed towards productivity

Two contemporary examples put this model into context and illustrate change that embraces complexity.

1. Safeguarding

Safeguarding is a set of legislation, guidance and practice concerning the welfare and life chances of children. The concept came about primarily because of a number of high-profile child deaths around the turn of the millennium. Enquiries found that these tragedies had been potentially avoidable but welfare practice and information systems dealing with children, and people employed to work with children, had failed to protect these children.

The Children Act 2004 (which implemented the proposals of the Green Paper – *Every Child Matters*) required key people and bodies to jointly arrange to safeguard and promote the welfare of children. The structural changes included the requirement on each LA to appoint a supreme leader to head Children's Services and to integrate all of the services for education and social and health welfare. These three services have a poor tradition of joint work and high mutual scepticism. The funding streams for these services also vary between central government and local authority sources. The legal emphasis on leadership now provides first order powers to orchestrate matters, ensure co-operation, and 'get things done'.

However, in the instance of safeguarding, corporate responsibility (as set out in the legislation guidance) lies not just with the figurehead or the service 'non-entity' but each and every possibly relevant service and all personnel within. At ground level there is now a clearer legal duty of care extended to every professional person in any level of contact with children, to understand their responsibility to look out for any risks to child welfare and if necessary act upon their concerns.

All agencies are charged to review the manner in which they work and to be proactive towards child welfare – not just be re-active in what they do. A key associated procedure is that when concerns of any nature arise about an individual child there is an administrative tool that provides the framework for investigating the individual child's circumstances – the Common Assessment Framework (CAF). Initially, all possibly relevant agencies might contribute to the CAF and can be called to the table by a local manager. Only as views are shared, and the specific needs of each child brought into sharper focus, is the involvement of different agencies prioritised or stood down.

Safeguarding illustrates complexity theory and the application of BPR in several ways. Currently the requirement on services to share information and work side by side is creating tensions as well as exciting opportunities and there is little chance to delay developments by quibbling about protocols. All LAs have to respond to the legislation, and although a number of different operational models are emerging to connect the different agencies they are all more complex (or fluid) than previously. Different service teams fear loss of skills and professional identity as they disassemble and reform in multi-agency groups. But those groups make possible imaginative and efficient collaborative work that, it is argued, will be timelier, and in forms yet to take shape. The BPR gains will come from the release of potential, supported by new IT systems and universal connectivity that provide cross service information. The intended 'valued-added product' is less human misery. Complexity can embrace sentiment.

Case Example: Restructuring Children's Services

The change made by one particular authority regarding safeguarding children arrangements is the creation of a half dozen small local safeguard areas each with its own *Integrated Services Manager* (ISM) and administrative 'hub' office supported by investments in IT. Each 'hub' is to become the work base for the different agencies to create a multi-professional source of expertise accessed by each ISM; the belief being that operational cross laterality and mutual training is the way forward.

The agencies most represented at each 'hub' include social services, education (welfare, psychology, learning and behaviour), youth, conexions and youth mental health services. Agencies are restructuring their previously discrete arrangements to different degrees. Housing, police and health are barely affected, but some separate social and education bases have been discarded as staff are relocated to 'hubs'. Some service professionals remain managed by their service managers or receive clinical supervision from within their core service, others are managed entirely by the area ISM.

Early experience suggests there is improved focus and effectiveness at child welfare, but the view among workers is that some of the present 'dual' management structure is complex and there are concerns about the integrity of specific professions.

2. Individualised learning

Performance monitoring has been behind the tests that children take at set ages in school, and league tables compare the results between schools. Again, the factors that contribute to good results are complex and often beyond any individual school's control. The league tables have increasingly been seen as too crude and arbitrary, and ever more contentious as the issues become better understood by the wider public (e.g. the different catchment zones of schools reflect different levels of local material advantage according to wealth and social class – possibly intellectual advantage as well but that is more contentious).

This case illustrates well how classical methodology and performance management can undermine practitioners, and deny their expert perspective and their professional skills and creativity, although as I write, this situation is being better acknowledged by the DfES. New instructions to schools will concern how they might test children only when they are individually ready. And school performance will be reported on the individualised gains, rather than the accumulated score, obtained at given points of standardised assessment testing (SATs). Paymaster authorities do not lightly give up measurements completely!

This change is contemporary with moves to see how the actual curriculum of each child might be more tailored to each child's learning needs, and more responsive to their individual pace, interests, and learning style. I guess you, and certainly I have our own preference for how to be minded with the world, as indeed do many children if given the chance; yet the teaching organisation that prevails insists children learn in small blocks of time, in large groups, and with standard methods for presenting knowledge. There is very rarely the opportunity for children to immerse themselves in one item in depth or explore across the extensive connections they might make.

Again, the use of IT not only makes it possible for teachers to track individualised learning, it is also increasingly the first media for knowledge exploration. This process is already well ahead in the USA where over 50 per cent of all school students have their records and performance and test results tracked by one company (Pearson Publishing). This company can also direct students individually to lessons within IT packages that will boost their learning. There is also a move in the language and philosophy of education away from *teaching* (didactic and authority-centred) and towards *learning* (person-centred).

Education also illustrates another interesting point. In the best classrooms, with high student achievement, leadership is very apparent. The class teacher determines the way the class works together and shares common purpose, how individuals listen and learn together, as well as encouraging daring and creativity – all BPR processes. Yet there is currently a severe national shortage of teachers willing to take up school headship. This has been linked to the poor government vision about the personal needs and processes of learners compared to the pressure of curriculum dictates and over-emphasis on audits of school performance. There is a long way to go; but perhaps a change is in the air?

And, as a footnote, Pearson is an example of a company that is remodelling itself to become a 'solutions provider', wedding its core business of educational book publishing to the new technology, and new business of handling powerful information.

Conclusions

Managers at the frontline may be the only managers the public come into contact with.

There is growing recognition about the necessary realities of 'customer service' in order to keep services truly competitive and the first choice service. Managers in such enterprises must not only be good administrators but able to recognise how they can influence change and how to generate it. The information they offer must be fresh, and is most valid or acceptable when expressed competently.

At the same time some administrative layers are becoming redundant. Workers and managers increasingly use IT to file reports and obtain information thus reducing the need for secretarial and clerking assistance (a good example of efficiency gains by Business Process Re-engineering). Correspondingly many services are experiencing a flattening of their hierarchical structures. Middle managers must be able to screen, decipher, and prioritise a two-way information stream, which widens the closer to the base level the information is received or generated. It becomes even more necessary therefore that the middle managers that remain are highly able people.

To be effective within enterprise development whether active in generating or supporting change or otherwise, managers must understand the processes that bear on them. This is particularly the case should they wish to challenge pressures. This requires sufficient familiarity with 'the lore' and the ability to be able to see and swim in the stream of ideas.

3. Make a plan

Effective leaders have some vision of what they want to achieve and the ability to let others know and understand it. This requires not only that they use engaging language but show personal and moral conviction that carries well ('walk the walk' as well as 'talk the talk'). Managers who want to 'get things done' must be clear about what they want and how it will be done; and that requires communicating well with the people who will make it happen. Leaders and managers who wish to inspire and motivate others have to put themselves out and about: they must have ways of connecting with 'the shop floor'. How much they value other views and are willing to make contact is the key to being informed and this is done most effectively when leaders have sophisticated language skills and can talk with –

or at least understand – others using their particular idioms and habits of language.

Example: How to communicate well

Stuart was the MD of a child care company that was going from strength to strength. The company provided fresh chances for the most damaged and challenging teenagers many of whom had high-tariff offending pasts or were chronically self-harming. The work was particularly risky and fraught with operational difficulties.

Stuart, who could comfortably command attention at the highest level at conferences (and market his company effectively to buyers) also had the practice of dropping unannounced into one of the company homes and working a shift alongside whichever team was on duty. He had the language skills and approachability that assisted making a quick rapport with staff and young people from all backgrounds, and he was adept at distilling otherwise unwieldy information. Consequently he was well informed and informative with those he came into contact with.

His 'drop-in' practice gave him great credibility within his company and allowed him to have high expectations. It usefully meant he could experience and talk about relevant issues at first hand with his young residents as well as fellow colleagues, and pass on directly his belief that even the smallest positive steps contributed to all high quality personal achievement as well as corporate progress. He ensured the continuity of key values important to both company culture and client success.

People will make judgments about you, and the organisation you front, based on what they see and experience. This means that what you do, and how you do it, is so much more important than anything you say. If you manage or lead any group of people you will get judged anyway, so you may as well be judged on the criteria that are important to you, and judged on exactly what your organisation is about. It is well worth ensuring the best control of whatever publicity and interest that may be generated for whatever reason, and this is best done if confident reference can be made to an existing statement that sets out your stall absolutely clearly. A *Mission Statement* does this, and I return to this point in the next chapter.

Mission statement

The chances are quite high that whatever your work you will have a description of purpose in some form (mission). It does not have to be gold ink on vellum, or stamped on foreheads. It can be a humble statement of intent simply expressed, and what's written down can describe the greater enterprise or just the bit you are responsible for. Generally, if there is such a statement it is somewhere on view or it is printed on standard documents such as a charter or prospectus, or similar.

Enterprises that lack a clearly agreed and well-declared mission wobble most. If there is no clear direction in which to head there can be no plan or map of how to get there!

Business plan

Subordinate to the greater mission is the map or plan of intention in current use. This will be called the *Business Development Plan* (*BDP*) or something similar. Even a simple BDP may well have several specific different goals that together describe how the mission will be achieved (the big aim or strategic overview). Each goal can be broken down into several things (*objectives*) that will need to be done. *Actions* achieve *objectives*.

Actions are only do-able when the objectives and overall plan is **SMART**:

- *Specific* – exactly what actions are planned – the actual new additions, intended differences, or new endeavour: not just empty adverbs such as 'better' or 'quicker' or 'new'.
- *Measurable* – the criteria for how it will be known that planned actions have achieved what they set out to do.

- *Achievable* – a pilot has been run or similar work done elsewhere, or there is sufficient evidence or accord among enterprise experts and experienced managers that every action is do-able within the given framework of time and resources and the deployment of work.
- *Realistic* – everyone involved believes the strategy is desirable and will have beneficial outcomes, and there is sufficient support for the actions from those who will be doing them.
- *Time set* – each action has a time frame of stages to completion.

The best BDPs result from shared work between key persons in the enterprise who produce a well agreed and highly accessible plan that is normally shared with everyone so that they can see the whole and understand its structure overall. A well-tried format is to use sheets with headings as the example below shows.

Typical key features of BDPs:
- The time scale of BDPs is usually annual or longer but will invariably also include shorter term objectives within it.
- The plan becomes more detailed the closer in time, and the 'lower' the level of action to be implemented.
- Plans can be assembled with as many levels as necessary to cascade down to whatever level specific instructions need to be given. When cascaded down to individual persons, the appropriate sections that apply to them can be individually highlighted.
- Senior managers will be responsible for the whole plan (e.g. achieve a position in the service marketplace that makes the service the preferred provider).

Enterprise Services Development Plan: Strategic Overview
(A frontispiece overview that sets out Strategic components or Goals)

Strategic Goal 1: Enterprise Services will develop . . . market . . . etc. (A sheet like this to detail each strategic development goal)				
Development Objective 1: Super Team will Complete . . . Implement . . . etc. (A sheet like this to detail the objectives within each strategic goal)				
Actions	Means or resources	Manager or person responsible	Target date	Performance indicators (monitoring arrangements – may be comparison with internal or external benchmarks)
Actions are the things to do that will achieve the Development Objective. Actions are listed with appropriate remarks in a table with headings similar to this example				

- Local managers (you?) will share responsibility to obtain one or more development objectives (e.g. to reduce the response time for initial assessment of new referrals to the service from 11 to 5 working days).
- The BDP will embody change of all kinds including concrete action, such as acquiring new buildings or equipment, and abstract action such as change to organisational methods (e.g. all new referrals will have an initial assessment using x-y-z and then allocated a priority rating using A-B-C).
- Actions can be scaled down to individual levels (e.g. the administrator in each local office will take on responsibility to develop IT tools to track work schedules and case allocations so that the objective concerning new referrals can be actioned. In three months the solutions will be investigated with the best local method found to do this going forward for whole service adoption).
- Parts of the BDP can be linked to individual and team *performance appraisal* as well as markers for whole service evaluation.

You may think examples of this kind of planning are not relevant to you: YOU ARE WRONG!

Let's say you manage a small care home within a much larger enterprise that sets out company strategy and goals. It's already been done! *No it has not*. Have you no cares? No ideas or small plans to improve what you do?

You or your team will have hopes even if these are only comparatively small goals such as resolving a knotty work rota problem, a desire for more training, a wish to improve some quality for the residents, or simply to redecorate ahead of the company schedule. All those sorts of ideas are worthy. Good for you! If you formalise your goals you have to think in detail about how they will be achieved: and you publish them – even if this is just putting up your plan outline in the staff room.

Do those things and you demonstrate resolve – that's leadership stuff, and what's more, your plan is more likely be realised as it stays in the hearts and minds of you and your colleagues. That's called 'making changes' (you may wish to look at Chapter 2.4 – *How to Manage Change*). And enterprises that really zing have as many ideas going upwards for consideration as there might be ideas going downwards for consultation.

You may worry that others will be pointed in their comments and make 'Oh! Look at him!' or similar derogatory remarks behind your back, or will ignore your efforts. If so, then you are possibly not cut out to lead or manage. People who get things done don't let what others th28-ink about them get in the way of doing.

Enterprises that develop rapidly have very simply-stated long-term aims but very detailed short-term objectives that will be reviewed and adapted very frequently – possibly monthly – sometimes even daily or weekly. Three points stand out:

1. Enterprises without a suitable plan waste their own and others' energy and resources. Direction is usually capricious and given by the most influential or powerful member at any one time.
2. Enterprises that impose a plan of any kind risk it being thwarted to some degree if there has not been appropriate discussion with the people who will 'do it' and views are routed back to its executive level (managers) so that the plan can be revisited as necessary until it is sufficiently shared and supported throughout.
3. Enterprises that make specific goals (*performance targets* or *mission*) such sacred cows or obsessional pursuits that they do not recognise or respond to other things as they emerge will skew reality and foster collusion. They will risk doing much damage to staff integrity, client service, and ultimately their own purpose for being.

4. Demonstrate skills

Leadership is mostly concerned with cultural change and influencing people. Managing is mostly concerned with getting things done. But leaders and managers invariably have a mix of roles, and how well these sit together in a comfort zone – within your comfort zone – may be seen by personal comparison to the table that follows.

For each of the 20 statements put a tick in either the left or right hand column to how you see yourself. Tally them up to see which column dominates: if you do tick both sides of a row it is no matter, the score will even out and the comparison value will be lower.

Maybe now you have a better idea of where you are on the leader–manager spectrum. However, high achievers are always prepared to go the extra distance – literally so in the instance of top athletes – and we recognise it is drive, passion or self-belief that separates those top

Leaders are/I am most like this	✓	Managers are/I am most like this	✓
1	A one-off person like no other		Recognisably like others doing similar	
2	Self aware: deft in tough situations		Structurally aware: deft at re-routing	
3	Inspiring manner: confident ways		Exacting manner: distrustful ways	
4	Long, wide view even beyond horizon		Detailed view of immediate terrain	
5	Imagine, invent and innovate ideas		Implement, illustrate and import ideas	
6	Decide what needs doing		Decide how to do things	
7	Seek philosophical ends		Seek practical endings	
8	Do the right things		Do things right	
9	Understand people		Understand systems and structures	
10	Challenge convention		Use convention	
11	Need to be followed		Choose to follow	
12	Believe the mission may fail if I fail		Believe the mission may falter if I fail	
13	Assume responsibility		Accept responsibility	
14	High EQ (emotional intelligence)		High IQ (intellectual intelligence)	
15	Rounded ability with range of skills		Expert ability with focussed skill	
16	Self-critical		Self-analytical	
17	Accept but not seek being liked or loved		Seek to be respected	
18	Have resilience		Will compromise	
19	Learning-agile (quick at any task)		Learning-selective (have preferences)	
20	Forgive and forget		Acknowledge and remember	

performers from the also-rans. People who achieve the most are willing to push out beyond their comfort zone. How far will you be prepared to go?

A closer look at the actual roles of leader-managers will help identify the things you might still need to learn or do better. First, note the different ends of the leader-manager spectrum and how the different comfort zones reflect a somewhat different set of skills.

Manager end

Managing requires 'hard' *intra*-personal skills. These 'hard' skills are the personal technical application that the manager has that gets things done at all levels of endeavour. Like all technical skills there is generally a strong belief that these can be taught. Certainly most managers gain from experience and progress to different degrees according to what they are willing to learn. If I did not believe that I would not be writing this book!

Leader end

Leadership requires 'soft' *inter*-personal skills of communication, and the visionary beliefs necessary to motivate and inspire others. There is a widely-held view that leadership cannot be learned in later life like a new technique to apply. This view holds that these attributes are based on morality and values in the adult that stem from the accumulated experiences of childhood and therefore are instinctive or intuitive. They mostly are, but not uniquely so. If that was only the case it would imply that adults are rigid and unable to change and develop themselves, which would deny everyone their human potential – and is patently not true.

I think that leadership qualities are not laid down like some kind of fitted mind-set in particular forms of childhood, but leaders do retain the receptivity and open-mindedness associated with childhood, and many qualities and beliefs about one's self and others are grounded in our formative years based on how we are treated and the values that are imparted. The qualities characteristic of leaders are found in people who make personal change throughout their lives and are open to learning and new ideas. Potentially anyone can learn to do anything, but to *excel* requires passion.

Leaders who excel are energetic because they are passionate about their ideas and beliefs. You can't *teach* passion. I will challenge that of anyone. But you may *learn* to be passionate. It comes from the interplay between experience, belief and the desire to extend your values into the lives of others. There are plenty of accounts of leaders who find themselves thrust into their position by a passionate opposition to some adversity or human injustice.

The skills needed for leader-managers, no matter what business they are in, include most of the skills in the following two lists. If you wish to make some personal appraisal, do not simply look at each item and stop there. You must be able to justify or say to yourself HOW the skill shows – what it is you actually do. For example, look at item 8 on the manager list. Can you write down, right now, the Acts, Sections, and Guidance etc. that impact on you, and can you put your hand immediately to any associated publication?

You may wish to award yourself 1 to 4 on each criterion (as suggested on the Leadership Attributes table in section 1, above).

Management skills – What *to do and be*

1. *First serve your apprenticeship out.* It's the experience gained from journeyman work that will inform your first steps as a manager – how you approach others and the actions you might make. You will need very good understanding about the work to be done. Your ability to manage will improve with experience and you can allow your responsibilities to grow as you become used to carrying them. This means, in the early stages, giving yourself time to develop. Mistakes made then will do less damage than mistakes made when you have greater power. Mistakes are OK – it's how we learn.

2. *Be thick skinned.* That does not mean impervious. It is OK to show you are hurt when criticised and pleased when praised. But when you suffer setbacks you should have enough belief in self and energy to pick yourself up and get back on with the work, and you resume progressing your ideas although you may do this differently. Thick skinned does not mean stupid.

3. *Keep proper distance.* You will have responsibility to ensure work quality and individual work loads. You will have a part in firing and hiring. You will have to discipline or redirect colleagues or disappoint them by not backing their pet idea. That can be difficult if you have cultivated cronies. That does not mean you can't party with your colleagues but like a maiden aunt be sure to leave before the party swings. If you have a close friend or life partner among your colleagues be absolutely scrupulous in your dealings with them – ensure these are so open that you are seen to be even-handed.

4. *Communicate well.* Give your team (and others, including the public if necessary) a very clear view of what it is you personally do, why you do it, and how you do it.

5. *Cultivate trust.* Encourage high trust because you always show sound sensitivity, honesty and integrity to others and their issues. You never misuse trust. You show the interpersonal skill and people awareness that makes others want to work for you. You always analyse or criticise self before you do others.

6. *Listen well.* Managers do best when they listen more than they speak. Other people are probably your best source of information. Ensure they know they can have your ear when necessary, and work to ensure you can understand their saying and meaning.

7. *Know what to improve.* Have clear minded and purposeful ideas about what might yet be done better, even if unsure for the moment how it might be done.

8. *Know the law.* Be certain about the legislation that frames the work you do.

9. *Manage Money.* Understand finance well enough to budget, and to manage securely the actual funds for which you are responsible, as well as manage invoice ledger costs if necessary (exchanges of costs internal to your organisation).

10. *Match work to workers.* Use effective assessment formats and procedures so that service user needs and the work necessary is continuously monitored ahead so that staff can be well deployed.

11. *Ensure your recognition.* Make sure your team know your key professional work skills and demonstrate or keep them practiced when suitable opportunities arise. When you have personally achieved something inform them and your line manager.

12. *Know your team.* Show good appreciation of the skills and capacities of colleagues and deploy them so that you get the best from them.

13. *Fair share.* Manage team workloads fairly by appropriate allocations of task. Never show favouritism.

14. *Encourage others.* Ensure there are opportunities for your team to take on responsibility and to find solutions themselves.

15. *Eye on the ball.* Be fluent and solution focused if problems emerge but without any loss of focus on the prime task.

16. *Even tempered.* When errors happen, do not be so angered that your focus centres on who was to blame, but ensure everyone who needs to (including your self) does learn from mistakes.

17. *Efficient.* Use effective monitoring methods for the 'productivity' of your team and individuals within it, and let your line manager know how you are all doing.

18. *Keep stock.* Know about the resources of the organisation you work in including any special skills of line and other senior managers.

19. *Inform and be informed.* Have methods to get information, discuss and review what you do. Regularly collect and interpret data including initiating new data streams when appropriate and provide this up the line in formats that are informative and assist strategic decision making.

20. *Collaborate.* When necessary collaborate well with, or activate, other agencies and community organisations and lead or follow as appropriate when in partnership.

21. *Safety conscious.* Be familiar with and keep to all necessary Health and Safety legislation, and the organisation's policies and procedures that keep your colleagues properly equipped, safe and not overly stressed for long, and that clients' and visitors' safety is never compromised.

22. *Embrace technology.* Be competently knowledgeable about IT (and any other appropriate technologies and use these to full advantage (you need not be personally deft at all skills).

23. *Keep trained.* Know your own development and training needs and be active in pursuit of these.

Leadership skills – How *to do and be*

1. *Enthuse.* Love what you do, and don't be shy about letting it show. Never be shy about speaking with passion. Be infectious. Let your dedication show. This is one of the most effective ways to hearten the commitment of others.

2. *Know yourself well.* Otherwise, you cannot delegate effectively. Achieve the most by concentrating on what you are good at, and play to your strengths. This requires honesty with yourself and with trust of others when you declare your weaknesses. Write down what you think are your strengths and weaknesses and ask a couple of close friends to comment.

3. *Choose people well.* You will not be able to do everything by yourself. When involved in appointments choose people who are not like yourself but will complement your skills or the skills of the other assistants you have. When delegating even small tasks choose the person best fitted and best able to do that task well.

4. *Know your team*. The closer you work with people the more you need to know about them. It helps tremendously to have some idea of their background, personal life and interests. This can allow you insight when they are struggling and need substantial allowance or support for a while, and will help you match tasks to the person with the right personality as well as their more evident skills. It is worth investing in your relationship with colleagues when possible. This is social chat as well as joining for coffee or taking out to lunch. It has to be genuine. Staff must feel you are genuinely interested in them, even if you use your PDA as a memory aid to keep track of birthdays, names of children, and partners etc. You should also do these things for any colleagues you find difficult to appreciate or work with: it is your responsibility to help overcome any personal mindsets that distance others from you.

5. *Pass trust on carefully*. Delegate only to people you know won't let you down. Your job is to select disciples with the combination of personalities and skills to form a powerful team. Delegate with confidence and with a clear brief then relax because the work is in safe hands. Leaders lose trust when they delegate to the wrong people and when they take on or keep something to themselves at which they are ineffective.

6. *Set goals*. Be sure everyone knows what the end result will be. Make the goal clear, achievable, and merit-worthy. People must know what you stand for, what you expect, and why they should follow your lead. The greatest leaders are known because they had clear aims and objectives. Mandela foresaw an Africa free from colonial control. Martin Luther King had a dream of racial equality. Churchill led the fight against Nazi invasion.

7. *Be brave*. Let your integrity show by saying how things really are and be not afraid to tackle important issues openly. Do not hide in an ivory tower, behind colleagues or within the mist of mutter and compromise.

8. *Keep learning*. No one can know it all. Look to how others lead and influence people; look at rivals and younger people particularly. Attend gatherings and conferences of all kinds that relate to the work you do. Learn from the mistakes you and others will make. Never reject an idea just because you do not understand it at first or think it might not work. Nor, of course, because of prejudice.

9. *Always question*. You need to constantly question critically to see if all is on course and it remains the right one. It's about being open minded. Never take things absolutely at face value. Commend people and make progress when you can, and when otherwise question what is going on. It is your job to spot difficulties early and not follow false trails, but to make adjustments and keep progress powerful.

10. *Be decisive*. Wobbling is not leading. Think through proposed actions and how things may change. This can take a while. It is nearly always best to set short achievable steps so that the route can be picked out as you go. Once you decide upon a move stick to it.

11. *Lead by example*. This is the core of respect. People are always more willing to do tasks that leaders have shown they are willing to take on or try to do themselves. (Is this why the strongest visual memory I have, of a highly intellectual and charismatic leader I once worked with, is of him dealing with a WC deliberately blocked with multiple rolls of paper and excrement?).

12. *Know when to leave or move on*. Leadership and managing others everyday is exacting and tiring over the long term, and sometimes new skills are needed. When the leader becomes 'slower' than his followers the whole enterprise can collapse. It is always better to let another take over when new blood will re-enthuse, especially if this is your chosen person. Or, you look around and realise that you are so in your comfort zone that the work is no longer challenging, and you are losing enthusiasm and passion. To continue may damage your self-regard and actual skills as well as be detrimental to the enterprise. Remember how Margaret Thatcher was ousted because she was unaware of her sell-by date.

Knowledge and understanding

No matter where you find yourself on the Leader-Manager spectrum the people who get most things done have additional understanding that allows them to view what they are part of with some kind of 3D or X ray vision. They have an extra overview of what they do. Just as a person who is good at leading and managing has insight and understanding about themselves, the most stable organisations are those that understand their internal working and what they are made of. Their leaders can see into the organisation body and know how the different parts work together. This requires an analytical approach and some theoretical understanding about organisations. Leaders and managers who do well are not only passionate about what they do; they can see beyond the concerns of the moment, and they understand ideas that give them a bigger view on everything. How well they do depends on how well they know the following:

- **Know what to do.** Understand what the prime task is, and how to keep focused on it (this chapter and Chapter 2).
- **Know how to do it**. Be able to understand the enterprise goals and objectives, and sort out the necessary priorities and logistics that get things done (Chapters 2, 4 and 5).
- **Understand yourself and others**. Understand how people can work well together and how the skills and attitudes of themselves and others make the enterprise work (Chapters 3 and 6).

Help with *what you need to know and understand* is provided in the next chapter.

CHAPTER 2

What You Need to Know to Manage Well

1. Know what you do

Prime task

Managers (and the organisation they work in) get judged on *what they do* not on what they say they do. *Does your mission describe your prime task?* With a simple or small enterprise with only a few people, or when high up in a big enterprise the *prime task* probably covers the whole mission. In most cases the enterprise will be sufficiently complex that the things that need to be done are broken down into smaller separate, but interrelated, chunks or tasks (i.e. through team or department work) that all combine to achieve the enterprise purpose. Whatever the setup, your prime task will also usually be composed of a number of goals or objectives all inter-connected in some way.

It may help to view these structures as pyramidal but sectioned according to how your organisation works – either a number of layered horizontal sections of different size, ordered so that each one rests on the next below (*command structure*) or a number of inter-supportive linear cells that radiate down from the top point to cover a section of the base (*co-operative structure*). These structures are not mutually exclusive. A local authority may be seen as a co-operative structure in the way departments such as housing and social services inter-relate, but each specific department will probably rely internally on a command structure.

Progressive and successful organisations work hard to maintain their purpose and prime task by being aware that their culture determines how they do what they do. They work hard to keep the qualities they wish for alive and vibrant. These qualities normally reflect the attributes in the previous chapter that describe effective leaders and managers. This is 'walk the walk' (OK, a tired expression but nonetheless effective). Statements, and catchphrases, and even necessary policies, are not worth the paper if they are meaningless tinsel. They are meaningful and vibrant and alive if they really do describe purpose and method. Mission statements can delight or delude. Check yours out.

If you are new to the enterprise, or a new manager, it is essential you take time to find out exactly what is expected of you, what the issues are, and what resources you have. Draw on the skill and understanding you have from previous experience and see how it fits. Remember this is why you were selected for the post – maybe there are really useful ideas and views that you can offer when you see how. This usually takes time, and the new workload can seem over-much to cope with all at once. Ask your senior manager to suggest how or on whom you can offload some routine work for a while to give you learning space. When dealing with matters do ask others what they would do, or what is normally done. No one will expect you to know everything, and advice will help you to begin to select or reject established methods and so begin to manage more fully.

To check the integrity of your mission or prime task with what is actually achieved you may like to do the Professional Review Activity below.

Professional review

Evaluate how well your team or group understand their prime task in the form of an *audit*. This may be done alone, with a colleague or with a small group. It is very useful to do this activity in conjunction with a senior or supervising colleague, and may also inform you about possible training or development needs. This can be a particularly useful exercise for a new manager as it provides an excellent means to gather a lot of helpful information about the work and your team. You can declare this to be a way you will get a clearer perspective on the work you have joined: and you will have a perfect reason to be excused comment but be able to listen and learn a lot.

The task is simple, but may raise issues that will need further resolution, and it is related to activities that are 'vision forming'.

Professional Review Activity

Use flip charts, sheets, or post-it notes, whatever is suitable in scale for the numbers taking part. Allow over an hour for questions 1–7, and at least thirty minutes for question 8 but not much longer as a first response will usually represent the core understanding: longer time for responses can cause the issues to become fudged.

Consider together the work you do. Ask the questions set out below, and write down the responses.

1. What do you think is the mission or prime task of the organisation you work for? (*If you do have a mission statement, do not refer to it yet.*)
2. What do you think are the work objectives of the project or team or work that you do?
3. What stops you achieving your work objectives, or how might they be achieved better?
4. Are there are setbacks? If so, name them, and state when they occur. What causes the setbacks, and what needs to change?
5. Has there been progress? What are the main areas, and consider what is driving them or making them possible?

Consider together the responses. You must come to a consensus or rough agreement.

6. Can you make generalisations; can you group them into categories? Can you prioritise issues?
7. What comparison is there between 1 and 2?

Write down the key points where there is high and low correlation. Only now, read or display your Mission Statement.

8. What comparison can be made between the responses to questions 1, 2, and 3 and any of the organisation's documentation (policies, plans, statements)? How good is the correlation? Where there is low correlation, can any compromises or differences be explained?

This next stage can be done later, when a suitable opportunity arises, or immediately, if there is urgent need to pass the outcomes upward. Again, write down the responses.

9. When comparing the responses to questions 3–5 above, with any external or fresh viewpoint, (inspection report, view of visiting manager, view of new staff) what differences are there?
10. Can these discrepancies be resolved, and if so how?

Later, there are some possible follow up actions:

- *Audit your resources*; e.g. assess the range of skills and abilities represented within your team. If you are a new manager, you might now set out what you think is the plan for doing things if there is one (BDP), or begin to make a draft plan (see Chapter 1).
- *Analyse by research*; e.g. produce questionnaires for clients and colleagues. Ask colleagues how well they feel clear in their duties and their ability to discharge them satisfactorily. Question the why, when, and how of the work undertaken. This may also include inquiry into things that are not done, but perhaps could be. This sort of analysis can help put dominant factors into perspective, as well as uncover situations that have previously been disregarded.
- *Audit performance*; e.g. go over the past 6–12 months, or begin to table current work in order to assess some aspect of service delivery. This is done by using measurable criteria, such as how many cases have been concluded, at what level of time and cost, at what level of conclusion, etc.
- *Work sampling*; e.g. look into one aspect of how well objectives are met, and by what resources contributed, to see if there is a sensible correlation between resources and task. This may produce better information, for example, a detailed list of expertise among colleagues. Sampling by case study will analyse in detail the processing and experience of a typical client and the information obtained can be extrapolated.

Getting to the core of problems when they emerge can require great sensitivity and require mediation skills and professional distance in order not to be collusive. An example from my own experience – although not with manager responsibility here – concerned my advocacy work for young people.

Example: Getting to the core problem
    In a particular secure unit, I began to receive increasing complaints from my young clients that restraints were too readily used or led to injury. The measure of this was such that I later found that the Social Services Inspectorate had noted similar concern.
    My discussions with staff revealed their view that the Home Office purchase of beds for child offenders, alongside children with social needs, meant that the mix of young people at that time was particularly difficult to manage, and the staff felt disregarded as

they were without any say regarding new admissions. They were concerned to ensure young people with histories of self-harm and aggression were sufficiently supervised and controlled, so that no incident, or inter-personal difficulty, got out of hand.

I moved from simple empathy with the young people caught in an insensitive environment, to recognising the degree of counter-transference between two sets of people, both 'captive' and facing the same fears and uncertainties about control and safety in the other set. The underlying adult issues I raised included staff training needs, the number and inexperience of staff at particular times, and a lack of therapeutic supervision in a regime subject to the methodologies needed to maintain safety, as well as obtain the trust needed for effective intervention work.

2. Know how well you do it

Once you are sure about what you should be doing, it is worth checking occasionally to see *how well you are doing it*. There are some different ways this can be done, and it is essential to understand how things done inside the enterprise impact on those whom it serves.

Obviously one check for public services is the inspection procedures that will be applied however the service is provided (LA, commercial, or voluntary sector). Also quality awards such as *The Investors in People Award* scheme and ISO 9000 can help establish the quality of an enterprise. Although experience suggests that there is some variability in how consistently reliable those awards are, they do reflect TQM principles such as effective systems for gathering information, and practice that affirms and values employee development.

There is a simple TQM approach for checking how well the prime task is done, although putting it into action might not be straightforward if you do not yet have reliable systems for gathering information. The approach is based on TQM principles or assumptions: these are:

1. Customers or clients are known as the *external market*.
   Your organisation is focused on doing an excellent job, and you take pride in this. The only valid way of knowing that, is that the people who need you are well pleased. You call the scale for this *customer satisfaction* (whether your 'customers' are clients or service users, or whatever).

2. You *measure* or test how well you do what you do (you check out customer satisfaction and track and compare the different costs of the work) and you collect the data. You use information from this so you know what to focus on next to make doing things better (you set new targets).

3. You do this because you believe what you do can always be *improved* in some way (e.g. worker or client satisfaction, less costly, more quickly or other additional quality).

4. The enterprise has an *internal market*. The different parts of your organisation only work well together when they are mutually supportive. Enterprises that are effective understand that their internal market must also receive high quality service.

I guess that items 1 to 3 above are immediately understandable, but item 4 less so. In the case of complex enterprises the mission or prime task is broken down into different things to be done. In these situations some of the work you do or information you have will almost certainly be used to support the work of others within your larger organisation, and similarly they for you. This requirement for service within the organisation is called the internal market. How well it is provided you could think of as the degree of mutuality, or *work integration*. When this is poor, it can be a great cause of internal dissent and can drag an enterprise down; more often, poor help to each other is just one of the many ways working together is actually just frustrating at times. But if it is tolerated it will have a cost.

Example: Poor internal service (logistical objective – see below)
   Sheila is an examinations administrator in a large FE college with satellite units. In the lists that lecturers send her of examination entries she frequently finds instances when students are not on her database. This is because the students were never properly enrolled when they signed up for a course despite the fact that the college is partly funded by enrolment numbers. The student records office blames lecturers; lecturers say

they did the paperwork, student records are to blame.

Whatever the source of the problem Sheila has to resolve the issues and align the records at the expense of her proper work, she has raised the problem several times with her senior management but the poor practice and her frustration continues.

The point here is that the better the mutual support, the better is the effectiveness of the whole enterprise. We think of soldiers, not cooks, when armies come to mind, although we have the cliché that an army marches on its stomach. This suggests we do intuitively understand that how well an enterprise 'manages' its endeavour does depend on all team members doing their part. In a sense you provide a service directly to your team. How well you manage and work for your team so that they can get on effectively and without frustration is the measure of that service. Thinking this way aligns you more towards seeing your job as a facilitator rather than a director.

A key feature of enterprises that function well is that they have a very clear focus on identifying client needs (very TQM). This usually means that both the internal and external markets rely on good data:

- Data is used analytically and expertly. The information is used to drive measures in solution-focused ways to redress concerns or create additional qualities to the service and its results.
- Data is seen as evidence of need and as a direction point for change, and not as material to justify blame.

The key feature of enterprises that are embracing complexity and undergoing business process re-engineering (BPR) is they have *flattened hierarchies* supported by effective communication. The flattened hierarchy means that high levels of mutuality are only obtained when the people within them really care and think about what they are doing. It is this quality of persons that makes it all work, and not an imposed system or rigid structure. BPR fluidity is obtained by:

- Initiatives and temporary responsibilities shared across the establishment.
- Junior colleagues are encouraged to be involved in high impact undertakings.

- Flexible teams – responsibilities are jointly assumed and independent of position, seniority, or rigid line structure.
- Responsibilities taken up by those best fitted to the task, using criteria such as enthusiasm as well as knowledge and skill, and not according to hierarchical position.
- Senior and middle managers believe an important part of their function is to support, encourage and develop junior colleagues.

Rigid Managerialism v. BPR Activity

This exercise compares manager instruction with team cooperation.

Clear and mark out a suitable rectangular space (a large carpet is ideal).

1. Appoint a manager.
2. The manager directs everyone onto a spot within the space so that they each connect with one or more other persons by touching hands or feet. The manager directs them so that the space is equally covered by people. *Time this*.
3. The manager introduces a ball into one corner. The ball must be passed from one touching person to the next but only as the manager directs until it emerges at the opposite corner. *Time this. Ask everyone how they enjoyed it?* (Sit and boo if no fun: stand silent, cross armed if middling; jump and shout with arms up if enjoyed). A possible extension is to ask a volunteer manager if they can direct a quicker route across.

Then . . .

1. Tell everyone to find a spot on the carpet themselves so that the space is fully covered and to touch by hand or feet one or more persons. *Time this*.
2. Introduce a ball at one corner with the challenge to see how quickly they can pass it to the opposite corner only through touching persons. *Time this. Ask everyone how they enjoyed it?* (as above). A possible extension is that they do it again, to and from random points, to see if they can beat the last timing.

When mutual support is effective it tends to be taken for granted as it is not seen. This is true particularly in little ways: for example, how a PA or other office staff might ensure there is conveniently always a few stamps and envelopes in your drawer because they know you work late at times.

Problems emerge when mutuality breaks down. The issues can be serious to the work sections concerned and the atmosphere can become very heated. Efforts to resolve problems may mean unions or professional associations become involved. This is particularly the case when teams who have strong pride and belief in what they do face unexpected criticism that their practice does not sufficiently support the enterprise.

It is then a good idea to review clearly how teams or practices are working so that the whole range of work done can be evaluated before tackling any issues. But first determine exactly what it is that your team is supposed to do: remember, objectives follow prime task.

Understanding goals and objectives

A common model for service organisations has three main objectives. How well the prime task is achieved will depend on how well the three objectives hang together (are mutual). The following model may need a little interpretation to apply to your particular work, but when the specifics of any one organisation are stripped out the generalised model looks like this:

Service objectives

Service objectives are linked most directly to the prime task and the aim is high-quality end results. How to achieve good results is often well understood in most organisations, but high-quality high-value enterprises are those that *keep on* doing well. The difference between these services and the 'also-rans' is that the also-rans seem not to understand or be able to maintain the need to keep inputting effort and resources in order to retain high-quality end results. In this context, service objectives concern how *consistent* prime task outcomes can be maintained. No matter how specific service objectives might be itemised for your enterprise, the following examples illustrate common factors that help maintain consistent results:

- Skilled and effective employees at all levels, and other resources as appropriate, are maintained so that there are sufficient persons with the right skills, or no waiting for or rationing of materials (i.e. always one spare Zimmer frame). *Client needs are consistently met.*

- Systems and manager attitudes encourage employees to develop their skills and act independently and out of role when appropriate to maintain seamless service quality (i.e. the bursar lays tables). *Clients never see any gaps.*
- An appropriate work environment is maintained so that energies are not diverted away from prime task (sufficient space and resources, administration support, technology, clean tidy offices, good relationships with colleagues, etc.). What is undertaken is done as promised – all interactions are personalised and based on valuing individual people within and without. *Clients keep their trust.*

Example: A service undertaking the care of adults with significant learning difficulties included the following operational objectives:
- Individual client needs are fully assessed and staff are sensitive to individual needs, and understand and contribute towards care plans.
- Skilled care or intervention when needed is immediately available to clients.
- Clients are encouraged to make independent choices; staff establish secure boundaries around clients and know how to extend these appropriately.
- An appropriately safe environment is maintained by staff who will keep to approved work routines and expected practices.

Impact objectives

Impact objectives are the straightforward results or outcomes of the work as it is perceived or experienced right now. How well is the prime task being done? The following examples illustrate common ways that impact objectives are framed:

- Customers or clients (service users) and the local community or service user group are at least sufficiently satisfied but ideally delighted. *The public speak highly of the service.*
- Formal inspection criteria are met or ideally surpassed. *Inspection reports positively validate the work.*
- Independent or professional association awards, and special designation or recognition (e.g. a teaching hospital). *Recognition or*

acknowledgment of quality is granted by other professionals.

- Comparative audits, such as unit or service costs, or case throughput, show that your service gives good value for money. *The service is measurably good.*
- People are changed by membership of the enterprise because there is a culture of improvement and service value. There is strong organisational response to new materials and technology and the developing moral and ethical codes associated with the work. The culture encourages everyone to seek and share ideas and information, to trust and inspire each other, and to be confident. *The enterprise culture drives service development and service quality.*

Example: A residential care service had the following impact objectives:
- Clients are very satisfied and they strongly believe their placement is the best for them.
- People in crisis recover – clients make tangible personal progress and develop healthy self autonomy.
- The company will maintain a list of standards, independent regulators, and organisations that offer only approved membership.
- The company will aim for profitability to benefit the quality of service first and shareholders second.
- The company will meet or exceed all national training targets for personnel.

Logistical objectives

Logistical objectives are the actions that ensure service and impact objectives; these mainly impact in the first instance on enterprise members. The actions include:

- Training investment ensures everyone is kept abreast of industry developments and ways that recognise client or customer views, and that needs may change or be better met by new methods. *Workers are consistently satisfied and proud to be part. Service user groups consult the enterprise as beacon exemplar.*
- The worker base is supported by effective recruitment and ongoing monitoring. Technical competence alone does not guarantee a worker is valued. Chances are high that the new employees most valued are also sociable people with a passion for the work and a keen

interest in self-development (also known as 'People Like Us'). All staff are properly trained and deployed, and there are effective procedures for selection, induction, monitoring and appraisal, and pay, conditions, and additional rewards. And these things compare well with similar organisations. *Employees feel special and valued.*

- The work culture is highly responsive, and there is a reflective ethos. Systems and procedures are efficient, and sensitive to possible conflicts of need, or change to service requirement. New methods are embraced and evaluated open-mindedly, and not automatically resisted or pre-judged. *The enterprise can evolve quickly when necessary.*
- Specific resources are obtained, made available, and maintained. The managers that head key sections within the enterprise are all excellent communicators and mutually compatible persons. The most universally common section with key logistics impact is financial management: other examples are; transport, training, and personnel. *The work never stops for lack of a nut and bolt or a clean towel.*

Example: A company providing residential rehabilitation had the following logistic objectives:
- New staff will be properly inducted – all staff will consistently keep to the operational arrangements that maintain resources (list of policies such as Use of Vehicles, Health and Safety, Off Site Procedures, etc.).
- Admission procedures are sensitive to possible conflict of client need – the process of selecting clients, the social mix, and individual progress from site to site, and through stage to stage, is always given due consideration.
- Resources are available and maintained – company budget holders maintain fiscal control and may expect support from the practice of colleagues (careful purchases and minimal wastage).

Most managers of course have responsibilities across these different objectives and will be working to a BDP that contains these objectives in ways that may be difficult to separate out into the parts I have modelled.

It can be that you are not clear on exactly what you are supposed to be doing, and not sure how to do what you think you should be doing. Lots

Objectives Review Activity

Allow only a few minutes each for items 1 and 2. Items 3 and 4 will take longer and may lead to some further research or inquiry before they can be resolved. Remember:

- In an exercise of this kind it is the discussion and debate that is worthwhile. How issues may be resolved is too variable to generalise about usefully except there will some compromise. Work with it.
- It is the mark of effective teamwork that members continue to contribute their best within the compromise.
- The mark of over-compromise or poor resolution is when individuals cannot sufficiently commit during the exercise or will otherwise 'vote with their feet' later and ignore any ensuing agreements or directives.
- Poor resolution or later problems are most usually because of dominance by an individual or small clique within the group and no one challenges this. Or is there collusion in some form?

The activity work sheets below are set out for service objectives. Make the sheets the size you want. If you wish to collate team thoughts on a flip chart, do it individually first, to avoid contagion of view.

The exercise may then be undertaken at some point for Impact and for Logistical Objectives, using the same format with appropriate change to the task headings.

1. Describe my/our prime task or service objectives in as few sentences or bullets as possible:
➢ . . .
➢ . . .
➢ . . .

2. How do I/we impact on our service objectives?
Complete the statements given:
  I. *We are best at:*
    This assists service objectives because . . .
  II. *We are worst at:*
    This detracts from service objectives because . . .
 III. *We could improve:*
    We will do this by . . .

3. Discuss and compare findings of exercise 1 and 2.
Reach the shared or joint conclusion as quickly as possible. Don't quibble over small detail. List agreed items. List any disagreed items. Resolve issues.

If this cannot be done easily, or there is sufficient disagreement to prevent an equitable resolution, agree to disagree for the moment.

This indicates the need to re-establish clear team purpose and is best done later to give chance for some thinking or for information to be researched.

4. Conclusion. Finalise in tidy language the service objectives for this particular team:
My/our enterprise service objectives are/purpose is:
➢ . . .
➢ . . .
➢ . . .

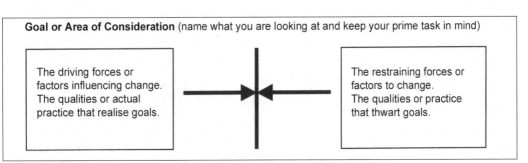

Figure 2.1 Force Field Analysis Activity

of enterprises muddle along in a bit of a hit-and-miss way. They are maybe not the best to work in but that's reality. It may also be that the three objectives do not seem to hang together well for you. Perhaps you feel other parts of the enterprise are frustrating your part in the work. And whatever the grander plan might be or be not, it's 8.30 a.m. and there's a days work to be done.

The main job, particularly for middle managers, is making sure everything works each day – the jargon is *ensuring daily operational matters are resolved in order to maintain service quality*. You might think of this as operational pressure, and sometimes . . .

- Prime task gets lost in the daily weight of matters. (The *Objectives Review Activity* is designed to help with this.).
- Knowing who you are gets forgotten. There is help with this below in section 3 on management lore.
- All that happens is fixing problems. You are a manager; that's what you're paid to do!

**If you are adrift,
put your hand on the helm!**

It is essential from time to time that you do step back from daily tasks and check out how well prime objectives are met however loosely these are set out – maybe even use this time to get a better fix on them.

Think how formal inspections do impact upon organisations that have let their practice slip in some manner without realising this. Effective inspection in these situations challenges the complacent and will often bring viewpoints up short – sometimes brutally. The *Objectives Review Activity* set out on page 26 will assist you to frame your objectives.

The activity can be just you, but is best done with a group of people. This may be your work team or a team of managers with different responsibilities brought together according to the necessary focus. The exercise is also very useful for training purposes and if used that way better in time put aside rather than during a routine staff or business meeting. The process may benefit from being led by a guest facilitator.

Analyse and review

One of the simplest ways to review how the work is being done is by *Force Field Analysis* as

illustrated by Fig. 2.1. This method can be used to screen the whole staffing establishment, or teams, or even individuals within the organisation. It is used to review the quality of their work or to look for possible pitfalls in planned developments. Simply use the headings given to frame thoughts and conclusions.

Hannibal's elephants kept going because the fodder foragers were good. To know what the fodder requirement is at any one time is the stuff of data. The *Data Streams Activity* Fig. 2.2 on page 29 will allow you to see:

- If your work is done well enough.
- What information (data streams) you have that tell you this.
- Where information sources *or* the actual work done might be improved.

The flow diagram as given can be used in two ways:

1. Using the list obtained at the Start Point apply the rest of the flow diagram to the overall situation in order to evaluate the 'big picture'.
2. For each item on the Start Point list, apply the flow diagram separately to evaluate the discrete detail.

When making your list at the Start Point, some examples might be:

- Service questionnaires.
- Numbers of complaints.
- Service costs per session or piece of client work.
- Incident reports.
- Fuel bills etc., according to what is being evaluated.

3. Understand management lore

I believe it is really helpful to have intellectual ideas such as that about objectives above. These ideas do offer a perspective on how you do the managing part of your work – the way you get things done. This normally means the way you work with and understand other people. I guess you may be thinking, emotional intelligence? Partly yes, and there is a section later, on this theme. This part is more about managementality, or the *lore* or ways of management that help managers understand the generic aspects of their work, and helps them talk to each other even

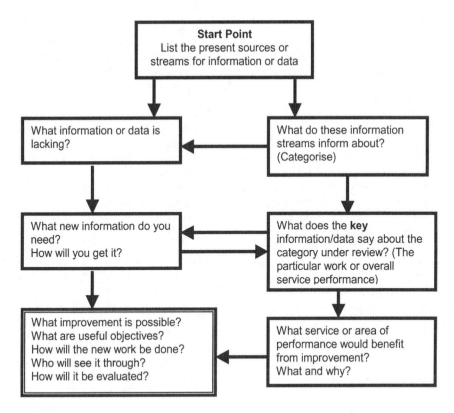

Figure 2.2 Data Streams Activity

though they may well not understand each other's service or industry. The lore always has some ideas that go in and out of fashion.

The following lore comprises key ideas of value, because, I think, they stand the test of usefulness and are not faddy. In sequence each has a key connection with the next.

Explicit and tacit knowledge

One issue that is always being raised is whether managers should be technically expert professionals (specifically skilled) or managerial professionals (generically skilled). The theory that differentiates these skills is called *explicit and tacit forms of knowledge.*

The argument of many workers is that the best managers are those who are time served, have done the work on the shop floor, and intimately understand what the work is all about. The argument of managers is that managing is an expertise of its own with its own special skills. This is why universities have business management schools. These managers believe experience and understanding gained from

managing a range of enterprises equips them well and helps develop the open-mindedness and inventiveness necessary to manage any enterprise well.

It is not an argument worth resolving as both skills can be equally valuable. And there are outstanding and very poor managers from both camps. The best manager, in any one situation, will have a balance, according to the needs of their job, between the two extremes; or when initially this is not the case, they can learn fast, and are not embarrassed to declare what they do not know or understand. I look at my career and see that my management skills began in tacit form until a crisis caused them to evolve rapidly, and they have since grown exponentially in explicit form. The wider are your experiences the more likely your explicit skills will develop most as these are much less specific to one particular form of work.

Tacit knowledge

Tacit knowledge is individual experience tied up in people's heads rather than readily found in a reference source or database. It is rooted in individual action, commitment and involvement; it is usually expressed by anecdote ('did I tell you about . . .') and consequently tacit knowledge is specific or *context tied*.

Managers have tacit knowledge in the relationships they have with colleagues and clients, and by their familiarity with their particular workplace or service, and the adjustments they personally make or orchestrate such as change to personal methodology and manner of working in order to provide quality service. Managers with high tacit knowledge are most likely long-stayed or have come up to management through the ranks.

- Tacit knowledge is locally specific, the depth of 'lore' and degree of expertise may be highly valuable but not easily transferable and of limited benefit away from the particular workplace.
- The manager motivates colleagues through relationships (good or poor quality) and high inter-personal activity (examples are 'first to the bar' and knowing names of colleagues' wives/partners/children).
- Examples of tacit knowledge include knowing:
  o Who best to ask to organise an office or team function.
  o How to get a rapid response from a crony in a support organisation.
  o Where the spare set of minibus keys are kept.

Explicit knowledge

Explicit knowledge is formulaic generalised knowledge that can be reproduced and is represented by all information media ('you do that like this . . .'). It is rooted in analysis, formal verbal and written language and modes of representation, and is *context related*.

Managers have explicit knowledge in their theoretical command over the work and the degree they are well read or informed and can theorise about what they do. This book supports explicit knowledge. Managers with good levels of explicit knowledge understand and can explain how their work relates to external issues and developments. Managers who have high levels of explicit knowledge are most likely to be career managers who are chosen from outside, are short-stayed, and have a management qualification.

- Explicit knowledge is transportable because the skills are relevant to many other organisations.
- The manager motivates by use of effective systems that provide support (examples are budgets and well protected supervision), and by fair appraisal, acknowledgement and reward (personal performance reviews).
- Examples of explicit knowledge include knowing:
  o What to do when there is work beyond the team expertise.
  o How to negotiate the protocols for work with a support organisation.
  o Where it is normally best to put a spare set of minibus keys.

You will do well to know how your skills balance out, and how they have come to put you into whatever manager post you have. And, importantly, managers work best when they have insight into the balance represented across the people they are involved with, both within the team, and without. They know the skills held among other managers above and across the organisation as well as those held among the people they directly manage. This is particularly required when decisions are needed concerning delegation or deployment and there are very key or sensitive issues of skill to be considered. You can do a simple exercise like the next activity, *Forms of Knowledge*, to help evaluate that skill balance.

It is essential that managers occasionally practice *self-appraisal*. Managers who fail usually do so because they have lost the ability to be self-aware, and not because they are lazy or incompetent. Managers under pressure tend to work harder. When you begin to burn the candle at both ends it will shine brightly for a while but soon burn out. You will lose energy and perspective. Just at the time you think you least need to do it is probably the time you most certainly should review your performance and effectiveness. It is not an idle task to fill a quiet moment.

The starting point is to get to hand two essential bits of information. The first is whatever you have that sets out your mission or prime task or BDP or whatever describes 'What is to be done'. This is likely to be a document common to everyone. The second is private to you – your job description. You then determine the validity between your current job description and the work to be done. In the same manner you can

Forms of Knowledge Activity

First, some work must be done so that those involved have a working understanding about tacit and explicit knowledge. The evaluation sheet shown can then be used in several ways:

- Solo: the person evaluates themselves.
- In pairs, each is given two copies of the analysis sheet and each evaluates their partner and themself, then compare.
- In teams, as above, with the group evaluating one member at a time.

Forms of knowledge analysis

Name: . . . .   by self/by: . . . .

1. List with a bullet type note the main knowledge attributes that can be ascribed to yourself/the other person by evidence of what you/they actually say or do – put these on one side or other of the central divide.
2. Consider how the items listed compare one with another in degree of expertise and complete the line balance (see 3).

Examples of tacit knowledge	**Examples of explicit knowledge**

(The sheet in this example is foreshortened)

|

10 9 8 7 6 5 4 3 2 1 0 1 2 3 4 5 6 7 8 9 10

3. Balance: evaluate the strength of each form of knowledge from 1–10. Represent this by a line drawn underneath each remark outwards starting from the centre position as 0. This exercise provides a visual indication of relative strengths. It is better reproduced with the items rewritten in order of descending value. The addition of each side and comparing the two totals is another interesting, if a rather rough way, to see how well an individual has balance or a particular leaning.

---

review the work of a colleague for whom you have responsibility.

The reason for this is that as people become engaged within their work they take on different and new aspects that are often not what they were originally employed to do. There is nothing inherently wrong with this. The roles people take on help groom and support the organisation they are part of. But they can lead people away from what they are supposed to be doing. It is again a matter of balance. The necessary understanding is recognising the difference between roles as informal appendages that grow and the core function that the original job description intended.

Roles and functions

Problems emerge when people become overburdened and this strains their ability to discharge their prime tasks, or may prompt disloyalty. The danger is that once an appointment is made that is the last time the appointee and their manager look at the job description. Manage people by keeping their job descriptions at the top of your filing cabinet. One worthwhile check especially if a new manager, or when economies have to be made, is to look at the mission or team task afresh and deconstruct and evaluate the actual jobs that need to be done and construct a 'virtual team' with which you can compare your actual team.

Problems also creep up because tasks are for some reason taken away from the people who should be doing them and done by others – this can make muddles or cause tensions, for example, when a competent colleague informally takes on a task properly the responsibility of their senior. The senior loses control and access to information, and colleagues may resent the arrangement. There is nothing wrong with changing job descriptions when this is fairly negotiated. Organisational change often requires a review of the work done by different people (more on this in Chapter 5). Just make sure that you manage it rather than that it manages you!

The *Roles and Functions Activity* sheet is used to discriminate between roles and functions. The sheet can be used at manager level or as part of the review process for junior colleagues, and like the *Forms of Knowledge Activity* can be done solo, as a pair, or in a group. It will of course particularly illustrate occasions when a person has work that has strayed or developed far from what they were originally employed to do. In this context realignment might be part of performance appraisal that leads to a new job description and a pay review (see also Chapter 4; *Work Security*).

Roles and Functions Activity

Write down the task or jobs you do, starting with the work that occupies or concerns you most. Decide which side of the line to enter the item.

Function: as given by job description or an uncontroversial task or responsibility.

Role: things done because you are best or only person, or told to do it.

When completed consider the balance and should anything change.

ROLES

*This example is foreshortened.
I like a diagonal line but it
doesn't matter how the
paper is divided*

FUNCTIONS

An essential quality check from time to time is to see if the enterprise is doing what it set out to do. Therefore it is important to keep a check on events and how the work is perceived, so that the personal or internal models of yourself and your enterprise match the way the external world actually impacts. You have to do this honestly. When managers try to manipulate the public view to show the enterprise in a better than real light, they risk being charged with 'spin'. Never risk public, service user, or member cynicism as it is a taint that is hard to remove. Remember, for example, how everyone now knows about the practice of seeking the 'good' days on which to bury 'bad' news!

But there is nothing wrong with public relation jollies to draw attention to enterprise success; and nothing wrong with being clear and loud about enterprise purpose and ambitions. Just make sure

you do not overreach yourself. Far better to announce that the enterprise has done better than hoped than have to explain why it has achieved less. The practice that helps ensure you are not caught with your pants down is to evaluate the *Claims Gap*. This is a bit like looking at roles and functions but in the context of the whole enterprise.

The claims gap

Service organisations in particular make claims or aspire to qualities that they do not always fully realise. Practice seldom exactly follows written policy, and ethos may not exactly match the mission as stated. It may vary locally from shift to shift and between different teams doing the same work, or prevail more widely. How well people work together, and how closely the qualities are shared that drive their mutuality directs the way service users are treated. The culture you are actually part of compared to what is claimed is a 'gap'. The 'gap' also lies between the enterprise aspirations and achievements – the difference between enterprise intentions and the actual experience of service users. All organisations make claims or aspire to qualities they do not fully realise, and the gap is not overly significant unless it so widens that it is questioned by dissatisfied service users or organisation members (not TQM).

The public claims and aspirations of enterprises are sometimes called 'espoused theory', whereas actual practice and associated individual beliefs is called 'theory in use' (after Mabey and Salaman, 1995). The degree of gap between the ideal and the actual situation reflects how well managers can deconstruct their own beliefs and mental models and show confidence and ability to think analytically and self-critically about what they do. This means a manager can see how the inter-relationships, systems and processes underpin the way the enterprise works, rather than that they might simply point to discrete events as evidence. Understanding the distinction between espoused theory and theory in use is an essential first vantage point to help managers think critically and to probe behind things on the surface and beyond immediate causes.

The feminist or ethnic case for better recognition and work equality in the 1990s included some Fire and Police services, and the military services. Some notorious matters were challenged, and exposed, within a number of organisations. Their need to encompass modern values and equal opportunities became the subject of investigative and undercover reporting for television and the press.

Claims Gap Activity

A quick check to see what 'gap' you may have can be done by reviewing, absolutely and honestly a period (perhaps the last 3–6 months), to obtain the following information:

- List the events or outcomes that fell short of what you (or your colleagues) normally achieve.
- List things you or your colleagues (or enterprise documents) claim in your dialogue with outside professionals, senior managers, or the public if relevant, *but* which you actually feel uncertain or uneasy or a bit untruthful about.
- List the occasions you or your colleagues failed to do as promised for a client or customer (including internally – the internal market).

Don't be too hard on yourself if you have an embarrassing list. Most people and enterprises that show high hopes and willing work do fall short to some degree: it's the size of the gap, and where it occurs, that matters. Again, it's a question of balance. Did you fall short because of hopes that were unrealistic (poor information?) or because of effort that was inadequate for some reason? Did the gap impact upon clients, or upon colleagues, or finances?

If the gap is unacceptable do one or more of the following:

- Review practice by formal and probing audit: and armed with clear and better information make necessary changes.
- Challenge complacency and any organisational inertia.
- Make generalisations from specific events so that you can:
  o Feel informed about the operational ability of colleagues or teams.
  o Judge the usefulness of systems.
  o Decide if particular practice is maintained, or altered, or better supported, or other intervention.
- Consider a conference or training to re-affirm the wider organisational intent so that this is:
  o Better shared.
  o More clearly understood.
  o More highly valued by colleagues/your team.

There is a connection, or integration, between all that has been covered so far, with how the enterprise finds its course. Enterprises sometimes make directional shifts: that's OK, if there are people at the helm and it is a decided course; not OK, if it represents blind drift, and suddenly the enterprise flounders.

Organisational cultures

Ultimately it is the people within them that shape organisations, and the individual personality of strong leaders and managers can become bound up in the way the organisation presents itself. The two may become intricately one. Management theory is used to describe why differences in organisation exist. It is essential that managers have sufficient appreciation of the culture they are part of, not only so they may be effective within it – which supposes the manager is happy within that culture – but also so that the manager can recognise developments and changes from within or pressures from without that may strengthen or threaten the organisation. One theory suggests four main types of culture (after G Jones, Henley Management College): these carry no comparative evaluation, but they do each serve different organisational purposes and involve quite different styles of doing things.

1. Communal culture

Communal cultures attract people who are passionate, creative and liberal. They are egalitarian and may support people who are not contributing, but equally, someone who wishes to lead strongly will be resisted. This culture may have a philosophy that is valued above achievement. It will usually have humanitarian aims, and may carry on with a mission even in considerable adversity. Some of the experimental communities that began to arise in the 1930s and of which few now remain might fit here (e.g. The Findhorn Community) as do co-operative ventures, and contemporary environmental and 'eco' organisations. Communal cultures can be defensive when their beliefs are challenged, and individuals may be sacrificed for the common good, although they will be missed and anguished over.

2. Networked culture

A networked culture is informal and flexible. People value helpfulness and trust, but usually have a weather eye open for new winds. Position and work is dependent on keeping a high profile contact with others. Some very modern commercial organisations are most like this, typically so also are consultancy groups, geographically dispersed organisations like a group of professional services, and some charitable institutions. Senior officers within local and national government departments can interact like this when multi-agency work is well developed. An individual who does not fit will be quietly ostracised rather than attacked.

3. Fragmented culture

The fragmented culture is normally not well represented by organisational structure. This culture may only exist to serve the interest of the one or two high-flyers who try to retain control. Those people who do well attract others as well as resources, but are frightened of losing their position; this encourages selfishness, and a pecking order mentality. Some research organisations are like this, as well as training and academic accreditation systems based on competing agencies. Individuals may use aggressive tactics to maintain their position, but these will be covert to disguise their true nature or intent.

4. Mercenary culture

A mercenary culture is most concerned about money or dominance. It is based on measurable outcomes of product or throughput. It will measure these obsessively, and parade standards and performance schedules. The work will be task-orientated and competitive. Dissenting views are not tolerated and people have to work together as expected to maintain results, rather than for any benefit of co-operation or inquiry. Yardsticks are used so that employees or divisions may be measured, and poor performers are castigated or cast out. The culture is characterised by the expectation that constituent parts will be self-financing. Ironically the most typical organisations include many of the varied but 'commercial' inspection and accreditation organisations that range across education, care, and other services: these have arisen over the past 10–15 years in response to government desires for performance reports – and a number of these only have existence while they can win government contracts (i.e. OfSTED education inspection teams).

Matching the culture to the manager

Problems arise when people do not recognise the features of the culture they are interacting with or are part of. Good observation, analysis, and maybe some intuition can guide judgement about the underlying pathology; all of this relies on adequate information. Consequently, most people are wary to some degree about new positions, and it is not uncommon for a manager to be seduced by surface style to join an organisation only to feel themselves then to be within a dysfunctional situation, because there is a mismatch between the organisational culture and their personal beliefs (a recent TV police drama, *Life on Mars*, has a running plot based on this phenomenon).

The importance of judgement in new situations is because people react when they become caught up in a system that is not working well, or they feel they have been duped into making a commitment that they find does not suit them. This is as true for employees as clients. Although the biggest area of worker risk is when they take up a new post, difficulties may well be greater if they only emerge some way into a commitment. Much of what you might observe on a first visit may be superficial, but determines what it might indicate. Equally, at a more subconscious level, your intuition will be working: learn to tap into it.

There are a number of considerations that can help guide decisions about committing to new organisations and new places, and help you to avoid the possibility of later disappointment. The surface style is still the best indicator of enterprise culture, and is seen in the people and their interpersonal style. Does the present manager have a Mutt and Jeff routine with his deputy? Is your reception flustered, or off-hand and not properly catered for? Is all the paper work ready? What can you judge from the quality of obvious features such as routines and furnishings? What would you wish for that is absent? Does everybody have a pleasant demeanour, and does this seem to be normal, or do you feel there is best behaviour on show, or worse, a crack-papering cover-up?

Similarly 'visit' your own place of work, and imagine how it may appear to visiting clients or other professionals. How are visitors treated by your colleagues: are they shown the cloakroom and offered refreshment? Do people say hello and offer a smile, or duck and shoot by? Are the women, or the men, fully integrated, or is there an apparent divide due to service and role differences, or perhaps resulting from more subtle and less defensible reasons?

How are others treated by your organisation? What seems to be important, process or product? Do performance measures such as targets, rates, and costs seem more important than the people they concern?

What is the staff view? How do they see the quality of features such as head office support, training, staff turnover, resources? Are staffing levels appropriate and are there arrangements to deal with times when there is crisis or conflict? Do they find line supervision clear and working satisfactorily?

Are your facilities cared for, are notices all current? Is there a consistent standard, or a difference between accommodation provided for residents or clients, for staff, and for the manager?

Truly effective and healthy organisations will not usually be let down or be dominated by one component. Everyone will appear happy in the part they play and all will share a common understanding that shapes efficiency, approach, and purpose, even allowing for different styles and personalities. There is balance and proportion. For example, successes are properly accredited and celebrated, and one failure is not unduly damned.

Managers should keep an eye open to see if everything about their organisation seems well integrated: this usually goes hand-in-hand with quality. There will be just appraisal for all employees and ways of quietly checking that workers, and clients, are satisfied. If there are very dominant features, are they healthy? Many organisations work well because of strong or charismatic leadership, but such regimes do not suit everybody or necessarily provide the best services. Equally, most enterprises that fail do so from the top down.

Directional shift – compass bearing

This idea links directly to the issues already explored concerning mission and goals, and is useful as it recognises the tension between simply doing the job for the service end results and doing the job because it's an enjoyable or worthwhile journey. The idea is best illustrated by the arrow diagram shown below.

Effective results are the measurable outcomes of the prime task. The arrow reflects the pressure to 'travel vertically' towards performance targets. The service will compare well on indicators for the amount of work done. Effective results are the stuff of bean counters and are usually achieved by high levels of knowledge and technical competence. The features that typify effectiveness are a fixed ethos, and a well regimented structure focused on outcomes that are seen as a product, whatever the type of enterprise.

Affective impact is the 'horizontal', emotional, outcomes associated with the individual, and possibly immeasurable, benefits of the endeavour. These outcomes are the 'softer qualities' experienced by customers or employees, such as:

- Feeling valued.
- Having a sense of belonging.
- What it feels like from having contact with, or being within, the organisation.

Affective outcomes are usually the result of belief or attitude, passion and inspiration; and are changes produced in belief, person or system by the process.

Of course, in the metaphor of the arrow or compass most enterprises travel simultaneously in both the horizontal and vertical directions. As a manager, it is up to you to keep this appropriately balanced. Bean counter managers will tend to resist too much affective direction as it is costly or will reduce measurable effectiveness.

To illustrate by using an extreme, the comfort and working conditions for the employees cannot be so luxurious or undemanding that too little work gets done. Or, more realistically, the numbers of meals delivered by a meals service becomes more important than how fresh and tasty these are, or there being no time for a bit of chat at the point of delivery. The chat may be valued by some service users even more than the actual meal.

The compass bearing will be picked up by activities like the 'objectives review' (above) and once you are aware of this idea, the compass bearing can become a matter of constant relevance and be seen as 'bearing' on all sorts of work undertakings. There are some easy ways to check out what is happening with enterprise direction in this context, by monitoring the exchanges between people and what their priorities are; examples include:

- How do front line colleagues regard and report on what they do – is this couched in terms related to effective outcomes or affective impact? Do they raise issues about clients beyond the immediate service remit?
- Do individual colleagues, or your team, have strong 'ownership'? Do they resist letting others work with their clients in case the work is not done as well as they wish? Or, by other actions or concerns, do they routinely do more than the bare prime task?
- By more formal evaluation: typically by use of a Force Field Analysis (see Analyse and Review above). Use each or either of Effective Results/Affective Impact as a heading or 'Area of Consideration' on the sheet you set out, and then face up the opposing tensions.

The direction of the affective-effective compass for your team will depend on tangible factors to do with the attitudes, expertise, and adaptability of colleagues and how well they weld together to reflect your organisation's culture and support its purpose (see also later in this chapter; *How to Manage Change*). The model *The Development Cycle of Organisations* (below) is an analysis tool to help assess the effectiveness of your organisation and the pressures that drive development. It can be reproduced to be annotated by you and the activity used in focused discussion with colleagues.

Development Cycle of Organisations Activity

Consider your organisation and how the factors in its development might overlay the model:

- The outer ring represents *pressures* – identify and annotate these.
- What are the strongest pressures? Are these all valid and embraced or should (perhaps could?) some be resisted?
- What will happen if any pressures become too great or too weak?
- The inner cycle represents *process*. What drives the speed this revolves at?
- What happens if the speed of development is too fast or too slow?

4. How to manage change

Know what the change will concern

Controlling change of one sort or another is fairly constant work for a manager, whether a small adaptation or a major restructuring. Change impacts on people in two ways. They work out rationally what the proposals mean to the work they do and how the change might make them

Figure 2.3   The development cycle of organisations

more effective, and they work out what it means emotionally – how it affects them and what they feel about it. Change links to ideas about directional shifts, and all change affects employees and will to different degrees test their bond to the enterprise. How well changes are made will depend on how you orchestrate and prepare for them. The bigger the intended change the more it will impact upon your team therefore the more it must be considered and introduced in a controlled manner. Sometimes however, especially when change must occur that may be unpopular it is best to act swiftly and not look to get consensus or support. In that case be prepared to deal with the fallout!

Most proposals for change depend on people abandoning some areas of comfort and routine, to familiarise themselves with and accept new arrangements. Change can be very scary to some and unsettling to most no matter how level-headed individuals might be and how empathetic they are with the needs of clients. If the change is to go through well the sceptics have to be converted or at least see that gains outweigh losses, the WIIFM principle – *what's in it for me?*). Key to managing developmental change is to know who will resist and who will welcome the proposals. Do not get cross with sceptics; they just deserve more of your time. Maybe you and your schemes are not convincing? Consider that sceptics may have valid objections, and also that these characters have beliefs that are not short-lived. Once sufficiently convinced and behind you, one former sceptic is worth two or three unquestioning followers who may have less about them to convince or be convincing.

The importance of preparing the ground with the people concerned before phasing in new ideas cannot be overemphasised, because getting people behind any proposal is by far more important than getting the details planned. Adjustments can always be made as the development rolls along – and others will help make them, but if people are not on board you sail alone. Always remember – *People before Paper*.

Considerations for change

Here are some of the things which it is highly desirable, if not essential, to consider before change is embarked upon.

Be sure change is merited

A core practice of being a manager is to continually review experience, and to look for opportunities to influence thinking or introduce changes, in order to improve the work. However, there will usually be conflicting operational and money pressures, as well as lobbying from different people or groups who wish to influence the way work is done, or don't wish anything changed.

Use your reviewing skills to make useful generalisations whenever possible from specific events. Each event by itself may not merit questioning practice, but the accumulative effect may be that a change is merited. For example, a service to schools that I was involved with suffered a small but annoying number of consultations where there were mismatches of understanding between the Headteacher buying the service, and the consultant advisors. A simple change was to include with referral forms a note about the normal consultancy process and protocols, and how the time would be used. The trick is to resolve different forces, by making, every so often, a firm and positive decision on matters you have been reviewing.

Focus on product not process

Ask questions:

- *What outcomes are desired for service users?*
- *Are changes necessary to achieve those outcomes?*

Only consider changes if the answers are positive.

Link change to mission or purpose

There must be a link to the enterprise's mission or purpose. This is a principle that is important – you could look a bit silly arguing passionately about service users benefiting from an office arrangement to recycle ink cartridges. On the other hand, there are not many desirable changes which won't have a benefit on the end product. Even small matters which make life a bit more convenient or save a bit of time have outcomes that are desirable, such as lower stress levels or increased functionality, so that service users do ultimately benefit.

If the change is at all sizeable, it should be either a local tweak to a greater plan or something that can be offered 'upline' and sanctioned within your BDP (see Chapter 1.3). You will have to decide how much the mooted change is merited, but it must fit within the overall enterprise direction of development and assist its purpose.

Anticipate problems

- With substantive change you must foresee any obvious problems and know how what you do will benefit; be sure you have thought through all implications.
- Ensure you have enough support from your seniors. Discuss with your manager first, if appropriate, and if the change is your idea (either personally, or from within your team).
- If the change originates from the enterprise as a whole (rather than your bit of it), make sure that it is discussed with you fully, so that you are able to support the proposal.
- If the proposal is a team decision, discuss it in a formal manner (at a meeting), ensure there is sufficient support for it before proceeding, and record the decision in written minutes.

Communicate well

- Decide positively for change or retention, and let everyone know the matter is decided. Do not return to uncertainty (and worry) unless something comparatively big brings the area of practice back into question.
- When substantive change is imposed without much team consultation, make it absolutely clear to the team what is the value of the proposal, and ensure they understand and endorse it.
- Explain, without jargon, using language that everyone will understand (explain service terminology), why the change is occurring, exactly what is proposed, how it will affect service users and the team, what is expected of the team. Don't assume they will understand the proposal fully, or support it all at one go. Invite questions.
- Use as many methods as is sensible, and an appropriate one for each bit of information. Give all information as soon as possible; if you are holding back until you have more information let people know this – make sure there is no opportunity for misinformation by rumour or innuendo. Use team meetings, briefings, or whole day conferences to get the main message across. Use other colleagues, working groups, and one-to-one discussion to canvass the details or deal with uncertain support or detail. Use memos and emails to update on small detail, or circulate answers to specific questions. Individuals will want to talk through their own concerns – make time to see them.

Take people with you

- Be passionate, enthuse, infect others with your belief. That's leadership stuff.
- No matter from where any proposal originates, or how big it is, those it will impact upon must be on board.
- Remember that colleagues at the front line have valid operational experience and opinion that must be included if change impacts upon them or service outcomes; and these people will also be the first to advocate for the service user. Do not forget to canvass this broad base of people and get their vote.
- Be absolutely sincere in any dealings with staff. If working conditions or service outcomes are part of any proposed change, include consultation with union representatives or professional associations as well as service user groups, at the earliest opportunity.

Understand the impact on people

Change usually impacts on people's emotional comfort zones, and they will need time to give up old ideas, practices and beliefs before they can take on new ones. People vary in their resistance to change. Some people react automatically from fear or stubbornness before they think matters through. Adjusting to change has stages, very like those in the grieving process:

- Denial. *It won't affect me. It won't go through – there are too many problems.*
- Anger. *It's unfair! Why me! Have they really thought about . . .? It works so well, why change it?*
- Resolving. *Maybe I could escape this by . . .? It will be them more than me . . .? OK, that is another way of doing it . . .*
- Depression. *Well, that's it then, nothing I can do. Why bother to get excited?*
- Acceptance. *Oh well, it happened before and I was OK. I've still got a job I like; it's maybe not so bad? Not everything is different . . .*
- Hope. *The training looks interesting; I could be good at that? I've just thought . . .!*

Plan the pace of change

- Make a scheme of work or plan with a time or flow diagram that shows that you know that developments are best obtained by a series of small steps rather than massive or rapid change.

- Allow sufficient time for new things to become familiar or embedded, before progressing to the next stage, but not so much time that the impetus is lost.
- Publish your plan for change as soon, and in as much detail as possible, and update it as frequently as is necessary.
- Set out the plan using a Time line, with important dates for the end of stages, consultations, actions and so on.
- Link performance indicators and service benefits to the whole or specific parts of the plan.
- Make sure the plan addresses the intended outcomes, how they will be achieved, what resources will be needed, and who will do what by when.

Stage the change on a secure foundation

This is valid whatever the scale of the intended development. Your stall must be set out before the goods are unpacked. With small scale changes the discussion might only be a meeting or two with one or more persons. When the scale of proposed change is extensive, and will take time to implement, then so also will discussion need to be gone through, stage by stage over an appropriately long period.

- Start with broad stroke themes and overall vision. Add on desirable outcomes, where and how change is seen as needing to occur.
- The next layer is more detailed, with targeted objectives, necessary actions and leads to a peak of individually specified actions.

Keep the effort alive

- You will have to persevere and keep focused, bring the errant on line, and feed back praise or thanks to the people who action the plan well.
- Let everyone know how it is shaping up.
- If something is going to be 'on the wall' for a while, don't let it get dog-eared or faded, either literally or metaphorically. Use a laminate or plastic cover. If the plan has hand-written annotations, don't let them get stale; incorporate any editing into print.
- Republish the plan when appropriate.
- Actively manage. Be prepared for some details of planning to change. Make new arrangements as necessary to keep the plan alive.
- Be prepared to advocate for your team with senior management if some detail is proposed

that you feel is not merited of your team, or not sufficiently supported by them.
- Chase up information where progress is uncertain.
- Report back to the team at the review dates.
- Evaluate the training and resource requirements, and ensure any necessary personnel development is timely done, and resources are on stream.

Use methods to manage change

Dialogue in hand

A well tried way to progress developments is the *dialogue in hand* method. A *dialogue in hand* begins with the announcement of an issue as valid for discussion but for which there is no fixed resolution. For more complex matters it helps to create some form of flow diagram framework with a time scale. Within the framework regular informal and formal discussions move the issues along with gathering points for views and information to be exchanged; the processing methods are organised, and decisions are taken at given steps.

This provides opportunity for the high level of consideration that makes for good support. The technique allows time for people to 'come on board' and gives them opportunity to help steer direction or suggest ideas. It can be essential for the best progress of many developments if these look to be at all substantial, or when there is only a problem and no obvious routes out. The time and pace of a dialogue in hand allows mindsets and old practice to be rethought or challenged if necessary, and ideas or proposals to be fully passed around, investigated, and thought through.

The impetus can be stroked along by the discussion methods chosen. Typical formal forums are:

- Regular short inputs at routine meetings.
- Working party discussion and report.
- Questionnaires.
- Client or other forums of consultation.

Essentially, everyone with a valid interest is kept informed and invited to contribute, and the intention is that a lot of discussion and thought will take place informally during day-to-day business. The method suits open organisations and those adopting BPR processes (see Chapter 1).

The key to a dialogue in hand is keeping issues alive and solvent, and understanding how the use of different forums and information routes combine and contribute towards ensuring the development process is open and even handed. Don't look to this kind of process if the wish is to exclude controversy, impress pace, or favour one person's preference.

Sowing seeds

Sowing seeds is rather like a dialogue in hand but much less formal. Sometimes it can be a good idea to quietly make a comment or ask a question of someone who you know will pass it through the team grapevine. Later the seedling can be grubbed out or staked up according to the team feedback you receive and if you wish to grow the idea on or not.

Let time work

Time for most managers is the most valuable commodity. It's very stressful to be put under time pressure to agree something. This is a common cause of resentment because of the fear of making the wrong decision, or the assault on personal values that can happen when feeling forced to agree with the majority or senior view. Remember your colleagues are no different!

All managers are usually under pressure to produce results or to trim budgets. And those pressures are invariably passed on. Some workplaces have an ethos based on a quick throughput. This may be couched as a business-like approach in the degree to which workers are expected to have an aggressive thrust towards dealing with the workload. Watch that the pressures do not become too onerous on yourself or your colleagues. Work will suffer when lack of time precludes proper foresight, or poor consideration of operational limitations: the biggest problem with time pressure is that panic solutions are most likely to come undone, and produce more work to do in the long term. Ultimately this can badly affect the quality of work and the sanity of the people trying to deliver it. Being constantly under time pressure can be an indicator that a senior manager, or yourself, cannot prioritise well, and probably works inefficiently.

Example: Prioritising problems
    Sally was PA to a boss who could not prioritise. She tried to remain at her job

because she was experienced and had a considerable interest in the client group being served. But she was never sufficiently in control of her work or sure when her day would end. Typically, letters to be done were given to her last thing in the day. Her boss would fuss in and out of her office on petty errands, and gave Sally tasks she would have started earlier had she been given them. He would arrive in a flap because he had visitors he had forgotten he had invited and Sally had to drop what she was about. He rarely delegated effectively.

Although her boss was considerate in other ways, he could not trust his own efficiency so neither could he trust others, and was always inappropriately checking her work. Try as she could to improve communication and manage her boss better she could not impact upon his ways. Sally found her work was invariably too frustrating, or not appreciated. Unable to show her anger directly, or confront her boss constructively, Sally too often left for home at the day's end crying, and depressed. Eventually she left.

There are always gains when developments are properly paced. Allowing time avoids knee-jerk responses if action, not reaction, is wanted. Being pushed hard for a decision can feel like aggression towards you, and if you concede unwillingly you may then blame yourself for not resisting; in all a pretty unhealthy situation. Think about that in your dealings. Although allowing time sometimes may let people come to a resolve contrary to your hopes, at least that is a more sure and honest situation. Time can also allow the subconscious to work, and for conflicting feelings to even out.

Example: Letting time work
    I once had the onerous task of asking everyone on the payroll of an institution to accept a 10 per cent pay-cut, including myself. This was one measure I wanted to implement to stave off a looming crisis that I had inherited and in a situation where generally I had good support from colleagues. First, I used the 'grapevine' to alert colleagues about the consideration, and I spoke to some key colleagues about the issues. This allowed for the shock response to be avoided and people had some time to

consider and discuss among themselves, and with their families.

A few days later I took each member of staff aside and put the situation to them individually. I explained that it would not be imposed and only implemented if there was sufficient support. When I was asked what would happen if the measure was not well enough supported I had to honestly reply that I could only make decisions when situations were certainties. I gave out formal letters, which detailed the main issues and hopes for reinstatement, together with a reply slip.

In the event only one person, Dave, felt unable to accept the request, and he had said that this would probably be the situation. Dave was good enough to come and tell me this was the case. I thanked him for his forthrightness and I accepted his decision and wanted no rationales for it. I reminded Dave that the outcomes of the canvass would only be known to me and that I would make arrangements so that his decision would both remain private knowledge, and honoured should the measure proceed. A few days later Dave asked to see me, as he wanted to accept the pay cut and in so doing support his colleagues.

Controlling time helps manage pressure. It is often wise not to give or expect 'immediate' responses; this form of pressure can be construed as aggressive, or if couched in dubious rationales is covertly aggressive. This is particularly so in group situations such as meetings. There may be other issues you cannot easily raise immediately, and a blanket refusal might embarrass or anger a colleague. Ready agreement, or refusal, might risk you or the other person in some loss of face, and a quick decision might make for more difficulty if you want to recant later. Pressure can be resisted by a polite and considered comment perhaps along the lines that a suggestion seems OK, but you'd like to be sure you can do things well and need to consider before deciding.

Deferring decisions even for a short while allows matters to be gathered in and weighed. Alternatively, a provisional but private decision held until your deadline, resolves your inner pressure, and still allows opportunity for fresh considerations. These forms of 'time out' also allow the subconscious to work, and for thoughts to surface that were not immediately accessible. Time pressure is debilitating, and resisting it when appropriate to do so – even if only for a very short while – is a sound way to assert your self-care. Doing this makes it less likely that commitments are given to a path that is later regretted or resented. Regrets are debilitating – take time over decisions.

Patience is one of the virtues that managers can be tested on, and the next chapter deals with such essential qualities.

CHAPTER 3

How to Show You Manage Well

1. Show humility

Some managers seem to think that their position magically confers upon them wonderful powers and vision. They believe that only they can be creative and imaginative and only their ideas are worth promoting. They get carried away with their majesty and, as in the story of the emperor who wore new clothes, it can take great courage or great innocence to challenge their self-view.

Unfortunately the collusion – or illusion – can bamboozle some leaders (or those managers up the line with the power to promote) and you will almost certainly have met someone who has been promoted past their level of competence (the *Peter Principle*). Sadly, some managers in this situation can be so devastated by the criticism when they finally recognise the truth (or it is dashed in their face), that what genuine confidence and skill they do have becomes crippled. Alternatively, those managers who thwart or pervert matters through ignorance or by deliberate manipulation become despised or even hated. In drama and literature such characters are usually associated with mutiny or the come-uppance part of the story.

There are career managers who by fortune and connivance, or occasionally sheer chance, do obtain heights they cannot then command well. These must be distinguished from those who are driven upwards and seek promotion not simply because of ambition but because they are able, who then become bored and want change or new challenge. They leave when there are no opportunities, or they will try to move sideways and seek a secondment or other ways to refresh or enrich their work. These sorts of move are very valid because, as well as providing a new scene, the change gives low-risk opportunities to test out abilities and gain experience.

There is nothing to be ashamed of if you are content because you enjoy your work and are effective at it. Many such managers do not seek promotion but get it anyway because they become valued as their abilities shine. Others are not encouraged up or away because their organisation does not want the upset that may follow from losing someone already managing well.

Wise managers know not to put too much store by any kowtowing, or on popularity or the habitual deference they receive. Managers who are self-aware and self-assured have an accurate take on their talents and how they might best lead others. They understand that leadership relies on power by influence, and they seek change through persuasion and rationale. They understand well that their post confers power by position and do not abuse that power or seek to extend it by unwarranted self-aggrandisement.

Remember the deal between leaders and followers described in Chapter 1 – you have power so long as you hold credibility with everyone around you. It is proper to acknowledge and be thankful for trust, and to have the humility to always recognise your power is ultimately conferred by others no matter what the culture is of your enterprise and how it structures authority. Treat others as you would wish to be treated yourself – that's valid for all managers – no matter whether they run a burger bar or a major institution. In practice, this shows in the way you are respectful of and considerate to others and show complete integrity.

Example: Manager Integrity
A while ago around lunch time I was at home at my PC, writing but not 'at work', when my team administrator phoned; apparently I should have been at a training centre. This was not too far away, and although some discussion ensued which left me still rather confused, I abandoned my desk and set off with my laptop and the necessary presentation – part of a sequence of training inputs from different professions with through-put repeats for a series of groups.

On arrival in the training room I found my immediate senior manager holding forth at the front, but I also unexpectedly recognised some people among the trainees. Within a few moments the situation became clear; this group had already received my input a week or so previously. My colleague realised she had made a scheduling error and promptly acknowledged it with an open apology to the persons assembled and myself. Between us all we then decided I make the best of an impromptu extra training session, and this somewhat salvaged our team reputation – my intended day by now well awry.

This senior colleague and I enjoyed high trust and plain speaking between us. Everyone makes errors occasionally, and the event was not personally unsalvageable – I just took other time off. However, a day or so later I still received a pleasant letter of apology concerning the event and thanking me for my turn out and input. That sort of honesty coupled with formality is not only good managerial etiquette, it's just plain, respectful, good manners.

Self-focus Activity

Hi.
If you are reading this book through sequentially and have got to here I would like you to do something right now. In a way it is to do with self-awareness, but has a particular focus that will make more sense when I return to the issue later (especially if you do as I ask).

- Think back to the last time you felt really stressed and aroused to strong emotion. You may have been dealing with either a confrontation or a very difficult issue. It may have been paper work, your partner, a meeting, or your car or traffic that stressed you. It doesn't matter what, except that you were most stressed.
- Shut your eyes and re-engage with *how you felt* (*not what you did*). What did you feel like doing? What emotions dominated?
- Get a scrap of paper to insert here or use pencil in the book margin.
- Write down a few words only to describe:
  o how you felt . . .
  o what happened to your body . . .
  o what you felt like doing . . .
Be honest.
Thanks.

2. Be minded and curious

Getting things done is all. Concentrating on the task is *mindedness*. If you are comparatively new to managing, you will want to prove yourself. Managing is like learning to drive a car. Passing your test gives you permission to drive, but it will take a hundred thousand miles or more before you are experienced. At the early stages it's OK not to feel confident and find you get in a muddle when you try to do more than one thing at a time. In fact, I very much advise you not to expect too much of yourself. If you are stressed about getting things done, you will wind up your colleagues, or become frazzled yourself.

You may have a new job, and you think you must start with high impact. The first thing to manage is the pressure you will put on yourself. Other people may already have unrealistic expectations of you. Your seniors and other managers may have expectations you feel are daunting; you feel you must have all the answers for junior colleagues. You may have also just become 'one of them' – you are now 'management'. The dilemmas and qualities you could only have an opinion about before, may now be in reach of your touch. Service users and colleagues will look to you to resolve those issues of scarce resources and how best to care; and you may be in a sensitive political situation through which it is now your responsibility to steer a course. The second thing to manage is the pressure other people put on you.

To help managers cope with these two pressures is the main role of any mentor a manager might have. How aware are you of yourself? If you are already very aware, hurray! That mindedness is valuable. Keep it always. So many people who have it at the outset of their leadership one day find they no longer have it; they lose touch with themselves and become adrift.

There will be a number of things you think you should do that may not figure well with the way you would like to work, but you will have some options and a number of your own ideas. You are keen. To be strong and effective, first prioritise the tasks and ideas you can progress that will benefit your position as manager. You must also believe very strongly that any of your actions or decisions are right: they fit how you personally see things (not just what you think is the company line) and *they must be do-able*. If you are true to self the enterprise will benefit. If your first acts as a manager are close to your heart and they get carried out, your confidence will benefit.

Take on, and keep to your heart, the ideas and the manner of working that *you believe in* (intellectually and emotionally). They must suit the work you do, and complement or confirm your personality or character and your interpersonal style. Ideally your style is strong, positively orientated and assertive. Workers soon despise managers who are negative, nagging, or doubting.

Remember there is a danger in trying to 'be someone you are not', and a danger that if too much is attempted at once something will fail – and too many setbacks will test your confidence. Only take on ideas about managing you think *will fit your personality, your outlook, and your values* about the work you do. That applies also to this book. It's full of ideas, but that does not mean you cannot be selective.

And *pace your development*. Allow yourself time to change from being preoccupied with 'doing' practice to being preoccupied with 'managing' practice. Adapt ideas and introduce your ways slowly: expect to learn slowly; expect to make mistakes; ease into your way of doing things until your manager skills are smooth and routine and you are no longer vulnerably self-conscious.

Effective leaders value getting things done. That may well mean not leading from the front but freeing up others to lead at times who will have different ideas. If you are promoted within your enterprise you will have to delegate old tasks and let cherished areas of work be taken over by others.

When new ideas and a willingness to experiment are welcomed, they must be accompanied by a tolerance of honest errors and well-meaning false leads. The thinking is no risk–no gain. Valued managers are those who do not take for granted the way work is habitually done and ask how it might be done differently. Probing and questioning is a form of constant appraisal that we normally call curiosity.

Managers have to make decisions all the time, and it is this aspect of the work more than any other that managers can be hesitant about. They know this is what people will criticise most. There is always an unwritten expectation of wisdom, and a challenge to be intuitive, and not reactive with knee-jerk or obvious responses. Sometimes the need for a decision looms so large the manager freezes in fear of it.

Managers who make decisions well, invest in others. They cultivate relationships and share their worries and uncertainties; and when decisions need to be made there are always other colleagues, or a senior manager or two, with whom they can mull over the issues and receive second opinion. This openness makes it possible for others to see your work in process and be sympathetic to the sometimes very difficult positions in which managers are put; and contrary decisions are less resented when the people on whom it will impact feel consulted. They can see you are minded to do your best.

Mindedness and curiosity has four truths you might wish to take on as a personal motto:

- Nobody is so perfect they can not gain wisdom.
- No act is so perfect that it is beyond question.
- Nothing is so well seen there is not more to discover.
- No good path is ever trodden un-followed.

Wise managers act like good parents. They take pride when a junior colleague comes forward with a fitting suggestion or develops a new slant to the way the work is done. They are happy to bask in the reflected light from the energy of their team. They use their authority and ability to act across the enterprise structure and assist, embed or spread good ideas. Enterprises that thrive best enjoy the supportive culture you will nurture. If you are hindered by plodding senior managers who resist and stifle your enthusiasm and inventiveness consider that they may not be worth working for and move on. Manage as you would be managed and free up others by giving them opportunity to speak openly. Invite comment and criticism. This is how any enterprising culture improves itself.

3. Be self-aware

How well managers do depends on how well they understand others, but to understand about people and how they might best work together requires good understanding about oneself first.

The most essential area of understanding for all manager-leaders is where they are on the scale between command and collaboration. *Command* is power by position. *Collaboration* is leading through influence.

Power by position at its most obvious is a form of high command or absolute dictate – and in most enterprises, and on some occasions, such as emergencies, it is necessary to be able to give an order and not get quibble back. This can also be the initial case when working with people who have little personal idea or talent for the job in hand. Power by position is usually obtained by direct authorisation from an even higher power (or by strength of character or experience). These positions are usually obtained by proving greater capability than others through a selection or screening process – getting the job. Alternatively, power is given through nepotism or cronyism, and although this happens it has even less guarantee of suitability.

Collaborative leadership is usually the much preferred style when working with teams; these managers use good example, discussion, consideration, and sound reasoning to get everyone pulling together. Their power is given by collaborative agreement. Leading through influence is often also a position obtained through selection by higher power, but increasingly by peer selection. However obtained, the position is usually only tenable if sufficient influence is maintained – managers who lose regard often find their position untenable sooner or later.

Your personal point between these two extremes can be viewed as a position along a scale known as the *command-collaboration continuum*.

The command-collaboration continuum

This is the idea that there is a spectrum of authoritarianism that ranges from being fully collaborative or democratic, to being dictatorial (and by extrapolation, so will be the enterprise you work in). Actually, any manager or leader can't be placed exactly on one point along the spectrum. According to their different style they will be to some degree mobile along the continuum when dealing with different issues as well as responding differently to the pressures of time and other urgencies. Like most people, managers and leaders can have mood swings, changes of mind, and preferences that might mean they let some issues become more open to debate than others. And managers do have to tell people what to do and sometimes this requires that they are insistent and able to overcome opposition. When a manager seeks fully collaborative agreement they may be facilitating rather than assuming proper authority, but at times that is appropriate.

Although your position on the continuum may not be fixed, I think you can check out your tendency. Consider the statements bulleted below, and how they relate to you and the people you manage. For each item do two things:

1. Decide if you agree with each statement as it applies to how you like to be treated. If true, what does it mean or how has it been shown to be true – think of actual examples of how you have been treated.
2. Decide if you agree with each statement because this is how you think about colleagues. If you think it the case that that is how you do treat them – prove it. Think of actual examples when you witnessed evidence or you have acted this way towards those you manage (the test is, can you voice it aloud or write it down)? If not true, do you wish it to be so, and how will you progress that?

- They do best when they enjoy their work and feel relaxed.
- They appreciate being seen as individuals.
- When their successes are acknowledged and rewarded, colleagues become more motivated and even better at what they do.
- They appreciate being listened to – it makes them feel significant when their views are taken into account.
- They like to be consulted – just being told how to go about their work can make them disown others expectations.
- They respond best to sensitive management – heavy-handed authority is often counter-productive.

At what point there is a suitable balance is for you to decide – every manager's situation is different. You are the expert at your work and will know what your appropriate position really should be.

Now, if you wish to be really tough with yourself, find a way you can independently present the *Manager-colleague Relationship* questionnaire to your team (this is on page 47).

If this form of questionnaire is surprising to you then the chances are that you or your enterprise do not use 360-degree appraisal techniques (see Chapter 5), or if you do, maybe there is room for more rigour?

Managers who are self-aware and assertive are comfortable showing manager qualities – they show some Art of Leadership that makes them accessible and understood by others. The *Art of Leadership* is typified by managers who:

- Judge their own or other's contributions by outcomes rather than the time put in; they believe in working SMART not hard (see Chapter 1.3).

Manager-colleague relationship. Put your name if you wish: [*Colleague's name*] ....

Please indicate your evaluation of [*Manager's name*] .... on the five-point scale. Write overleaf referring to the item number if you wish to add explanation or comment. Your views will be respected and kept confidential. Thank you.

1: excellent/concur completely; 2: very good/strongly agree; 3: satisfactory/agree;
4: adequate/neutral; 5: poor/disagree

	For each item rate how your manager does	✓
1	Gives clear expectations about my duties and responsibilities	
2	Supports my professional development and career progress well	
3	Gives clear expectations about my tasks and who does what	
4	Encourages me to be imaginative and solutions focussed	
5	Meets my need for appropriate information	
6	If professional differences emerge, helps to resolve these satisfactorily	
7	Gives me respect for my views, skills, experience, and specialism	
8	Communicates clearly with me	
9	I am always adequately consulted on developments	
10	Good at seeing when my experiences might illustrate the general case	
11	Takes responsibility for logistical worries, and lets me get on with work	
12	Creates an environment of mutual trust among my colleagues and I	
13	Always notices and commends me when I have done well	
14	Makes decisions confidently and asserts leadership when appropriate	
15	Lets me make my appropriate decisions and supports me in these	
16	Helps resolve any concerns between me and others (clients or peers)	
17	Keeps a balance between roles and functions and work share	
18	Monitors my situation to avoid my work overload or excess stress	
19	Can articulate well, verbally, and by written report	
20	Is approachable and even tempered – sets good professional example	

- Keep in touch and spend time with individual staff, and service users when possible, to talk and share experiences about the service.
- Observe other colleagues at work and invite colleagues to see how they work.
- Think *process before product* – how was it, not what it was.
- Network and compare; they keep contact with other professionals outside the organisation, and not only in identical or similar work.
- Self-refresh; they take occasional days off routine or take on a new role occasionally (i.e. redisplay the staff bulletin board, volunteer to accompany a resident outing, take on a small project).
- Swap roles occasionally with colleagues. Ask someone more able than them to do a particular task, and maybe trade one of theirs with them.
- Are able and prepared to do anything they might ask of others – although they often acknowledge that others can do it better!

Managers who are self-aware and assertive also know:

- No quality system is 'self righting' – it must be managed.
- Quality is a journey not a destination.
- A long climb is best achieved by small steps.
- If they admire the view from the top, or gloat over what they have achieved for too long they are in danger of 'falling off the mountain'.

4. Be aware of stress

Facts to consider

Stress kills. But stress also gets things done. Stress is where dragons be – in the land beyond your comfort zone. It's quite a good idea to be alert and hold your sword up when challenging dragons, so some stress is OK if it keeps you focused and energised. Knights that laze around behind their castle walls don't usually win fair damsels, so prizes worth getting usually mean going out of your comfort zone and into the gloaming. But chase dragons all the time, especially if always going for the biggest and fieriest, and you risk losing your wit and charm. Your sword arm will be tired, your mind will be hardened, and your white horse exhausted. Chances are, one day, you will get toasted.

Although the dragons are all gone, if confronted we retain those primitive responses, and this may be just as well as our modern world does have a whole new set of threats that can unexpectedly confront us. Most work places have some degree of stress, and it's OK if it just keeps everyone on their toes and things get done. Managers need to be well informed about stress and how to monitor and mitigate when the balance tips towards abnormal levels, not only as it may apply to themselves but also to those they manage.

The Health and Safety Executive recognise undue work stress as undesirable for employees, and have a set of expectations which, if ignored, lends weight to any employee grievance. Contemporary statistics (Sunday Times Magazine article on work stress 16/7/06) inform that 45 per cent of us regularly lose our temper at work, 64 per cent have experienced 'office rage', and up to 60 per cent of all absences from work are caused by stress. In an illustration from one service group – teachers – examination of the problems brought to a recently set up dedicated help-line counselling service (Teacher Support Line) found that a third of calls concerned conflict with a manager; and research from the Department for Education and Skills indicates 45 per cent of ill-health retirements from teaching are related to psychological problems.

It is the statutory duty of employers (*Management of Health and Safety at Work Regulations 1999*) to assess health and welfare risks to employees and take practical steps to protect them from reasonably foreseeable dangers including the risk of developing stress-related illness caused by work. RIDDOR 1995 regulations prescribe for 'any act of non-consensual physical violence' done to a person at work; and requires a report on any incidents that result in an employee being off work for more than three days. The definition of 'violence' includes emotional stress as well as physical injury, and the legislation is clear that suffering as a victim of violence (including verbal abuse) should never be considered as 'just part of the job'.

Social care work is well recognised as stressful and it shows in high levels of sickness generally and stress-related illness particularly. Research results generally over the past decade are agreed that managers and social workers experience the greatest stress followed by residential care workers, then home care workers. The greatest sources of stress at work, in order, are: workloads, change, staff cuts, overlong hours,

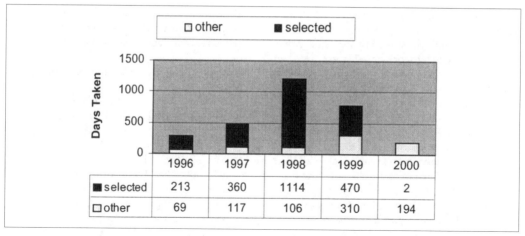

	1996	1997	1998	1999	2000
■ selected	213	360	1114	470	2
□ other	69	117	106	310	194

Figure 3.1 Sick Record group T: accumulated

and bullying (TUC survey 2004). The workers who exhibit the most stress are those with particularly responsible jobs or who work alone, and those who work with children and families, those with mental health problems, or with severe learning difficulties. There are also periods in life when people are particularly vulnerable to stress or depression such as when experiencing bereavement, domestic relationship difficulties, or physical ill health. These are important issues for managers to be aware of and are proper for consideration during professional supervision. Neglect can be costly to the organisation as well as the individual; there have been some landmark court cases concerning stressed social work employees who have won substantial compensation because their plight had been ignored. In stressful work, it is a reasonable expectation that there are appropriate supports in place such as professional supervision and counselling; good training; and senior managers who will acknowledge and respond to difficulties.

On the other hand, people who are well motivated and get plenty of job satisfaction take fewer sick leaves. The absence record is always telling on this issue. If you are a manager new to a team one of the first things to do (even ask at interview) is to look at the sick record. Is the average only a few percentage points from the maximum number of allowable days, or a very much smaller or bigger percentage? If you are an established manager this is one of your benchmarks, and if the situation is poor understand better why that is (assuming the record is not skewed for an exceptional reason).

The sick record example shown in Fig. 3.1 relates to the case of an employee who claimed successfully for compensation following stress related illness and dismissal. The 'selected' group is mental health and stress-related illness in a particular residential child-care institution.

I created this graph from the LA personnel department sick records in order to give evidence as expert witness to the case. The particular institution had been undergoing change externally imposed by the managing LA since the early 1990s. This was against the advice and experience of the institution managers who were outmanoeuvred or re-deployed by remote managers at borough offices. Had a service manager within the responsible authority also begun a similar graph the inordinate growth in the 'selected' trend would have been clearly visible from 1995 – perhaps someone did? Certainly the particular LA ignored, until far too late, the massive loss of morale and actual harm (including physical assaults) that was occurring to many employees, and which was evidenced within the sick record detail. Note how the graphs shows massive drop in the amount of reported stress or mental health illness in 1999–2000. This is because the most exhausted people were levered out by redundancy or dismissal by mid 1999, and if ill through stress employees were becoming reluctant to register this as the true cause – none in 2000. This very unhealthy and poorly-managed institution closed soon afterwards.

As a manager you have a duty of care towards your junior colleagues to ensure their workload and work difficulties do not become unmanageable to them. Factors such as job design, team and organisational characteristics, or too little say all cause employee stress but are manageable. The main reasons for work-based stress are when people are too pressured or overloaded; and when they are not consulted and have change imposed. Change can occur at such a pace that workers suffer from 'initiative fatigue'. Each idea may make good sense, but people can only cope with so much change – otherwise it becomes confusing and tiring. Managers who are in touch with their colleagues who have to apply the new ideas ensure each development is well consolidated and followed by a stable period, before the next initiative – they take a paced approach to planning. Similarly, stress and burnout can result from a number of low-level factors with an accumulative effect that has been overlooked; or by a 'tipping' factor' such as a particularly irritating development or a difficult phase of work.

It is not always difficult to remedy the processes that cause employee stress, except when the solutions require more resources or major operational change. In those instances stress may not be easily or quickly relieved – but it can be acknowledged, and that is always a considerable help. Acknowledgement brings issues into open discussion and the support of colleagues is invariably helpful. Also, if everyone finds everyone else is facing similar problems it can bolster team spirit. There are some very effective ways to acknowledge stressful times for colleagues: these range from simple direct support such as extra time off, help with childcare, or extra resources etc.; to greater investment, such as subsidised gym or crèche facilities. There are commercial companies who will routinely provide relaxation therapies, such as t'ai chi, yoga, head and neck massages.

When there is no money for such options, imaginative acts come into their own. A cash-strapped but caring manager can make effective gestures without incurring high cost. Ideas abound, but some examples are:

- Aromatherapy materials, or a decent coffee machine to scent the staff room.
- Surprise cakes occasionally.
- Joining staff for coffee or lunch breaks.
- Meeting fieldworkers for coffee from time to time to ensure they have a break.
- When there is an unexpected slack moment, directing someone to go home early or not come in.

- Personal letters of acknowledgement and thanks posted to home (addressed to both persons when the colleague has a partner).

Example: A highly supportive response to stress:

This concerns a situation when a group of colleagues approached their manager and offered him respite from accumulated stress.

A director of a residential institution for young people with very challenging behaviours had the onerous job of closing it for reasons too complex and not immediately relevant to this account. It meant new placements had to be found for the young clients, and he and all the staff would be made redundant. It was an exceptionally difficult and distressing process. The director had been very active in trying to turn fortunes around before he had to face closure, and he had become worn down over a number of months – his wife reported how she had taken him to a lively jazz concert but he had fallen into deep sleep within minutes of being seated.

A small group of his senior management team resolved on a plan to cover the director's duties and progress the matters already in hand. They approached the director with their advice for a week's leave. There was good mutuality and trust, and after some hesitation the offer was taken up. The director and his wife booked into a Lake District hotel a half-day drive away, and from that respite he was able to return with recharged energies to complete what had to be done. Those magnificent colleagues were mine.

Managers aware of colleague stress will be:

- *Transparent and honest* – Recognise stress when it occurs and say what they can or cannot change.
- *Sturdy in attitude* – Take up issues when necessary with senior managers; protect the work from external pressures; protect individuals from threats, and do not ignore poor performance or a weak team member.
- *Calm in manner* – Reassuring; unflappable in crises; not panicked, nor suddenly reactive through worry.
- *Person centred* – Will value reflection; has person-centred practice with thorough investigation before decision or action.

- *Identified with team* – Participates by sharing issues, consults and delegates; and supports staff when problems occur, including representing team pressures to senior managers.

Monitoring stress levels, at its simplest, means keeping an eye on the welfare and wellbeing of colleagues, but *do not rely on memory or casual enquiry* – keep a note of problems, and keep the kind of records that will provide you with appropriate information from which you can extract information similar in context to the 'sick record' case exampled above.

A person who is frequently absent on Mondays may be indolently recuperating from playing in Sunday League football, or actually be reluctant to face work pressures because these are becoming unbearable. An uncharacteristically morose attitude could be because the person is naturally rather dour in the low-light winter months, or because they feel they have let down a client in some unnoticed manner and they are still fretting about it. People who suffer most from stress are often the most conscientious.

The same approach, and note-taking can, be used to inform your caring concern for a colleague, or to point up your responsibilities over them, but there is a great difference between how the two actions are undertaken. Be aware that this kind of record, no matter how responsibly it is done, can, in some teams, be seen as unwelcome monitoring. It all depends how you use it, and the manner in which you keep it confidential, or not.

Good care of colleagues is also shown when supervision is properly maintained or other support is available, but often that is not enough. Don't wait for, or rely only on the formal arrangements. If you think a colleague may be getting stressed – check it out. It is well recognised that colleagues are valued as a help in times of stress – whether work-based or personal – in addition to friends and relatives. Be that good colleague! As soon as possible, find a moment to ask them how they are. If something needs better resolution, and it can't be done on the spot, arrange a mutual time to discuss the problem. That in itself is very supportive, and the colleague may well be given a boost by the recognition that there is difficulty, and it will be discussed. If necessary, bring formal supervision forward or arrange for it, if not normally provided by you. Always make a written file

note. This is good personal practice, but perhaps more importantly it provides additional evidence of good support practice should the matter for any reason give rise to a later enquiry and you need to demonstrate proper care.

How the issues are dealt with separates the *affective* and supportive organisations from those that seek to be merely *effective* and care less about the cost to employees. You must seek help when you feel stressed, you must tender help when you see others stressed. Sensitivity to stress is a core attribute of a good manager – it requires a good understanding of our common reaction to all forms of confrontation.

Stress arousal

We would not have evolved as a species without the capacity to survive in the face of danger. Anthropology and psychology have brought the associated mechanisms involved into most people's understanding, that is, the notion of 'fight, flight, or freeze' as instinctive reactions when under threat:

- *Fight: as self-defence.* The objective is to overcome the aggressor or threat. Normally timid people can exceptionally be roused to a frenzy – perhaps to protect someone or something they love. It can result in over-reaction, either in words or physically.
- *Flight: to get away.* Walk, run, or jump. This may well involve action not normally done, or valued work materials or possessions left behind.
- *Freeze: present no stimulus.* Freezing is also a natural defence mechanism. It does not invite chase as flight may, by avoiding fight it presents as submissive, and it protects from the probable harm of unprepared defence.

Physiology explains why we have one of these Stress Arousal reactions. Our sensory input is handled by a kind of control centre – the amygdala (actually near the brain centre). When alarmed the amygdala bypasses the areas used for reasoning, and connects sensory input directly with parts of the brain used for action. Reactions become very autonomic. We breathe fast and shallowly. Very rapidly the oxygen supply to the brain is lessened but the flow to muscles is increased. This causes the ability to calmly sequence thought or respond to other stimuli to lessen, but the ability for action to increase.

That no one is free of their own physiology raises an important area for self-awareness. At the beginning of this chapter there was an *Activity* that asked you to identify your feelings when very stressed. This exercise, quite accurately, shows your dominant form of dealing with stress – your usual reaction or instinctive response. See how well the feelings and wishes you remember (and I hope noted down) fit one of the three classic forms of stress arousal: fight, flight, or freeze.

If you did not know before, then I hope you may now have some greater insight into your character when facing challenge. There are links here for why anxiety often spills out as aggression; it has similar physiological effects that impact upon body reactions and drive the person into defensive action.

Fight response

Sensations felt	Body's response	Felt like doing or does
angered	tensed up	shouting, swearing
maddened	energised	hitting, thumping
frustrated	heart thumps	slamming (phone, door)
hurt	make a fist	having a row
buzzing	teeth clench	getting cross (someone different)
tense	'sees red'	doing faster (eating, driving, working)
electrified	breathes hard	sorting it, (whatever it is) right now!
single-minded	stares	wanting to get even
its their fault	sits up, stands up	looking for someone to blame
boundless energy	forgets to eat, drink, smoke	
energised, decisive	cannot sleep	

Outcome:

- Thoughts focused on who to blame or punish for the problem.
- Action made *towards* others

In a work situation, will get angry or defiant, when things are not going as they wish.

Flight response

Sensations felt	Body's response	Felt like doing or does
alarmed	knotted stomach	escaping, going home
anxious	eyes shut	hanging up (phone)
worried	breathes fast	telling other party to go away
shocked	legs twitchy	resigning
unsettled	feet tapping	putting off till tomorrow
fearful	needs air	reporting in sick
nervous	feels distracted	displacement activity (looking out
is it my fault?	craves food, drink, cigarette	of window, pacing room)
it's not fair		letting someone else sort it
energised, but indecisive		comfort eating, drinking, smoking
		disappearing (literally, figuratively)

Outcome:

- Thoughts focused on damage limitation, and how to escape.
- Action made *away* from others.

In a work situation, will leave early and be upset when things are not going their way.

Freeze response

Sensations felt	Body's response	Felt like doing or does
denial, disbelief	faint	nothing
confusion	sick	unplug phone
stunned	weak	avoid callers
speechless	unable to move	avoid issue
whose fault is it?	sobs, cries	stop to rest on way home
total lack of energy	ears hiss, buzz	take time off work
unable to do anything	slumps in chair	fantasises about problem
helpless	feel physically ill, in pain	disappearing
	lose appetite	
	sleep a lot	

Outcome:

- Thoughts not focused, but blurred and churning.
- Unable to process thought into *any* action.

In a work situation, will become quiet, and not participate when affairs such as a meeting don't go as wished (can look like passive aggression).

Your particular response is one you instinctively display if you become unexpectedly threatened in any way. Typical scenarios are:

- Being hit by another car when you are already late for something important.
- Being robbed.
- Getting on the dais to do a presentation and finding your PA (100 miles away) has loaded the wrong material into your laptop.

This response is also highly likely to be your habitual way of dealing with repeated low level challenge; all the awkward and problematic stuff that gives you a bad day and holds you up or must be dealt with. If this is too frequently the case and your proper work, and your usual demeanour begins to suffer it must be rightly recognised as too much work-related stress. The same problems and processes of course, can occur in your colleagues.

Initial or instinctive responses underpin attitudinal aspects of personality and have the potential to come to the fore only when the person is threatened. But none of the classic responses to stress arousal outlined above are actually helpful in dealing with sudden threats or enduring problems; and certainly professional people, whoever they are, or whatever work they might do, are expected to control their instinctive reactions and ensure some thought before action.

The ability for considered action rather than raw *re*-action improves with experience and age, and is enhanced by the forms of training and skills development that can assist in this regard – and I hope reading this is one of those.

One form of training that is very evidently right at the centre of these issues is training on restraint. All the training models (e.g. TeamTeach) acknowledge the way we may become rapidly aroused and risk losing professional effectiveness. They emphasise the importance of mutual support, clear methods for step-by-step control, the need to remain within self-control and by achieving that, remain clear thinking.

We differ in our resistance to arousal and how resilient we are at withstanding stresses. Some people cope daily at work with comparatively high levels of stress arousal that others would find intolerable. Some people cope with emergencies better than they do routine problems. A repetitive state of alarm can cause a person to become highly sensitised to the source of their distress, and their ability for higher cerebral function in given contexts or environments may eventually become impaired. This is why people who have been in tight spots for a long time but have managed well may suddenly make a bad decision. Some behaviour may become quite automatic, and continue long after the original trigger source is gone.

Whether the stress is at work or at home the results are much the same, and there are common physical and psychological symptoms of stress. Stress arousal can be of short or longer duration, and similarly different in the degree of arousal; normally the events that give rise to these different states are also somewhat dissimilar. Stress arousal can be:

1. *Exceptional and infrequent, but high arousal.* Typically, this is a sudden physical emergency such as a domestic or vehicle accident, or an aggressive confrontation such as being mugged.
2. *More frequent, but less exceptional arousal.* Typically, this may be work that deals with acute situations involving people or events that vary in intensity but to which indifference is not desirable. Examples are found in the emergency services, police and custodial work, and in some driving, restaurant, and similar time-pressured work.
3. *Repeated, low-level, arousal.* Typically, this is otherwise normal work but the clients or customers are problematic or demanding, or the available resources are stretched.

1. Exceptional high arousal

The life or death emergency or sudden physical confrontation that causes high arousal is comparatively rare for most of us. The physiological changes of high stress arousal are instant. The body floods with noradrenalin which activates the sympathetic nervous system to directly increase heart rate, release energy from glucose and glycogen, and increase muscle readiness – particularly the heart. The body is readied for action, and anything not immediately useful is shut down – including higher order thinking skills. (A well-proven example is how in emergencies people on airplanes try in panic to press a button at their side to release their seat belt – they have temporarily lost the knowledge that these belts simply pull apart at a central buckle. The more impressed knowledge pattern relating to car seat belts dominates).

The changes in blood circulation from a pounding heart bring the adrenalines in a rush to nerve endings, and fingers and toes tingle. Endorphins (a natural opiate) are released and injuries can be endured with lessened sensitivity to pain. Cortisol is produced that depresses the immune system. The face pales as blood goes to

muscles, and the mouth may go dry, the person may be unable to speak or shout out. Some body processes such as digestion begin to shut down. An urgent need to use the lavatory may be felt; a relic autonomic reaction from when lighter body weight probably assisted quicker escape for our hunter forebears.

High stress arousal can produce some unusual sensations and responses, and a number of things can happen along a continuum of physiological symptoms. People report a variety of sensations, such as tunnel vision, seeing only the object of their attention, and sensitised hearing. Values and behaviour can alter and treasured possessions may be thrown away or held tight when on the contrary it is more sensible to let them go. Action may be taken that even puts life at risk.

People in exceptionally high arousal states can produce unusual surges of strength; and this superhuman power might be used for harm or good. Exceptional feats can be achieved – there are accounts of people lifting cars to free their trapped children – and occasionally people who are normally mild and physically frail will unexpectedly fight aggressors – elderly people go on the attack when confronted by intruders.

Traumatic or high impact events usually leave the body trembling. Much of this is the 'chemical aftershock' from the hormones that have surged through the body, and the person will most probably be unwise to try immediately to resume whatever was being done before. Taking 'time out' to compose is advisable to assist a return to the normal personal state. An aroused person is at risk of mishandling situations and returning to the heightened state unless time is allowed for the body to process the chemical charge. Going elsewhere for a period, for some fresh air, or to cool the face with a cold splash, allows the body to settle and the mind to assert better control. In most work situations high stress arousal should be followed by a de-briefing to offload feelings and review matters such as decisions or risk issues surrounding the event.

> Example: Post traumatic stress
> A colleague and I once had to escort a young man on a journey in a car. I thought I knew him quite well, and the circumstances behind the journey had a long and complex history. I was driving, and my passengers were in the rear. The young man suddenly

attacked me from behind. The driving wheel was kicked from my hands, and I came close to losing control of the car as a determined assault was launched upon my colleague and me.

Once I managed to stop, the situation was safer, but my colleague and I were barely able to contain the young man until the police arrived to assist. Everyone sustained some hurt and bruising. The car interior was considerably damaged, and the roof and interior distorted from the kicks it had received. Afterwards I was exhausted, shaking, and somewhat disabled. It was a good half hour after the police had gone (with the young man and my colleague) before I got sufficient command of myself to drive. It became a long and trying day.

It was some days later as I drove along the same stretch of road that my unresolved emotions unexpectedly surfaced. I had to pull up, and I was unable to drive for a while – a form of post traumatic stress. I had to recognise that my feelings and reactions had not been properly dealt with, and during a difficult, already stressful, period the incident had been 'too much'.

In high arousal situations the key symptoms to monitor in oneself or others are:

Facial expression

- Facial expression
- Eye contact
- Voice and words
- Posture
- Proximity
- Other body language and gestures
- Physical changes

The face shows feelings that are universal and cross-cultural. We all recognise puzzlement, or anger, or surprise in others. You should:

- Avoid showing anger, uncertainty, or fear. Try to show concern, tilting head to one side indicates the listening stance.

Eye contact

Staring eyes are aggressive. Shut eyes indicates a wish to exclude or deny the other person. You should:

- Keep a natural eye contact as in normal conversation. If the other person is making you uncomfortable by staring, centre on the forehead; break eye contact only if an excuse or other interruption comes to hand (to consult paperwork or someone else etc.) and say 'excuse me a second'.

Voice and words

Anxiety can cause the voice to be raised by pitch and volume – sometimes the initial response is a strangled squeak. You should:

- Try to keep your voice even and language simple. Avoid authoritative comment and overtone. Use the person's proper name.
- **Never** use language that could be construed as threatening, abusive, or racist.

Posture

Sudden change of posture is alarming, some postures threaten. You should:

- Keep your hands and arms relaxed and by your side. You may feel more comfortable and safer standing than sitting. If so, do this casually and ideally before any verbal exchange.
- Avoid muscle tension, pointing, or a folded-arms posture.

Proximity

It is aggressive to move up closer than the usual cultural body space between the parties. The need for personal body space increases in conflict. You should:

- Keep a comfortable (and safe) distance.
- Do not crowd the other person: if you are crowded, avoid backing away as the space you make may well be encroached upon, you may get backed into a corner.

Other body language and gestures

Some people are more receptive to body language than words. You should:

- Avoid raising or wave your hands or arms, or making sudden movements that may be seen as threatening.

- Avoid tapping, excessive head nodding, fidgeting, pacing, walking faster, repeated behaviour (folding and unfolding documents).

Physical changes

These are not all readily apparent in others. Typical physical change caused by arousal includes:

- Rapid breathing, flushing/blotching, sweating.
- Dry mouth, teeth clenching, jaw jutting, hooded look.
- 'Butterflies', feeling hot or sick.

2. Frequent, less exceptional, arousal

The more acute symptoms of stress such as a pounding heart or need to pee can occur at the time of 'threat'. However, people can have the symptoms of frequent but less exceptional stress without any immediate connection to the recurring trigger events. The symptoms can occur at any time once a stressful period has been ongoing for a time – days or weeks or longer according to how susceptible the individual is to stress. The symptoms include:

- Cardiovascular: pounding heart (palpitations), blushing, sweating.
- Respiration: asthma attack, difficulty speaking (including squeaky voice), hyperventilation (feeling breathless).
- Muscle: tension aches in shoulder and neck, worse than usual handwriting.
- Immune System and Body: sudden sneezing fits, fatigue, sore throat/cold when usually immune, unexpected fungal and similar problems (thrush, herpes, body odour, dandruff, zits).
- Gastric or Metabolic: loose tummy, increased urination, no appetite, dry mouth.
- Mind: headache, feelings of anxiety, forgetfulness, being irritable or short tempered, sudden unexpected loss of composure (typically tears or anger), waking at night with worry on mind, moodiness, post traumatic stress symptoms (flashbacks, avoidance behaviour).
- Psychological: impulsive grab for alcohol, tobacco, chocolate, high carbohydrate food or other substances, dysfunctional sex drive (impotence or new behaviour).

3. Repeated low arousal

Recurrent low level stress caused by operational difficulties and confrontations at work are a major, but unrecognised source of stress. This is because they are not readily apparent but being so chronic they can lead to eventual mental or physiological collapse from which recovery can be a similar long haul. Chronic symptoms result from long periods of continual stress (months or years) or when otherwise healthy tension has reached a fatigue point but the situation has remained without relief. The symptoms include:

- Cardiovascular: high blood pressure or heart problems needing treatment.
- Respiration: worsening asthma.
- Muscle: tremor, tics, resistant postural problems (chronic tension aches in shoulder and neck, stooping).
- Immune System and Body: chronic tonsillitis, propensity for catching colds/flu, skin and hair problems needed treatment, worsened eczema or arthritis, allergies, emergence of chronic fatigue conditions including ME, weight gain or loss.
- Gastric or Metabolic: bowel problems, chronic indigestion, food cravings.
- Mind: frequent migraine headaches (usually at weekend or after end of duty period), anxiety states, irritableness and short temper, depression, obsessive behaviours, personality changes and out of character actions, alcoholism, character change, emergent mental health problems.
- Psychological: persistent cravings leading to addictive behaviour for substances such as alcohol, tobacco, food; prescription medicine and illegal drugs, sleeping difficulties, impotence or sexual addictions, upturn in dangerous activities (sports or lifestyle).

The best way to deal with all the different problems and pressures that cause stress in people who lead others is to have some insight into the mechanisms which cause them, and to have a guide (perhaps this text) that helps you check all the necessary parts are in place and working OK.

It is essential that you are aware of your own level of arousal when faced with a stressful situation, and aware if accumulative stress is making you over or de-sensitised or damaging to your long term health. It is professional to monitor your own internal processes and to realise that stress arousal may risk you acting or speaking without proper thought. If your workload is too much you must not be hesitant to ask for help, or seek support through your work counselling service (if there is one), your direct senior manager or via supervision.

Similarly, managers concerned for the wellbeing of staff must look out for the same loss of equilibrium in persons they work with. It is particularly important to be aware of junior colleagues who are fielding abusive service users. Verbal abuse and violence of any nature is absolutely not tolerable. Also, you should look out for colleagues who seem to have lost empathy or belief. They may begin to comment how ineffective the work really is, or be disparaging about service users, or about colleagues who they think are letting the team down.

The process of reaction is common, whatever the level of stress arousal, but the outcomes differ according to who we are, and how commonplace or unexceptional the situation is. The form of each person's reaction to arousal reflects the brain patterning that has taken place over time by all previous associated experience. This can be very evident. Classic examples are:

- The child who flinches when adult proximity surprises them because they are used to being hit.
- The person who is automatically defensive in conversation, because they are used to being blamed by partner, parents or boss.

The reaction can be instant or develop over a few minutes. In slowly unfolding threats the reaction may take place over minutes or hours, and, exceptionally, may take much longer. The reaction can be seen as distinct stages, as a chain that ends in a final action.

The reactive chain-to-action process

There are five stages to this process.

1. Trigger or event stage.
2. Appraisal or thinking stage.
3. Emotion stage.
4. Evaluation stage.
5. Action stage.

Trigger or event stage

An operational problem or an interpersonal confrontation causes arousal. The person is made alert. This is the antecedent to autonomic response and emotions. If this happens routinely in certain circumstances before any actual threat is evident or real it is a symptom of post traumatic stress. In the trigger stage:

- Persons routinely in stressful situations become conditioned to the triggers and learn to recognise them quickly. They become more routinely alert, and quicker to notice triggers (although probably not consciously so); you will think of them as always 'wound-up'.

Appraisal or thinking stage

The brain deals with information by pattern matching. If the event matches past events, a view or experience is subconsciously recalled; the past events are matched to associated emotions and a mood or reactive feeling quickly surfaces such as feeling ignored or challenged. A sort of 'here we go again'. As a habitual cognitive connection the emotion may be dysfunctional or quite realistic depending on the particular person and the prevailing circumstances. In the appraisal stage:

- Persons routinely in stressful situations cannot help but learn to show conditioned responses. They will habitually respond to the triggers in the same way. Occasionally what they think mismatches the particular case. They will be aroused when it is inappropriate.

Emotion stage

Emotions settle to drive the response. If angered, some warning signs of ritualised behaviour will be displayed (e.g. raised voice, aggressive eye contact, exhaling forcibly). In the emotion stage:

- Persons routinely in stressful situations risk becoming desensitised or over-sensitised.
- Persons may habitually protect their empathy and personal emotions by resisting how much they engage their emotions. They may make cold or aloof responses. They may begin to talk about clients disparagingly.
- Or persons may be overwhelmed by the accumulative transference of past high emotion onto the particular case and become too highly

or unhealthily identified with the issues and lose perspective with the particular case.

Evaluation stage

This provides a fleeting, or longer, moment of reflection – how do I respond – what do I do? Personal moral values or professional standards will override instinctive responses, unless the person is severely tested. In the evaluation stage:

- People severely tested can give way to their emotion and react according to their personality and how they are dealing with their stresses. The action stage may be immediate when an event causes higher than normal arousal, or with lower but persistent arousal action will show as a gradual shift in attitude and behaviour.
- People routinely in stressful situations but de-sensitised, habitually respond in the same way – they do not insult a wearisome complainant. They do not throw their PC through the window when it crashes again. Nothing is worth such effort. They make themselves storm-proof and ride out the moment, knowing it will pass.
- Some people will have high moral or religious values and these will prohibit them from re-acting inappropriately (except if they lose that inner control, mayhem can follow).
- Some people need or are restricted by awareness of consequences which they will avoid by subduing their behaviour: typical consequences at risk include loss of dignity; being hit back and hurting more; disciplinary action; arrest; points on driving licence.
- Some people will reframe their thoughts (they may have had training or counselling in interpersonal skills); typically they might think the other person is having a worse day than them, they might use breath control or 'going to a calm place' or 'counting to ten' thinking techniques.
- **The evaluation stage is the last point at which support or intervention by another person can be made whether it is a client or colleague who needs the help.**

Action stage

This is where behaviour becomes evident. Pattern matching at the appraisal stage and weak evaluation produces the prejudices, attitudes or manner that typify that person's behaviour including defensiveness, resignation or anger, direct strong action, and even capriciousness. With high arousal the ability to make rational thought is much diminished and behaviour can become instinctive, driven solely by the strong emotion or within an addictive or habitual pattern driven by the adrenaline charge. There is some medical evidence that some people become addicted to the natural morphine produced by their body and increasingly engage in the high arousal activity that produces it; be this dangerous sports, excessive exercise, fighting, or criminal behaviour. People who have strong prohibitions at the evaluation stage show high personal self discipline and behave in more socially acceptable ways and make skilled or empathic action. The range of behavioural actions in the action stage include:

- Usually beginning occasionally, but becoming more frequent, a person mismatches the particular case to their rational experience. They over handle, or misjudge situations. They may get a reputation for being 'hard' or indifferent, or for jumping to conclusions (go into 'fight' mode). Occasionally they buckle under an over-flood of feelings and may become withdrawn and depressed but more likely they become habitually angry and short-tempered. *They become cynical.*
- People routinely in stressful situations who are self-protecting (or in flight or freeze mode) will do the minimum work necessary and protect their personal energy and resources. They may pass the issue along on some pretext that they can't deal with it. They will be the first to withdraw from a difficult client in service situations where the police or security personnel can be called instead. They may call in sick and award themselves a day or two of respite. *They become unreliable.*
- People who are highly conscientious and highly identified with client or service problems (and may also become disassociated with service realities), will increasingly launch into inappropriate over-action. They may offer services or personally do too much for the client, or speak or act un-professionally; they may project dissatisfaction or anger onto other agencies or co-professionals. These are the people who rush away from difficult meetings and situations in frustration with tears and anger. *They become burned out.*

- People who understand themselves well, know they are well supported, and have personal and professional confidence, take appropriate action. *They act reliably and appropriately.*

Dealing with exceptionally difficult people or situations can put even the most professional persons at risk of passing beyond their own behaviour boundaries, and they begin to project re-active anger or a defensive attitude, often in private first. If somehow this is made public it can precipitate angry or discontented responses and the situation escalates.

With personal confrontations, do absolutely remember not to respond with your own anger. If the other person has poor personal control they will be better managed if you are calm and rational and assertive rather than aggressive. Beware that you do not act in any way that could be interpreted as bullying.

Bullying

It is now widely recognised that bullying can occur in the workplace and that along with sexual, racial, and disability harassment, bullying is usually expressed as some form of discrimination and will almost certainly be unlawful. All these forms of persecution, together with denial of opportunity, all share similar features. If proven and significant in affect Employment Tribunals have the power to grant unlimited compensation to the victims. Within the first few years of this millennium there have been several very high profile instances of women in quite senior positions with big city companies who have proven in the courts that they have suffered bullying and discrimination.

It is important to realise that general forms of grievance procedure are not always appropriate as they do not sufficiently protect the worker or the employer. Some issues are such sensitive subjects that, as well as the different specific anti-discriminatory law, all organisations are advised to have non-harassment and equal opportunity policies, and the advice when necessary of someone who specialises in employment law.

It is people who have a management or supervisory role who are most frequently accused of bullying. Most bullying does not occur as sudden attack, but by underhand comment and insinuation or disregard. A manager may not realise their actions can be construed as bullying.

They may think they are robust or they provide 'strong leadership' when in fact they make demands without sufficient thought to how well expectations will be received, or how staff may need to be differently supported.

Managers with a bullying manner will make threats or question job security, or bully through discrimination such as overlooking individual interest and abilities in favour of boring or low status work. These actions are very unsettling and difficult to challenge. More direct bullying is ridicule or demeaning comment, particularly if this is done in front of colleagues or clients. When managers deliberately use tactics such as unfair deployment, rudeness, aggressive and intimidating manner they are also usually unapproachable and react threateningly if challenged. They are always underhand or unsympathetic to reasonable requests. If union officials or senior managers become concerned they will try to misdirect matters and obscure the facts.

When bullying is hidden within the culture and attitude of an organisation it produces a higher than average staff turnover, high absentee rates, low morale or negative attitudes, and poor work results. Bullying is one of the most stressful pressures an employee can suffer because it can be difficult to establish the evidence for it. Evidence can be amassed by keeping a record of incidents together with witness accounts, and what specifically what was said or done, and by retaining any relevant email or letters – too often this advice comes too late.

Also, because formal accusations of bullying occur infrequently managers are often unsure about what to do. The factors around sexism or racism somehow seem more in the public domain and the issues more widely understood. If bullying is alleged it must be treated like any other complaint and looked at in isolation from personality differences or other subjective interpersonal issues that might be seen as associated by the complainant. The person complaining must be assured the matter will be kept confidential and investigated with absolute rigour in a manner that will be fair to them and the accused. When bullying occurs people are often reluctant to speak up. They fear they will not be believed, or their view will be belittled or they will be seen as a trouble maker. Other people may admire the bully or find what they do to others is acceptable to them. The greatest fear of the victim is that the bully will continue to intimidate with added vindictiveness and make continued employment impossible.

The point is – bullying is counterproductive: bullying attitudes and behaviour reduce all the positive potentials in people. You may wish to think that your enterprise is too small and cosy or otherwise immune from risk; the real risk is a financial one. The potential monetary cost can be so great it is sound commercial sense to ensure there are adequate and active policies. It helps if there is an Anti-Bullying Policy as this serves as a warning as well as making it easier to acknowledge and report should it occur. You may wish to review the anti-bullying or anti-discriminatory policy you have, or otherwise ensure they are drawn up.

There is one type of bullying that is particularly undesirable – passive aggression. Managers (all people) who act this way make deliberate punishment or retaliation hidden within what seems to be normal working and proper management decisions. Typically instructions or information is restricted or only passed on at the last minute. If questioned the manager will have an excuse – very often one that implies others in turn have let them down. The person or team subject to the manager's anger may be bypassed for all sorts of small or larger considerations. They may be set up as a scapegoat, or their actions denounced as a poor example. They may be secretly ignored, or carefully victimised. Very serious matters can be disguised within apparently proper actions.

Example: Bullying Manager
I was providing consultancy and support service to the managers of a medium sized company providing very successful child care in an area of exceptional need. The MD asked me to provide external supervision to the Training Manager, Mary, who I knew to be excellent at her work, highly motivated and conscientious. Mary had become very stressed and had been off sick for periods. During supervision it was clear that Mary's stress was centred on her line manager, the Operations Director (OD), who was also the person who normally provided her supervision.

There was revealed from Mary a strange history of 'cronyism' and 'grooming' from the OD – at an early point the OD offering to set up a break-away company with Mary in a key role. Mary later had to make formal complaint to the OD about serious breaches of practice in another's manager's work – although she saw this person as a crony of the OD. Mary felt this was a turning point. From then on she suffered what she described as a series of misdirections, disregard, and personal put-downs which if fully true, I could only construe as bullying. One tale sinisterly put about by the OD among Mary's colleagues was that her stress was related to problems with her partner at home – a gross indiscretion, and untrue.

On the other hand the OD had only lately been recruited; she had law qualifications and experience within the Home Office regarding youth offenders and child welfare. She was a formidable presence, being quick-minded and well-informed, had made effective changes, and had become seen as key to company progress.

However, to process her concerns Mary set out and documented what was in effect a whistle-blowing grievance to take to the company board. This assertive action re-focused company attention. And to cut to the end, the OD left rapidly, with her career fully deflated. Her convincing career 'history' had in fact been found to be largely fraudulent. The OD's calculating attack on Mary was because Mary as training director had company policy and practice in her veins and was probably the one person who might unseat the OD – as so she eventually did. Had Mary fully buckled under the stress she would have left (she came very close) and the OD would have wickedly won her job security.

5. Be assertive

One of the most common difficulties new managers face is how to tell people what to do. They are too anxious. The manager may be too sensitive, anguish about it, and then fail to give unambiguous direction; or they overcompensate and their manner becomes unnaturally arrogant and their style appears authoritarian. The proper balance can be difficult to find. The necessary behaviour trait is called *assertiveness*.

Being self-assertive begins with self-awareness. If you wish to have the attributes and manners of a respected leader it is essential that you feel good about yourself – not haughty and infallible, but 'good enough' yet looking to improve. This knowledge comes from a clear and unbiased self-view that is possible when personal demons have been shaken off, and is reinforced by the regard and actual comment made by persons you value among both your work colleagues and from your private life. Normally the most powerful persons at work on your self-view will have been – and maybe still – are your parents. Believe it!

Our culture values modesty and is embarrassed by complaint. We do not readily draw attention to our personal achievements or difficulties. The quiet stoic remains an icon, yet the demands faced by managers at times can seem incompatible. The dilemma of managers is, if they give in to pressures they feel like a dogsbody; if they reject pressures they risk being branded as unco-operative. To be effective for their organisation managers need to be effective for themselves and their team, and keep the pressures balanced. Even managers who are accomplished at diplomacy and keeping control of pressures can have problems when everybody else seems to outmanoeuvre them, or colleagues or senior managers come with demands they can't meet.

The assertive solution is not to be emotional but to present the case of their own or the team's workload, and let the facts stand for themselves. If strongly pushed to take on too much by senior management remind them that the initiative is theirs and you would like to support it. But will they also decide what you should forego in order to take on the extra work? Get into hard negotiation.

Managers who are properly assertive about what is valuable are also clear about their attitude to the prime task and are able to say clearly by what systems or methods it will be best achieved. They enjoy the autonomy and power necessary to discharge their responsibilities: 'they know what they are doing and demand they are allowed to get on with it'. Their teams and relationships tend to be cohesive and stable because they communicate well within and without the workplace, and can appropriately represent individual and organisational needs. Neither are they shy of claiming their achievements.

Work that is unseen cannot be appreciated, nor is it helpful, or just, to see another manager carry away the accolades for something you began because you did not claim its beginnings as yours. Appreciation must start with

self-appreciation: first acknowledge what you are doing well and celebrate it; draw attention when you are pleased with what you, your team, or individual colleagues have achieved, and keep seniors and others in the enterprise updated with items of good news.

Assertive persons show themselves to the world as positive thinking and unshakable in their values. They demonstrate the actions, stance, and language of a person with high self-worth, and when combined with deference and respect for other viewpoints and values, this does not alienate others.

However, not all open-handed approaches get a positive response. Sometimes other people are too aroused to 'hear' your sensitive responses. And in some situations your own anger may slowly build up. Eventually you might over-react. Or if contained, your internalised anger may turn to depression. If you can express your feelings and remain in self-control it will assist you to be psychologically and physically healthier. Being non-assertive because of other concerns, or if you over-control yourself for fear of loss of temper your emotion must be swallowed up or contained differently. Any of that leads to stress.

There is nothing wrong with being angry if there is good reason. Your feelings are yours to own and act upon: they are valid. It is on what you say and do that you will be judged. Actual loss of self-control of course will bring problems, but sometimes it is perfectly appropriate to appear cross. The trick is to play-act your anger. There is a famous occasion when the Soviet leader Khrushchev made a point at a world summit conference by taking off his shoe to thump the table – except he had gone to the meeting with an extra shoe for table thumping!

Of course this kind of planning is not possible, or ideal, in every situation, but it is possible at times; and planning to be deliberately angry is a useful skill. It will help you present to others your boundaries or expectations as well as represent an honest reflection of the results of their behaviour on you; but you keep your real anger threshold safely ahead. You don't have to *act* temper. Anger is best seen when controlled. This can be communicated comparatively easily by telling people you are angry. Use simple clear speech and emphasise your points with short punchy statements. Keep the exchange as brief as possible. Also use some simple body language such as standing, direct gaze, and holding eye contact for longer than natural. Neither will you need to swear or be disrespectful in any way, anger can be well communicated without loss of dignity or personal standards.

> Example: Planned Confrontation
> Years ago when I was first teaching I had a class to whom I wanted to give a 'blasting'. I planned the event knowing the lesson in which I was next likely to meet disorder. I prepared senior colleagues, and when their back-up was assured I was able to call them in, ostensibly in temper to reinforce my authority. But fully in control I read the 'riot act' to my class. I was then given a clear mandate in front of the class about what I should do if I had problems again.

To avoid going the whole distance is a professional skill. Because you are part of the dynamic in an encounter, your overt, and subliminal communication is part of a two-way process. How you respond, and what you do, can make the situation better or worse. Invariably a substantial loss of your control will cause the situation to deteriorate rapidly. The other aroused person or persons will already be subliminally alert to all the clues you are giving out.

Looking at interpersonal exchanges raises the issue that our own dealings with others can trigger reactions that lead to conflict, or conversely are soothing and empathetic. There are some simple ways we can frame or take an initiative with our interpersonal exchanges which can actually help protect us from adverse reactions or deteriorating situations. The idea of 'aggression-proofing' is an everyday awareness for some professionals – particularly those working in the area of mental health. There are some key ideas, and simple practices, that build or help show your proper assertiveness.

Positive personal practice

Assertive managing requires a high level of awareness to what is happening in your team or what you are responsible for at any one time. This is particularly the case when the nature of the work regularly produces risk issues. There is always a duty of care to both clients and staff. The manager who does something – who intervenes – is being assertive. There are attributes that will help ensure your intervention is seen as properly assertive and not over-bearing or ineffective.

Here are some assertive manager attributes:

- *Be seen to manage.* Show you have noticed what you have noticed early – whether it is good or bad. Make a comment as soon as reasonably proper, and as necessary and appropriate.
- *Be seen as calm.* Respected managers avoid their own 'personal edges'. They know what arouses their temper, and do not go suddenly from 'cold to hot'. When annoyed they clearly signal their degree of annoyance at appropriate points by telling colleagues that they are annoyed; why they are annoyed; and what the colleague has to do to put matters right for them.
- *Keep your agenda but be seen to be considerate.* A useful survival trick is shifting the focus of negotiation when under pressure to agree or to make a decision, especially when stuck in a board meeting or with a senior manager. Delay, by playing for time, or using a get-out. For example, deal with pressure by saying you will have to consult with colleagues or another manager before you can give a definite response. If you have to say no, return with an offer of something else, and preface this with cooperative comments such as: 'I'm sorry I couldn't do . . . but I could . . . I've looked again at my diary and it is just not possible, but I know you are concerned about . . . I will be seeing . . . Would you like me to . . .?'
- *Use assertive language.* The way a manager speaks and uses words conveys assertive command; the 'best' managers will only manage poorly if they do not make themselves unambiguously clear. Consider the following suggestions.

When dealing with problems:

- The manager's proper power is reflected in the context of words that are clear and direct. Use expressions like:
  o *I want, first . . . second . . .*
  o *do this now, the problem is . . .*
  o *tomorrow by lunch, will you . . .?*
  o *Tell me what you think about . . .*
  Do not use expressions like:
  o *It would be nice if . . . ,*
  o *We like it when . . .*
  o *I wonder if . . .*
  o *soon please, do you think you might . . .?*
  o *I wonder if you have an opinion on . . .*
- The instruction content of language must be precise and specific if you want people to do

what you have in mind: say exactly what needs to be done to put things right or whatever.
- Stay relaxed. Keep an even tone and pitch of voice, and use appropriately matching body language.

When praising colleagues: be specific. Generalised comment is nowhere near as effective as providing a comment that explains why you are pleased. This helps colleagues build self-perceptions about their own skills and reinforces good attributes. Use the person's name. Examples of specific comment are:

- *Jo, you've done that quickly – you are efficient – it's always helpful when I get these figures on time. Thank you.*
- *Nasima, that's an excellent illustration of the kind of problem that's been dogging the team – you've an eye for detail.*
- *Thanks for that memo note yesterday Jay – that kind of initiative is very helpful. I felt well informed.*
- *I'm pleased with what Jon and Sarah have achieved for this client – good collaboration is absolutely essential if clients are to get maximum benefit from this sort of multi-agency work.*

Below are several little mnemonic routines: each provides a structure for reviewing the work of managing. You may wish to choose one to add to your repertoire of ideas that help you to stay focused.

Managing is HARD

H   What is **happening** in the team, to the work in hand? Flag up to yourself anything unusual or any practice or demands shifting away from norms.

A   **Assess** the risks:
  o What new or additional difficulties might arise from current activities?
  o What was any previous experience or what is known about particular clients or colleagues that may have particular bearing?

R   **Review** the facts, and what your thinking is, and make a professional judgement to continue without any further intervention or enquiry – although you may make a diary note.

D   **Do** something appropriate.
  o Assertive managers act (not re-act) through considered intervention: they

may make general enquiry to see if all is going well, or draw particular colleagues aside for deeper discussion, or make other intervention. Or they may choose to do nothing for all sorts of reasons, including allowing more time to see how things might unfold more clearly. This is an 'action' only if this is a deliberate choice.

Alternatively you may prefer the 5 Phase Formula or get similar help from CEDRIC to assist your work.

Five Phase Formula (FFF)

1. Evaluate: what is going on?
2. Communicate: say what is going on and what needs to change.
3. Review: has your intervention made a difference?
4. Inform: go back to the colleague or team and tell them either that they have done or not done what you have asked.
5. Conclude: give praise, or inform about possible consequences. Repeat if necessary.

CEDRIC

C   'See' what is going on.
E   Evaluate it.
D   Do something: intervene or instruct about what needs to done.
R   Review: has your intervention made a difference?
I   Inform: say what has been done or not done as you asked.
C   Conclude: praise or thanks, or repeat from *Do* or *Inform*).

VOCALCOP

Vocal Cop is a mnemonic to help with your body language, when you should keep your arousal cues low. This is particularly valuable when dealing with clients (or colleagues?) who are likely to react aggressively:

VO   **Voice**: low and quiet.
CAL   **Calm**: careful movements and careful words
COP   **Command positively**: 'do this . . .' Use assertive attributes and language as described above.

Collaboration and assertion

Tackling colleagues about issues is for some managers one of the most challenging things they have to do. Taking up difficult issues in particular is felt by them as being confrontational, and so they hesitate or unassertively duck their responsibilities. Or when they must deal with a matter they become so anxious that ironically they do mishandle them by being too officious. Yet the skills that make criticism a potentially constructive action are associated with managers who are empathic.

The art of getting things done through people requires all members of a team to work effectively by communicating openly with each other. It is essential that their manager takes the lead in this and speaks frankly, and everyone else is encouraged to state what they think and feel, without fear of a negative response. Being able to acknowledge and share group and individual difficulties with others is one of the most effective counterguards against stress. This presupposes a level of openness and trust that makes critique possible, something that teams and workgroups can take a lot of time to develop without a good lead. Managers have the foremost responsibility to set the quality of the exchange and ensure issues can be taken up within their team; and also to assist individuals develop their skills, understanding and abilities to work collaboratively. The quality of the work is certain to depend on this.

When team members can resolve internal problems openly and appropriately this creates a healthier atmosphere than holding onto resentment, or complaining indirectly to the manager. However, when managers as well as colleagues can be reluctant to take up issues, the reason may typically be:

- The manager is too optimistic or deferential. He is unrealistic about how robust is the self-esteem or professionalism of others, and avoids criticism in case it sets them back. (*Mr C Nobad*).
- The manager has a strong need to be seen as supportive and understanding. His needs outweigh realism. (*Mr B Nice*).
- The manager thinks a problem belongs to someone else, or should have been sorted before they took on the job. Or they are just lazy. (*Mr Y Me*).
- The manager is fearful of counterclaim or strong characters. They are unassertive and

uncertain how well what they have to say will be received and they shirk away from difficult inter-personal meetings. Issues may be ignored, rejected, or doubted. (*Mr O P Goesaway*).
- The manager makes light of problems even to the point of laughing and joking. This makes it difficult to get him to see things seriously. He's ignorant of others' worries. (*Mr G Up*).
- The manager is too busy or too stressed to take on more. (*Mr O Dear*).
- The manager can't understand the issues presented by others or be empathetic to them. He has a completely different view. (*Mr I C Noships*).

Taken along a continuum, the ideal situation is to always directly confront the person involved; the least desirable situation is never to tell the person directly. Quality collaborative work is based on giving and receiving critical feedback in constructive ways, and team members do this routinely. When more serious issues of competence and service quality have to be taken up with one colleague it also requires a little forethought on practical matters and how you will deal with what you have to do. Key things to consider include:

- Prepare the colleague by telling them the purpose of the meeting is feedback and that there are difficulties to talk about.
- Ensure there is a safe and private room and that neither of you will be interrupted.
- Prepare well so that the facts are safe from dispute. If your position as manager is undermined by defendable counterclaim and argument it will become quite difficult to draw back to firm ground.
- Use calm but assertive language (see above) so that you do not bury your concerns or muddle your message by confusion through euphemisms or half-truths, nor get agitated.
- Do listen to what the other person may put forward as influences on their behaviour or reasons why they have not achieved what you hoped, and hear any requests they might make for support or allowance.
- Keep to your agenda and facts, and keep the meeting as short as possible.
- Do not bring in your own problems or relate your experiences or anecdotes to soften or ameliorate the tone – that just confuses.
- Briefly balance the negative content with short pointers towards the other person's usual ability or degree of commitment.

- Be crystal clear about what needs to be done, how and by when; and how it will be checked out or acknowledged when done. Ideally, make a written note of agreed action points and give your colleague a copy.
- Finish by asking your colleague to comment on the process and to confirm it is resolved.

Related to this issue is the fact that critique is too often understood as only meaning uncomplimentary comment, although everyone should understand that evaluation or review can be negative or complimentary. Critique is most useful when fulsome in detail. Although it is the detail that is used to point up criticism, it is precisely the detail that provides the useful information from which change can be made and equally, when positive, for which repeat can be sought. Managers who are alert to these concerns will ensure team reviews include a balance of comment and recognition of good work, and that critical comment, good or bad, is made in the context of what can be learnt from it – it is focused on solution. How best to give and receive professional comment is well worth considering.

Handle criticism

You won't manage anything well unless you can handle criticism. Answer the following *Critique Questionnaire Activity* to review your self understanding. This may also be used with colleagues, either in pairs or small groups, to review individual or team response to criticism. Coloured Post-it notes are useful: put individual thoughts or responses on them, and then group similar ones together in answer to each question.

Critique Questionnaire Activity

1. What has been my/our experience of negative feedback given in an inconsiderate manner?
2. What has been my/our experience of negative feedback given considerately?
3. What forms of critique prevail here (see Archetypal Forms below) – if it is variable why so?
4. Which form of critiques is personally valued most?
5. What are the reasons why or situations when I/we personally resent receiving criticism?
6. What are the reasons why or situations when I/we personally hesitate to give criticism?
7. What are the consequences of not letting someone know when you are unhappy about something they have done (up, down or across 'the line')?

8. Feedback: what are the ultimate conclusions? What must be done? How is it best done?
9. Personal Assertiveness: write down any new personal development you hope to make as a result of this exercise.
10. Swap your note on 9 with someone you trust, and agree when you will review your personal intentions for each other.

It is 'critically' important when taking up negative issues with a colleague to make clear the service quality reasoning behind what you say – unfortunately this is too often ignored or taken for granted. It is one of the main causes for others to feel 'got at', and for the person giving criticism to get a reputation for being disapproving. There is more on this in Chapter 4.

It is also important to understand how the different forms of *critique* can be seen as a pattern of archetypes. The archetypes are given below but not evaluated. It does not necessarily mean one form is inherently better than another; they are just different, and will suit different forms of enterprise structure, preferences and needs. With insight and understanding about the forms of critique you may better be able to influence how comment is given and received, as well as understand better the pressures or driving forces that gave rise to the particular comment and the manner it was said.

There are a number of archetypical forms of critique, including:

- line manager
- peer
- self-critique
- upward appraisal
- external appraisal

Line manager

A line manager can be hierarchic, controlling and directing but can cause the appraised person to feel patronised, or threatened or inhibited if faced with a sense of judgement – it is all down to the quality of communication and the degree of interpersonal respect encouraged within the organisational culture.

Peer

This critique removes 'threat' of management, encourages less confident people to speak up, and is effective if it encourages self-questioning and experimentation. However, it can make it more possible to moan as well as come up with zany or innovative ideas. Can be collusive (too cosy or blame-placing) if not rigorously even-handed. May be best kept to open meeting discussion.

Self-critique

This offers limited opportunity for debate, and is a very sophisticated professional skill.

Upward appraisal

This allows senior managers to gather the range of viewpoints, and allows them to see how their management is received. Is obtained from forums such as staff meetings, work-party groups, questionnaires and evaluation exercises, suggestion boxes.

External appraisal

This comes in various guises:

- Professional peer or consultant report; and non-managerial supervision. Especially useful in small organisations.
- Inspection reports and verbal feedback. Although this tends not to be individualised, it can say a lot about the qualities of senior management, as well as the quality of the work generally.
- Various forms of feedback from service purchasers and service users. User appraisal is often given very voluntarily by young people! It can be difficult to orchestrate client feedback in an organised way without being tokenistic, or just getting a 'wish-list', but invaluable when done well (e.g. *Warner Report* practice on staff selection, service user groups, advocacy services).

Finally, a central point about assertiveness is how you appear to others. There are certainly some managers who are only comfortable hiding in their offices. Managers who enjoy excellent communication with their people usually have a MBWA 'qualification' (management by walking about). Even if you do not naturally feel assertive there is a simple way you can appear to be so – and then become just that.

Make out you are comfortable, confident and assertive by using one or more of the Famous

Five techniques. These work in all interpersonal situations and should be practiced with whoever you meet, be they colleague or clients – for many managers it's intuitive or natural practice already.

Famous Five

1 Friendly face

Always make the first overture: always say the first hello, or make a comment or enquiry as you walk about. **Never ever** pass someone by without acknowledging them at least by a smile. This helps establish the value of you both as individual people. If possible acknowledge them by some small enquiry. This sets the tone for any interpersonal exchanges that may follow:

- Your initiative shows confidence – and that you are in 'power' – and this is 'your place'.
- Noticing others makes them feel significant – it lifts their mood and self-esteem.
- Initiating friendly contact reduces the likelihood of poor reaction if later you have a negative exchange.
- Gives you a chance to check they are OK – gives them a chance to say a word.
- Protects you from possible projected anger (transference) that can result if others feel ignored or slighted.
- Reduces your stress.

2 Choice

Should an issue arise during MBWA or be brought to your office, you have choices:

- Do not ignore it, but you don't have to deal with it on the other person's chosen ground. Either deal with it then, or acknowledge that there is a problem but you will return to it later and make arrangements when and where to do so (this can give both parties some time for thought).
- If an exchange becomes confrontational acknowledge the fact and offer a positive alternative or different follow-up. This can give both parties an exit, and give thinking or calming time. It's their choice to take it up and they need not feel rebuffed by your power.

3 Signals and body language

Use positive signalling and body language to show your presence:

- To show you are actively listening, use 'mm' and 'I see . . .'
- Paraphrase when possible.
- Do not interrupt – you may be busy but if you show it this is very annoying to a person who has a story to tell.
- If they are very aroused allow them to vent their emotion: just listen, let them speak until they run out of words and breath – then you can assert control.
- State the obvious. This shows you are listening but doesn't concede any points, i.e. 'I can see you're very angry/upset.
- Use positive listening signals such as:
  o Coded 'looks' such as pulling a face or raised eyebrows – pick up on mood; give nods.
  o Open and relaxed body posture.
  o Keep normal personal distance and space.

4 Neutral comment

If you have negative comment to make, begin the social exchange with neutral or unrelated remarks. Similarly if there is tension that would benefit from relief, attention can be diverted if you comment for a moment or two on something else that is socially acceptable (someone else passes by; an unrelated event catches attention).

5 Avoid a void

Don't ignore a situation that is clearly worsening. Do something!

- Your slow or hesitant management may be seen as weakness or incompetence.
- People may think you don't care.
- Lacklustre responses can:
  o Increase distress or anger of some clients.
  o Give incompetent or lazy colleagues or difficult clients reason to think their behaviour can continue. And when you finally do deal with the problem it is the more resented as the offending habits or attitudes will be more deeply entrenched.
  o Increase the anger or dissatisfaction among colleagues who are working hard and may be making good the gaps you are not dealing with.
- If you are stuck as to what to do, at least acknowledge that there is a problem and arrange to deal with it later – this gives you time to think or consult, but you must do as you said.

The value of a smile
It costs nothing, but creates much
It enriches those who receive, without impoverishing those who give

It happens in a flash, but the memory may last forever
None are so rich that they can live without it
None are so poor that are not richer from a smile
It creates happiness in the home, fosters goodwill in business, and is the countersign of friends
Yet it cannot be bought, begged, borrowed or stolen, for it is something that is no earthly good to anyone until it is given away
And if it ever happens that someone should be too tired to give you a smile
Then give one of yours
For nobody needs a smile so much as those who have none left to give.

Anon.

CHAPTER 4

How to Promote Positive Practice

1. Communicate clearly

Nothing is more important to a manager than communication. When arrangements between people go awry, the first suspect is poor communication. If you wish to manage well begin with communicating well; mean what you say and say what you mean. Always plan thoroughly what you want to say, and even in the briefest discussion engage brain before mouth. As a manager your words carry additional power, and although any misunderstanding may have potential to turn into a problem, the most irritating thing is when you think you have given clear instruction but the other person thinks you only recommended or hinted at something which they promptly ignore. If that happens it's your problem not theirs. Managers who get things done don't give ambiguous instructions (see also Assertive Language, Chapter 3.5).

Enterprises that achieve their ambitions have managers who connect well both within and without their organisation (also see Chapter 2; internal and external markets). They understand and manage the flow of information by making sure they give and get information easily and use the most appropriate method depending on the situation. They also understand that communication may be biased or contain hidden agenda and they are careful how they interpret what they read or hear, as well as selective in the manner they connect with other people.

Good communication depends on the skill to say something well **and** to know the best media in which to say it.

Your arm provides an analogy for the usual arrangements for communication. Small nerves lead from your fingertips upwards to merge and be gathered at ganglions found at your wrist and elbow, before taking a highway route to your brain. Messages from your brain can pass between brain and fingertip, but hit your funny bone hard or sit on your hand until it 'goes to sleep' and there is either message overload or shutdown at a ganglion point. Nerve fibres are the communication modes analogous to speech, paper, or electronic media; the ganglions are the focus points or synapse analogous to the front desk, your PA, or the team meeting.

Persons with urgent or vital information are easily frustrated if not angered when they meet poor administration or non-prioritising call handling. The good intent and morale of colleagues is thwarted when there are not good opportunities to discuss issues, when meetings and briefings are routinely cancelled, or these occasions become too brief, too busy, or one-directional. The communication pathways are only as good as the reception points.

Some communication can be extremely direct and bypass the usual modes (nerve fibres) – like looking at a fingertip to see why it prickles. *Management by walking about* (MBWA) and talking with people produces that kind of direct bypass, and very high IT connectivity can emulate it. If you routinely do MBWA, connectivity is raised as people will get to know your pattern and look out for you and make direct comment – just make sure you or they make a proper record of any important or formal things.

Communication modes are the methods for connecting, and the prevalence of any one will vary according to the enterprise culture, the nature of the work and how dispersed people are. The formal modes for work communication include:

- Talk, normally without evidence (e.g. *Can I have a word?*), such as small line-managing instructions, briefings, telephone conversations.
- IT communication, not printed to hard copy and only retained on electronic file if thought important – email, letter or memo attachments, and text messages.
- Planned talk, that has written evidence such as a meeting with agenda and minutes, supervision with written record.
- Paper documents, such as memos, printouts, letters, circulars, office diary, bulletins and suggestion box, etc.

Informal modes include:

- Talk: gossip and rumour, crony network, chat around the coffee machine.
- Other: unsigned remarks pinned to the notice board, unofficial email, graffiti.

Managers must concern themselves when necessary with the informal modes as well as official communication. Consider the following points:

- How consistently are different forms of information associated with particular modes? (With changes to instructions, do you send a memo to your colleagues but does your senior manager ring you up?
- Are all the available modes as effective as desired, or could improvements be made? If new referrals and memos are normally emailed to field workers, what arrangements are there for someone without PC access?
- Which mode is most acceptable or effective with your colleagues and how well does it reflect the culture of your organisation? Organisations with a lot of worry, gossip or rumour usually have a history of inconsistent communication – for example, people may collude over an issue by email or direct gossip, but not directly confront the issue or the 'responsible' person directly.

Synapses are the points or gates where information passes through. Even organisations with high internal connectivity will impose some structure to guard the security of particular information and to regulate the flow of information to ensure recipients get only what they need and everyone is not weighed under with information irrelevant to them. Consider the following points about synapses:

- Do you deal with one synapse or are there different 'gatekeepers' or points of focus for different types of information – if so, are the differences clear?
- If different synapses, is there a one-point override access somewhere when the information is electronic (it may be security controlled)?
- How well generally is information gathered in and re-distributed at your main synapse? This may simply reflect on your personal systems and efficiency, or that of your PA or reception staff.

Most communication is talking, and managers do a lot of talking with colleagues about internal matters. All communication, written and spoken, is composed of style and content. Communication has to be given and received. A lot of people are surprisingly unaware of their manner or style of speaking, and that this can considerably taint the content. Managers will not get wide-based respect without taking account of who they are talking to and how their comment might be received. Use the what's your style checklist to appraise self or others.

Reflect how well your natural style always suits what you do, and how well you consider who you are communicating with. Is there any room for improvement? It is equally vital to consider how the other person may receive information. There are some things to remember about people you speak with.

1. Verbal communication, speaking face to face, is potentially the most powerful and effective form of communication, but it can be valid on matters of importance to keep a record in one of the following ways:
   o Send a memo or thank-you letter to summarise discussion and table any decision or instruction.
   o Make a diary entry of the discussion and any key instruction or comment. There is legal precedent that if you can show this is your usual practice it will support your word in court against the word of another who has not made such an entry.
   o Make a written note of the conversation and put this in the personnel or client file as appropriate.
   o Ask another person to act as witness and remember what you said.
   o With permission, tape-record the conversation.
2. English may not be the other person's first language. Find ways to check their comprehension without being patronising. This may be vital if for example the situation concerns any medical or legal procedure.
   o Speak plainly and clearly.
   o Avoid metaphor or management-speak, which may all be gobbledygook and not as clear as daylight.
   o Avoid jargon. Ensure the meaning of any special word is understood.
3. More than half of verbal communication is body language.

What's Your Style? Activity

Consider the following checklists honestly and appraise your skill, or ask someone you trust who knows you well. Underline or circle items in pencil that match your style – tick 'W' or 'S' if writing differs from speech. At least one from each of the following three styles or 'communications sets' will be apparent in all your speech, though only the first two sets apply to how you write.

Manner tends to be:	W	S
• brusque and abrupt (over assertive?) • tentative and hesitant (under assertive?) • apologetic • pompous and haughty • patronising (over explication) • uncertain (requesting manner) • too conversational (instruction can be lost in other comment) • commanding or authoritarian (military) • quietly authoritative • consultative		

Content tends to be:	W	S
• specific and economical • all waffle and repeat • generalised (not clear on specifics) • rational argument mostly • emotional motivation mostly • balance between sound case and emotional appeal • in discussion: mostly what you say/or mostly what you ask/or both equally (choose one)		

Level of Attentiveness is generally:	S
• Fully attentive to the other person (you pick up on body language as well as actual comment). • Half attentive to the other person (you appear alert but your mind is elsewhere; you hear key words but lose the rest, or only focus on what you think is important). • Not attentive to the other person (you are brusque, or ignore their reactions).	

o Ensure you look at the other person and they can see your face.

o Do be un-stiff and use some silent 'Italian' (gestures) with your English words.

o If talking over the phone, make extra sure of mutual understanding, by following any other points, as may be relevant, from this checklist.

4. You can be misheard by anyone at any time, not just because a plane passed overhead or the other party has a faulty hearing aid.

o Asking the other party to repeat back to you what you have said is the simplest check here.

5. Your position of comparative importance might stop the other person from questioning you or asking you to repeat yourself.

o Ask them if they agree or have any uncertainties they want to ask you about.

6. People do forget what they have been told, especially if they do not 'want to hear it', or the information is given at a time of trauma or upset or moment of busy preoccupation, or if there is a lot of information to impart:

o These are the kind of situations when a reminder, or a written note or a follow up letter is helpful (in the right tone).

7. The other person may nod agreement but actually disagree and will ignore what you said:
   - Be prepared – you may not know this until something surprises you.
   - If you doubt a colleague, check it out later.
   - If a procedural matter, reinforce your point with documentation.

The danger of not being fully focused on what you say or write is that compromises and assumptions can creep in to detract from the quality of what you do. When things go wrong the testimony heard in so many enquiries is from people who did not get a message or were not included in new instructions. Managing properly requires vigilance to ensure the content of all communication is congruous with the enterprise culture and purpose, and sets out exactly what is required. You might think the next checklist reminds you of a job description – good, it is!

Be clear about how you:

- Expect or work to reach agreement about who does what to include duties, responsibilities, punctuality etc.
- Direct the work of junior colleagues with unambiguous purpose, necessary preparation and discharge of tasks, and responsibility boundaries.
- Give exact requirements to colleagues, teams, and other managers as necessary to ensure excellent internal service, and refresh information as appropriate.
- Resolve any 'gap' differences (see Chapter 2) that might emerge between the organisation's purpose and the actual work done by the team. The issues may include individual or team performance, boundary maintenance, resources, legal matters, health and safety.
- Model respect for other people's skills, experience, and specialisms.
- Respect the views of every team member when consulting to canvass a 'dialogue in hand' (see below 3; *Manage People Well*).
- Deal with any differences of view that may emerge, so that these can be openly discussed and team members are confident their views will be heard.
- Resolve any concerns between colleagues and service users that are brought to you (from within or without).
- Deal with any individual view or comment that needs to be enlarged or clarified so that the team might learn from it.

- Be responsive to the occasions when it might be best to shield colleagues from unnecessary organisational worry, so that they can stay focused on their work (based on competence about finance, budgets, and management structures).
- Keep confidential boundaries so that you can maintain an environment of mutual trust.
- Present your decisions in an open-handed manner so that your confidence and assertive leadership is evident.
- Are seen to do things. When you undertake any action yourself particularly when assuming a new responsibility, do these things without delay or quibble, and inform the people who need to know what you are doing.
- See the difference between roles and functions, keep the awareness alive and discriminate between these when necessary, and monitor the situation for yourself and colleagues.
- Say what you want – well, say it whether verbally or in writing.

Communication with other agencies

Managers and other personnel have to work with members of larger networks and other organisations when involved in partnerships, and when there is a duty to inform or liaise with other agencies. If these matters are to happen at all, let alone happen well, the quality and timeliness of communication is vital. Just consider how often the news comprises services or professionals who did not communicate well enough with each other or made assumptions. The national record on child protection over the recent past unfortunately provides too many cases in point.

How well the team or organisation is professionally regarded by other agencies and get their help and co-operation will in large measure depend upon two things. Firstly if the team is able to set out its concerns grounded upon positive practice, and secondly if it is able to show an active track record. Credibility with other professionals is considerably enhanced in multi-agency or partnership work when a team can show they have already acted well and at length, and have come to the end of their expertise or resources. A team that can negotiate through troubles as easily as if dealing with welcome situations will also be well marketed and well managed; and in turn this will reflect the quality of internal attitudes, processes, and procedures. On occasions it can be a severe test.

It is always good practice to:

- Be informed about or understand the goals which influence the behaviour or decisions of people from other organisations.
- Understand the organisational constraints under which others must operate.
- Recognise that relationships with other organisations may be complicated.

This may be because:

- Failure on the part of others to understand what your team is primarily concerned about, and what it can or cannot do (the team must be sure first).
- Actual communication difficulties (different priorities, language or jargon, as well as logistics).
- Differences in stance and attitude towards the service users based on being informed by a different philosophy or professional model.
- Differences in stance and attitude because one team or organisation may be handing over to another, with concomitant feelings of failure or resentment, or disbelief that the handing over is for the best.

Personal authority

When anybody communicates poorly face-to-face it is usually because of difficulties with assertion and confidence. People who are otherwise valued colleagues can mar what they want to say by choosing the wrong moment or using an inappropriate tone. You will have met people who do things clumsily such as raise major issues in the middle of your coffee break when you are relaxing, or fail to brief colleagues fully so that they make inadvertent errors, or whisper to someone at length by the water machine in such a conspiratorial manner that all other conversation stops.

Information is going to come from what others say to you; therefore to receive more you will need to transmit less. If you talk the most you practice speaking not listening skills. Managers by their position are already vulnerable to inadvertently dominating exchanges between themselves and their colleagues. It is comparatively easy to lose sensitivity to others or preclude their opportunities to speak. Managers with good personal authority understand how their effectiveness can depend upon receiving

information more than giving instruction; and they tend to talk less and to hear, see and understand more. This may be the only way to add to what you already know.

On the other hand, silence is often perceived as uncomfortable; particularly perhaps in team meetings, when someone if not you will fill the vacuum. Too often people are wary of silence and are only at ease when conversation is flowing and they allow the meeting to be led by those who are more vocal. There may be a palpable pressure to come to conclusions. In these situations slowing down, or reducing the dominance of another or oneself, can allow space for deeper thought and better decision-making.

You might wish to consider how you compare here. Your manner as a manager in meetings of any kind is crucial; your making no comment can be seen as silently aggressive or disapproving. This can be awkward when you particularly do wish to hear from others and not influence matters yourself; you should either declare that, or to avoid seeming too withdrawn or too noncommittal counter with an interested but relaxed demeanour. Be aware of your body language, and sit in an open-arm, open-hand posture, make use of encouraging nods, lean forward to show concentration, and use 'ums' and 'I see', and 'and?' Ask for a point to be expanded or exampled (see also Chapter 3; *Assertiveness*).

Silence is a counselling tool that emphasises that the other person has the important things to say. Too many questions or too much comment can overly direct the flow of thought, or subvert it as the other person either resists or gives way to dominance, or senses they are not listened to. Silence should be comfortable between friends, and cultivating silence is the skill that makes listening possible. If you lead interviews, case planning or similar meetings, providing a moment of silence is especially useful. If necessary actually propose a minute or two of silence for everyone to settle or review their minds before proceeding, particularly at critical points. Often it is only then that someone will make comment that would otherwise have not been heard. Pregnant pauses give birth.

When receiving information always have regard from whom it comes, and how it is couched. You may think that you are above the petty politics of others, or that your team eschews anything other than open mutuality. The reality is that other people do try to play 'power relationships' from time to time for different reasons and may hide their true motivation behind a deceptive front.

I don't mean you should cultivate cynicism but any critique should be able to 'stand free'. This means that all colleagues should be able to subscribe to it – all share the same beliefs. The continuum of accord ranges from total to none. Imagine the extreme case when you or a colleague makes comment that is met by complete non-acceptance. Then the breakdown of agreement is very evident. It is less evident when the dissent is less strong or not voiced for some reason. Sometimes in those situations this happens time over, and the distance between people grows but does not emerge until an issue that highlights the distance comes to the fore and brings to light all the prior unvoiced opposition. Without warning, relationships and cooperation are soured; if that happens to a team you manage it's distressing and can be difficult to put right.

It is a distinguishing mark of professionalism that conventional or the first-thought views on issues are challenged. This attitude means that issues are always looked at afresh each time, and only what is absolutely evident is considered. This is very hard to consistently achieve within yourself or with a team as we naturally carry our previous experience with us and are normally reluctant to overturn our preconceptions that may have been painfully impinged upon us. To carry some bias is very human in character, but sometimes whole teams can fall into comfy kinds of collusion that distorts clear view; and these effects can be at work in dealings with other colleagues as well as clients.

A useful exercise is to screen your own or the team practice for possible bias: this can be done as a professional development activity by taking each point in turn to discuss it and see what examples are volunteered. When this is done in a fully open and non-defensive manner it will investigate common viewpoints and inform about equal opportunity beliefs as well as help you sound out the validity of your personal authority. Here are some common forms of bias:

Seeing a halo

One outstanding good characteristic or a positive reputation is held foremost in mind. It dominates viewpoint and colours truer perception:

A colleague is held in high regard because of years of good work. A new person on the team may question the view because they see an old hack who they think does not show the credited qualities. This brings them into conflict with team members loyal to the 'old hack'.

Seeing horns

This is similar to seeing a halo but with a bad characteristic or negative reputation:

A service user who used to be problematic is still regarded and treated as such although this may not have been the real case for some while. The team may accredit themselves as better at managing the client and not recognise that the client has changed.

Long sightedness

This is about overlooking things nearby. The focus is on others or more distant issues at the expense of what should be evident because it is so close:

Everyone complains about what they see as poor practice at the 'central office' when dealing with their information. The office issued a new format for information three years ago but gave up asking this team to submit the new form when they repeatedly didn't. The original got lost, and no-one now remembers it. This real example is included because it also illustrates how the introduction of IT can remove at a stroke considerable potential for problems to occur or remain unattended.

Short sightedness

Seeing and responding only to the obvious problems and ignoring underlying issues:

Treating a elderly nursing care resident for depression without making any effort to recognise and act upon the cause, which may be remediable (assisting the life partner to visit more frequently, or stay in privacy overnight).

Rose-coloured glasses

Overcompensating with people because of the halo you gave them:

As manager you ignore some poor case work done by an 'old hack' crony and rationalise this as case overload.

Seeing in monochrome

Losing passion, all things become equal value:

This is caused by overwork or depression or both, or loss of belief and self-worth as the work is not properly acknowledged (by your enterprise, peers, or society; also perhaps by pay or indirect respect for the work).

High contrast vision

Your personal rather than professional standards sway you (and sometimes the other way in your domestic life!)

A colleague is less well respected by you because their command of English grammar is poor, or their accent is distasteful to your ear, or you just don't think people who ride motorbikes (or swear or smoke or whatever) can be properly professional. At time of writing a case example in the news concerns a doctor who told a patient seeking advice on abortion she was selfish to even consider it.

Seeing the same

Preferring people of the same race, gender, class, appearance, etc. as yours.

'Old school' type and similar prejudices favour your view: personally I always think highly of fat grey-haired bikers who wear specs!

Tower-top view

Going for the big view before the detail is established. This is a bit like monochrome sight, but from impulsivity or pressure, or a haughty management style:

Without consultation, faggots are removed from the menu because too many remain uneaten when served. Actually many of the residents like faggots but a while ago the supplier was changed, and now they are not as tasty.

Blind political correctness

Being so alert to imagined sensitivities that exist only in your febrile mind that you deny common sense and conventional wisdom:

You say 'sight disability' when your client tells you forthrightly that she's completely blind.
You banned the word 'faggots' from the menu after your holiday in America.

People in healthy cultures talk with each other a lot and are aware of bias, and they make regular comment to each other in direct ways including praise when merited.

2. Motivate and inspire

Your challenge is to ensure your people enjoy their work and get high satisfaction from doing it so that they remain interested and committed. The ways this is best done are all linked. The factors your team members need include work security, feeling involved and well regarded, some autonomy coupled with confidence in doing what they do, and confidence and trust in your management because you consult and help them be involved in decision-making.

Work security

There are several issues about work security. *Basic job security* is the essential starting point, and the key to ensure people are committed and not de-energised by doubt that their job will continue. Although factors around issues of job security may not be in your control, there are plenty of instances where the energy and imagination of a local manager saved a team's future by astute marketing or bargaining to gain new sources or a wider remit of work.

Job security

The local manager may often find it is really difficult to keep a fine balance between maintaining the desired number in the team and ensuring all the necessary skills are represented. Practice can become poor because of over-reliance on agency staff, or because the quality of the team has fallen although the number in the team can appear OK. There may be a temptation to ensure the team numbers are generous: however if the number is too big there may be problems if the work shrinks or become more fluctuating. It de-motivates staff teams if they become too idle or redundancies have to be made.

The 'sick record' example in Chapter 3 showed how high sickness rates and low morale result from when experiences are ignored or poor work practice is not remedied. Bad management not only affects service quality it can wreck the health and careers of good people. You have a first-line duty of care towards the people you manage. As the local manager your detailed knowledge about your team and expert understanding about the work will give you credence and authority if you have to be assertive with senior managers on issues of team establishment.

The need to keep team skills balanced or respond to work fluctuations is often met by taking on additional persons on temporary or part time contracts, or the use of agency staff. These people can be outstanding as they often bring fresh energy and new skills into the team.

But they will not have the sense of belonging nor normally the drive to put in that bit extra at a moment of need. Even if otherwise willing, unfamiliarity with work details may mean they can't easily see or know how to deal with any loose ends, and it can be unfair if too much is expected of co-opted personnel. The advantages are that as you come to know individuals they can form an excellent pool from which you can source applicants for permanent posts.

Most likely you will resist too much outside help or too much expansion because you know a tight team of competent persons with good communication and good resources can do much better than a larger number that includes people less competent or less well equipped.

Example:
At Agincourt in 1415, six thousand English soldiers won a battle against the French whose army was three times the size, and of whom over half were killed. The English army was the better trained and more veteran. Their archers were also equipped with the powerful long bow and were exceptionally well deployed.

The pressure to keep your team fully competent can at times place a high demand for training. The introduction of any new technology invariably requires personnel to develop new skills as well as embrace new work patterns. The obvious example is in the ways that internet communication, IT equipment, and mobile phones are making new forms of working much more possible, and a number of service industries are beginning to follow commercial practice and equip personnel to routinely work from home. This can be particularly effective for peripatetic forms of service, and when professional work is mainly carried out elsewhere than on company or service premises; for example, reports can be written to laptop at odd moments of the day and emailed back to the centre. When there is reduced need to go to a work base, the working day is more efficient and the amount of travel can be lower.

Keeping the team well established starts with appointing the right people and is maintained by supportive methods of appraisal and development. It is your job to pick the right people. A quite common cause for staff turnover begins at the appointment stage because there is a failure of proper understanding between an applicant and the interviewers. The new person finds they are in work somehow different from what they imagined and they leave (see *Psychological contract* below and more in Chapter 5, and *Roles and functions* in Chapter 2).

Emotional security

A second form of work security for your team stems from how you manage. A great deal of work satisfaction comes from the emotional security of knowing you do the work well because you know how to do the work. That means the operating arrangements are perfectly clear and well prioritised; there are accessible and effective frameworks set out in policy and codes of practice; your expectations are reasonable and consistent; and there is good communications, including you being accessible when a colleague needs to consult you. And the same situation is enjoyed in your necessary connections within the enterprise, across the decks and up to the bridge.

Psychological contract

The third form of work security is recognising that here is a 'psychological' as well as a formal written contract. Much of this is implied by attitude and manner during selection processes. The employer takes the lead by implying what it will be like working for the enterprise. Everything is not always made explicit or written up, but the applicant will get a picture of how they will be treated. They will form a view about their prospects for promotion, training and development, job security, how welcome they will be as a new colleague and what perks or employee care arrangements there are. The employer will get a picture that includes the less formal professional and personality traits that suggest whether the applicant will fit well into the team and be an asset to the work.

If too much is assumed one of the parties is likely to be disappointed. Otherwise the psychological contract binds both parties through commitment, trust and loyalty, and as time progresses like any partnership the bonds are forged deeper.

Your enterprise must provide good opportunities for the aspirations of its people if it wishes for their strong allegiance. Being bound together in a good common purpose satisfies the needs of humanity for belonging and to feel good

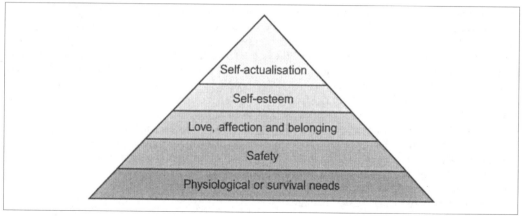

Figure 4.1   Maslow's Hierarchy

about what they do. Understanding this 'psychological contract' may be helped by reference to *Maslow's Hierarchy of Needs*.

Maslow's Hierarchy of Needs

Maslow's well-accepted idea is that everyone aspires to have their different needs met, and these are represented as stacking levels in a pyramid of sets. The third level is the need for love and belonging, as found among friends and companions, in a supportive family, by identification with a group, and in an intimate relationship. It is at this level that adults who have left their birth families behind can have many of their companionship and belonging needs met by work.

We talk of people who 'are married' to their work. I spent a long period working within a residential therapeutic community and only afterwards realised how much personal sustenance and companionship I received from belonging to the group and enjoying very close but proper familiarity with colleagues and clients alike. I know that my personal and professional development benefited immensely from submersion in an environment of constant process, that was at once both liberating and demanding. Cults take advantage of similar needs to belong, to bind their members. Some enterprises put so much emphasis on being 'a family' that they can become rather unhealthy and too cult-like in how they tie their people into a corporate identity and discourage outside contact. Keeping a sense of one's self separate from one's professional identity can fulfil a paramount need for personal well-being.

Example: Retaining identity

My wife also worked alongside me as domestic bursar in a therapeutic community for several years, and at times, as is the nature of living therapy, there would be open community meetings when one or other of us might be verbally attacked or come under some scrutiny or criticism (or praise – but that did not bring problems!). On such occasions our relationship could be tested. Across the room we had to relate to each other as colleagues and perhaps side with a resident's view or champion a cause that the other found awkward – such as an issue over food where I might agree with a resident, and my wife might be constrained by budgets. Once when she experienced theft of personal possessions I publicly chastised her for carelessness and ignoring policy on items of personal value (also a cheap trick to increase the guilt of the resident under suspicion).

Keeping credible boundaries was essential if we were to maintain our separate professional identities, and keep our shared relationship private. Some residents found it puzzling that we could compartmentalise our relationship and not be cosy together all the time or be mutually protective. I'm sure at times situations were manipulated to test us; what residents never witnessed however, was the private talk and consolation at home.

Maslow's fourth level is the need for esteem. Feelings such as adequacy, competence and confidence build self-esteem, and these feelings result from the recognition by other people of your abilities. This in turn gives you feelings of prestige, acceptance and status. If your self-esteem needs are not met, you feel discouraged and inferior. At the apex is 'self-actualisation', the point where the individual can find their own beliefs and life solutions. The layers described relate to all work but are particularly richly represented in social service and care work which has a long culture of valuing both co-operative and individualised attributes.

Managers are no different in needing their needs met. Although the greater opportunities to determine matters can normally offer managers enhanced opportunity to 'self-actualise' that is not true for all. The constraints of some responsibilities and the way they have to be discharged can mean a manager has fewer choices or opportunities to self-determine than his junior colleagues. Nevertheless if you feel well established and well regarded you will be able in turn to show regard for your colleagues, and more able to maintain and encourage their loyalty by treating them well and promoting their opportunities and experiences.

Regard and acknowledgement

Giving praise when it is earned is a significant managerial responsibility, and essential to motivating people. Although no two people are the same, everyone benefits from having their work acknowledged, it's central to job satisfaction and building professional self-esteem. The trick to get the best from individuals in your team is to find out what motivates them and manage them so that they can work with interest and enthusiasm. It is then usually easy to find reasons for praise.

There is a powerful reason why managers should use praise; it answers the core human needs described by Maslow. The field of behavioural psychology has time and again shown how praise for the desirable things people do is far more effective at moulding behaviour than negative comment about the things they do badly. Therefore it is very effective whenever possible to accentuate your notice or remark about anything creditworthy. This will promote positive outcomes from the ways individuals and teams undertake their work and help perpetuate their thinking and practice in those directions. Smiling faces, positive feedback, and good cheer all help to boost morale that will provide personal and team energy for even more good

work. And ideally, you too must also be acknowledged by your colleagues and your senior managers.

You must consider how you acknowledge the people who work for you. How much you are positive or negative is very often a matter of personal choice, or it reflects your tendency to be dour or cheerful; or where your outlook fits along the line of pessimism-optimism. When you praise, what you say has to be credible and be given in an acceptable manner.

Giving praise

Do not give blanket praise either to a team, or in a generalised way to an individual:

- Be specific: say exactly what has been done well, say why you have noticed it (usually because it progresses the work in some way). Say what you feel about it, and why particularly you are pleased. Comment focused on how a client or the service has benefited will help you avoid patronising overtones and help make the praise stand free of any personality bias.
- Be immediate. If praise is to affect or reinforce desirable behaviour it has to closely follow the praiseworthy event or action. Stale praise is worthless.
- Allow the other person to accept the praise comment but do not expect a response.
- Move on to the next subject or literally walk on before embarrassment or further explanation gets in the way and confuses the message.
- Give praise generously when it is merited and as frequently as appropriate (for example, trainees will need it regularly as confirmation of their progress, older hands will appreciate it from time to time so they know they are not taken for granted).
- Praise can be given to individuals in your team, and to the whole team.
- Your colleague peers and senior managers will appreciate praise especially if given as comment that you acknowledge or understand what has been achieved and what energy it may have cost, or you enquire how it was done.

Receiving praise

- Take it as it is meant. Feel good. Make sure you understand what is being complimented. Do not look to justify, explain or dismiss the praise. Most of us are not used to receiving praise, so it takes a bit of practice.

- Thank the person who is praising you. Tell them how you feel. This will encourage them to do it to you again.
- See who you can praise in turn!

Praise can be fulsome when merited, but remember that not all people respond in the same way. Some people will cringe if public comment is made, others will enjoy the limelight. Some people will be concerned how their peers will view the praise. As manager be cautious not to single out one or two team members continuously for praise in front of their colleagues who do not enjoy the same approval. That's a good way to split a team.

There are employees in the UK, mostly in chain stores and large companies, who enjoy *bonus schemes* and *incentive payments* – and of course there are the big city bonuses. The general view is that although these work for a period, or will add incentive for a special project, they do not work over the longer term. Not everyone will wish to keep up a high level of competitive effort: a one-size-fits-all approach ignores the fact that people are motivated differently and their ambitions differ accordingly. People not cynical initially, will become cynical, if the scheme does not deliver their hopes.

There have also been attempts – most notably in some London boroughs – to introduce *performance related pay*. Generally employees as well as many managers are not convinced of the value of these as a means to motivate people to do their best. The idea that people in public services who don't enjoy direct rewards might be missing out or not best motivated is questionable. In fact, the reverse is often true. Although most commerce recognises that people do best when they are paid properly for their work and according to the degree they contribute or shoulder responsibility, commerce also works on the basis that people like to be recognised for their achievements and are self motivated by being given space for trust and initiative.

Public service by nature concerns people, and consequently there can be a much greater awareness of the need to appreciate employees and keep them informed and involved in order to motivate them. Some public services are exceptionally good at valuing their own people by fostering a culture where belonging is highly valued, and individuals feel respected for who

they are rather than what they do. But this is variable; there remain sections of public service work where outdated attitudes prevail and good work is taken for granted and only poor performance is commented on. Unfortunately still, too many individuals who experienced as normal in childhood critical comment from parents and teachers, accept and perpetuate these attitudes without demur. The interpersonal culture in our islands continues to be predominately rather shy of giving or receiving praise and deals with it differently than do other cultures, such as for instance that in the USA.

Particular effort should be rewarded by managers, if at all possible, despite that in public service work this is not normally as easy to arrange as is the case with many commercial organisations. The reward need not be massively costly but with good imagination it can be better than tokenistic. When acknowledgment includes symbolic reward it has far greater psychological impact than word alone.

Possible methods of recognition includes:

- A compliment letter or short personal visit from a senior manager.
- A bunch of flowers or box of chocolates.
- 'Mention in Dispatches': e.g. make public comment during staff meeting; or inform senior manager or other visiting professional in front of the colleague.
- Putting a commendation note into their personnel file (give a copy to the colleague too).
- Offering to send them to a corporate event or conference, particularly if chosen or asked to accompany you or another senior person.
- A short write-up with photo in your enterprise publication or web site update; or much the same offered as material to your local paper.
- If their work commitments allow, within a reasonable time of the praise-worthy event, excuse the junior from duties and reward them with a shorter day or afternoon off.

High-worth style

Your style of management is the main way through which your staff may feel valued and secure. Ensure you invite participation and show that you place high worth on what your colleagues bring to the work, and encourage similar attitudes to be shown among team members. When people are highly valued by each other the desire to assist the team and have impact with colleagues or clients can provide a much stronger and meaningful source for motivation than not letting standards fall because of fear of what management might say or do. The best teams have informal ways of monitoring their own performance among each other.

Show that you value colleagues by welcoming open discussion and consultation (see *Meetings* in Chapter 5). The process of debate and consultation can be more important than any one chosen solution. Collaborative processes show that staff values and ideas are respected and ensure high ongoing interest and participation; and when the resulting decisions are shared rather than imposed they will be more strongly supported. All manner of managerial responsibility is valid for open debate. Among the views of colleagues will be ideas and valuable experiences that can inform strategy as well as usefully tweak less grand operational detail.

Even if you have a preferred solution, don't close down opportunity for colleagues to better it. If your own preferred solution is posited first or elaborated by another person the trick for an astute manager is to ascribe its ownership to the colleague, not yourself, i.e. 'Let's go with Jane's idea . . .'.

A readiness to extend trust and be open to the new ideas of others helps your junior colleagues grow in professional expertise and self-regard; and when genuine mistakes are made or something is tried in good faith but doesn't work out the person or team is given the grace to learn from the experience and is not condemned. That way you get trust back.

3. Manage people well

Team building

The problem with teams is that everyone uses the term (as I have) and makes assumptions, when in fact teams are as variable as chocolates (to paraphase *Forrest Gump*). To illustrate this three 'teams' are compared below. You may wish to think about similarities and dissimilarities; for example, the clients of each team are all dependent but in dramatically contrasting ways. There are also other comparisons possible that are not given.

School staff

The team is long established and must sufficiently share a wide range of personal beliefs and values in order to be highly mutually supportive, assume a role, and be highly agreed about 'clients', but each has very different technical expertise that defines their actual work (different subject specialism). Although on one site, the group is dispersed and 'out of contact' most of the time. Nevertheless they meet formally and briefly each day and at least weekly, and can make informal contact easily at least twice a day for extended periods (lunch and 'after school'). The team has a corporate identity whose strength influences the opportunities for pupils to experience similar 'belonging'. This is reinforced by 'end of term' social events. The management structure is fairly rigid. The client group also acts as a group (and sub-groups) and collectively can range from 'delightful' to 'consistently extremely stressful'.

Hospital accident and emergency team

Each person has a different technical expertise and the work done is highly integrated. Each must understand and keep to procedures but not necessarily share personal beliefs and values in order to progress their work with clients successfully. The team enjoys high connectivity when actually working together at any one moment but is not well established except for brief rolling periods, and members vary and change according to a shift-work pattern and other deployment factors. Most meetings or training occasions occur outside the group and are centred on a specific technical expertise. The management structure is complex and the work is invariably stressful as the work involves physical trauma and the clients are individual distressed strangers.

Peripatetic care team

Members in the group share similar beliefs and attitudes concerning clients that shows in attention to the client's physical needs and empathy with them. Aptitude, initiative, and trustworthiness are higher order requirements than a particular technical expertise. The 'team' is highly dispersed and only meets infrequently. They are managed centrally by one manager with whom they will have high mutual trust, and have a higher degree of contact than with other colleagues (unless working in pairs). The client group is so many individual separate persons with different personalities but similar needs, each becoming (probably literally) intimately known to their attached worker on whom high trust is placed.

Understanding Your Team Activity

People singly or in teams do the work that the enterprise sets out to do. To understand the nature of your team, here is an activity list to help you.

Take the Mission Statement and the overall expectation about the task or what your people are expected to do – break that down into components or items of work. Take a big piece of paper and set out a diagram that illustrates the number of people needed and what they each do (start with your job description) and show the interconnections and supervision routes. That is an *Establishment Diagram*.

Compare it with any establishment diagram you have already inherited in whatever form it is available – when there is one to hand already don't assume it's accurate without checking everything fits. See what you are currently working with to include the personnel numbers, the available skills, and the actual work currently done. Compare the shortcomings, the over supplies, and other discrepancies. Hopefully you can either continue to live with the compromises you are making, or you can begin to address them in some order of priority. You might do all that in your head, but making a diagram can help the thinking process and will help you take any issue up should you need (see *Manage upwards*, below).

Once you have an idea about the nature of your team it follows that many of the devices and theories related to team building may not necessarily be relevant to your 'team'. Ideas such as *structuring* (Forming – Storming – Norming – Performing) might have little to offer a peripatetic care team but much to offer the staff of a newly commissioned or amalgamated school.

Groups that are formed to work together in any format but without clear leadership tend to go through the same process. At the outset they will be energetic but 'chaotic'. There may be a lot of ideas generated but they will be poorly considered. Gradually the group will move from chaos to formality. At this stage the roles and function become resolved but may be rather rigid (the avoidance of the 'chaos' that may return if agreements are broken), but how the work is done will show discernable pattern. The group may regress or challenge some of its functioning at some point, until finally everyone is fully participative and in tune with each other. This last 'skilful' stage means that the mutual regard

and recognition of team strengths allows any awkward procedural matters, that were necessary for the team to emerge from chaos, to be quietly dropped, and the team will have the strength and co-operative skills to take on greater challenges.

It can be much more worthwhile to let teams process themselves in this manner than highly manage them. The outcomes of the training exercise in Chapter 2.2 (*Rigid Managerialism v. BPR*) normally illustrate this to be the case. From this, learn that managers might often do better to step back (hard for some) and act as facilitators to team development rather than arbitrarily architect its structure. The resulting team can be much sturdier and more resilient.

SWOT Analysis Activity

A valuable way to see what development your team might need is to use a SWOT analysis. This instrument has many applications but is particularly useful to initially evaluate a team and its work, no matter what its nature. SWOT stands for:

S   Strengths – individually or corporate, personal or systematic, within and without the team: compare work to be done with your resources.
W   Weaknesses – as above.
O   Opportunities – what can yet be done, what is changing for the good, what is untapped or unexplored, look within and without the team?
T   Threats – what is out of your control within or without the team, what are the limitations or hindrances, what possible developments would worry you?

Make notes how and as you wish (traditionally a sheet of paper is quartered), all at once or over a period. You may give the exercise to team members and convene to compare results; when you have a clear view, act on it, or research further as appropriate.

Assuming your 'team' is an integrated group there will be certain moments – they tend to sneak up on you and I hope you have experienced one already – when you suddenly feel centred within a wonderful performing circus. Your team is flowing powerfully around you and you can sit back and enjoy the spectacle. The performance finishes to a perfect crescendo. All is done, and the applause thunders. Hurray! Such moments can carry you for years! But however well all is working around you the team will eventually begin to fragment and the show will creak and falter for a while. You train people up and they move on or retire. When one project ends it only frees you up to begin the next. The work revolves daily much the same but also evolves to bring new demands or pressures, and somehow your team group must rediscover its focus.

A manager's work is never done; it is like the *task of Sisyphus*. As a punishment from the gods for his trickery, the mythical Sisyphus was compelled to roll a huge rock up a steep hill, but before he reached the top, the rock always escaped him and he had to begin again. It can feel like a Sisyphean task to be forever rebuilding your team or doing the work. If that distresses you then you have missed the point of being a manager. If we understand the world using a 'chaos' model (see Chapter 1) then we understand it is not natural for anything to be ever fixed and static.

If your world view is that the best human endeavour is the release of human potential then you will be happy also with the idea that as a manager you have a responsibility to help the personal progress of those you manage as well as a responsibility to the enterprise and getting the work done. When we lose a team member because they spin off out of our tent it should be a cause for celebration. When we are challenged to bring in a new routine to the show we should see the change as a welcome development and an expansion of our expertise and experience and not as another onerous task to cope with.

The French philosopher Camus wrote that it was absurd we should ever think of perfect order as a valid hope. He wrote 'The struggle itself is enough to fill a man's heart. One must imagine Sisyphus happy.' Or if it helps, think how the journey is always a greater thing than arrival.

The best teams are dynamic and it helps to embrace that fact by your attitude and actions. All teams have a culture that can't usually be easily distilled but makes them unique. How you develop the group will influence that culture, and one of the keys to effective bonding is to ensure individuals have a good understanding of why and how others work in different ways and what they might learn from that. Managers influence the culture of their teams most through the way they line manage. The ways to foster desirable team spirit are:

- Intervene only as appropriate according to your teams needs and the work to be done.

- Remember to keep prime task and service users at the forefront of all considerations, and the team focused on the task in hand. This will provide clear objectives and a good sense of purpose and the common focus for all discussion and development. A good team will share, understand and be committed to the objectives and have high success.

- The best teams are often composed of people with very different skills and personalities especially when teams are multi-disciplinary or inter-agency: e.g. an introverted office based person good at administration compared with an extroverted field worker good at energising the community. Your job is to keep them functional and successful by fostering good contact and interaction while observing respect for, and boundaries between, different social and technical types, giving directions appropriate to their part in the team and by explaining and maintaining the boundaries of individual autonomy (team, and individual colleague).

- If a problem arises deal with it as quickly as possible and particularly if it is an issue that may threaten team morale. Generally support and advise first when the team encounters problems, but step in authoritatively when necessary.

- When good work is done make timely acknowledgment or congratulations to the persons concerned and feedback the information to the team.

- Enable everyone to learn from each other (see Internal Links below).

- Keep an eye on the skills represented across the team so that you are not caught out by a skills gap when conditions or personnel change.

- Assist loyalty and bonding by opportunities to get together informally. This can happen at conferences and training away as well as seasonal bashes or fun days at paintball or whatever is the group preference. Teams that work hard deserve to play hard.

- When a team is dispersed by the nature of the work or located across several sites, counter isolation with protected times for occasional or more routine meetings where there is some comfort and space, and away from phones and service demands.

- Do not dominate meeting agenda with your management concerns. Get team members to report and discuss their work. Use a rota for all members in turn to air ideas or special interests that could advance the work.

- Champion any claims for equitable reward or acknowledgement particularly on issues of pay parity.
- Encourage the personal career development of team members.

Team maintenance

Assuming the team spirit is good, you cannot then relax and think it will continue. Your 'establishment' or team will be composed of a variety of persons and although everyone will benefit if you deploy and relate to them well this does not mean the same for everyone. Each colleague is a person in their own right and working with you will not be everything in their lives.

Each person will respond to you differently. Old hands will want respect for their experience and will not thank you if you manage them too prescriptively. Less experienced staff must be given closer supervision even if they might prefer otherwise, and one of the key skills of managers is to know how quickly to relinquish close direction and extend trust to new people.

There is also a honeymoon effect that occurs with many new people. At first everything is new and exciting to them and for a year or so they are enthusiastic and eager to please. Two or three years later these people are usually working at their optimum, well bedded into the team with a full share of the work. They have benefited from all the training and development that has been offered, and each day has become routine; just at that point they may begin to think the fun has gone and perhaps they should look to move on.

There is pride to be found in providing first class training and it has marketing potential, but when well trained people leave it can be costly. Managers must consider how to retain employees they wish to keep. The first factor is the general attitude and culture to which a manager will contribute rather than create. People are less likely to leave when they are confident in you and the enterprise, and they feel valued because the culture is positive, cooperative, and open minded. Success is acknowledged and celebrated, experience is broadened, and people are supported in their professional development.

The second factor is individual work arrangements, perks, and understandings that help tie them to the enterprise, and do not figure in the official policy for employee benefits. These are matters much more within a manager's sphere of influence, if not actual control. Examples include: extending flexible hours or time off arrangements, to support parenting or a carer responsibility. Typical small perks are free lunches or occasional supplies of refreshments or cream cakes not always directly associated with particular work occasions or successes; Christmas bonuses and small cash payments on occasions of marriage or the birth of a first child; time off on days of particular special personal occasion or need, perhaps to attend the graduation ceremony of a family member, or the funeral of a close friend. Individual duties can be enhanced by additional responsibilities or periods of secondment or organisation representation, and possible ties through sponsorship to obtain higher qualifications linked to an extended contractual agreement.

The arrangements are highly variable but all depend on the manager's receptivity and personal knowledge about their colleague. People seldom ask for favours but value them highly when they are given.

You will also have in mind the different expertise and experience represented across your team when you allocate tasks, and on occasions when work is done in pairs or small groups you will consider what will be the best matches. It is absolutely essential that partners have compatible personalities and that they can work together as well as have complementary skills.

However, beware if this is too cosy or they have a friendship that detracts from work. It is surprising when colleagues work together how often they are so distracted by each other the prime task is compromised. Two examples come to mind: I read about two peripatetic care workers who were so engrossed in their own conversation during their visit to a bedridden client that the client's need of company and social exchange became second place. And recently I attended a presentation to introduce a new initiative. The day was run by two colleagues from the same service one of whom I knew as rather zany if a bit driven to humour at all costs. The style of the presenters was consequently something of a Mutt and Jeff act that overshadowed and distracted from the message.

Motivate through competence

There are a number of practices that a manager may have in their repertoire that help keep people involved, valued, and committed, and the core notions behind Investors In People and similar awards centre on personnel development. The key factor in issues of motivation and competence is the ambient culture. You will meet people, or you may take on a team that are resistant to personal development, and they may need to be gently unstuck and reassured before they can progress. Usually their experience of training or new responsibility has been threatening because it was pitched in a negative or authoritarian manner – a form of 'you need to learn this or else . . .' The culture of competence is that training and personal development is seen as a right and a core experience looked for and embraced by employees.

You may wish to compare the following checklist of ideas with your usual ways to encourage individual and team development. The ideas given are intended to spark imagination and are not necessarily conclusive.

Motivating Checklist

Internal links:

- Use experienced colleagues to help induct and train up those less experienced. This partnering can be general, for specific items of work, and when work pressure allows simply to widen knowledge with an experience not normally possible.
- Give persons who have held particular roles for a long time a period of 'time off' to simply refresh or to refocus on a work-based research project.
- You devolve a responsibility for a set period (ensure your colleague has all they need in order to take it on).
- Set up a voluntary 'working group' to explore a work-based issue not routinely monitored but where some research and consideration might have beneficial outcomes.
- Ask colleagues with particular skills or knowledge to make a short 'educational' presentation to the team about their expertise.
- When tasks are sufficiently similar arrange or allow two people to swap their work for a day or a week. They then meet and compare notes.
- When a gap unexpectedly comes up in a work flow see if any more senior colleagues can accompany a junior for a period with an informal 'professional discussion' type follow-up. This works best if both parties indicate they are keen – but the ground work can be laid in preparation.
- If the usual supervision arrangements are hierarchical turn it over for a period in favour of peer supervision, or allow this method to run for a period between volunteer partners (the usual records and checks must be maintained).

External links:

- Encourage anyone who has the ability as well as a story to get it published in a professional journal, including yourself on behalf of yourself or the team.
- Look for opportunity for a team member to give a short presentation or run a workshop at a conference or an interdisciplinary gathering.
- When examples of outstanding work occur see if the local press or radio are interested.
- Keep in touch with parallel managers in other services and look out for opportunities to pair up personnel or do combined work of any nature.
- Deconstruct core skills of the team and individuals to see what consultancy may be added to team repertoire and appropriately marketed.
- Arrange representation by a team member on a service user group or advocacy service or similar associated organisation.
- Invite a secondment swap with personnel doing similar work in other enterprises or across authority borders.

Set objectives

There is no magic to this. Have to hand the enterprise's Mission Statement, the Strategic Plan, the Action Plan appropriate to your work, the establishment plan for your team, and the job descriptions of each member. For any one person or any one action component does any new objective or what you ask or expect all tie up – are there continuous and integrated connections? Are they SMART? (Chapter 1.3)

Delegate

Delegation spreads opportunities and helps everyone gain experience. It can relieve you when your workload or stress levels have become onerous or free you up to focus better on your primary responsibilities or difficult current issues. Delegate whenever and whatever you can, but you must be sure the other person is keen to take on the extra responsibility and that they understand well why the task contributes to the work and how it fits within the team activities. The motivation and self-value of the team will grow the more they feel in command of what they do, and similarly, tremendous job satisfaction and self-esteem can be obtained when individual colleagues have opportunities to decide upon and take forward their own initiatives.

Obviously delegation within teams must be even handed. Particular individuals with too much to do may feel overburdened, or if one person is too often selected they may become seen by their team mates as unfairly favoured. Use a planned approach to delegation so that the delegated tasks have a clear connection to developments, and the persons who are selected are best fitted to do the work. Delegation done in this manner is actually suited to presentation with a team or organisation development plan. This approach also formalises the fact that most managers will have persons in their team who are better at certain forms of work than the manager is. Formal planning also ensures best that any uncertain accountability is dealt with. Open recognition of such realities supports organisations that seek to be fluid and cooperative and helps them express and resolve their complex nature.

The best forms of delegation come with overall responsibility and decision-making clearly attached. These include problems without obvious solutions, or things that need to be done but are without an obvious specification as to how to do them. If a person is free to decide how something is done they are more likely to be careful and to put in the time and effort necessary to do it very well. This usually requires that you spend time ensuring your colleague understands *why* something is important and *not how* you might see or wish to shape the solution.

You delegate problems not given tasks. Telling someone to do a specific job in an explicit way is deployment. Delegation must be done for positive reasons and not done in any manner that may be seen as too burdening or characteristic of a lazy manager. Generally that means you do not normally delegate a routine low level task unless the colleague will clearly benefit and wishes to take it on, and similarly delegation can come about from helpful offers from supportive colleagues. But any tasks that are very readily transferred should be examined. It may be that they could already belong to someone else and should not figure on your job description but someone else's.

You must examine your own motives as well as evaluate the competence of your colleague on occasions when you delegate. Proper delegation matches the interests of the individual's career development with their competence so that the delegation is meaningful and do-able. Very often the best way to do this is through forms of appraisal and supervision, and the delegation balance to look for is that it offers more opportunity to the other person to make career progression and gain personal confidence than it offers you relief from task.

The next balance is between support and control. You will need to give appropriate support and supervision but without taking control or making the other person too dependent on you to progress independently; they may need additional training or resources. This can be a fine decision to make. Keep too distant but extend too much trust too early and the person may flounder and fail, and everyone loses: or if you are reluctant to release controls it may be seen as a lack of trust and a curb on the other person's potential capability.

The ways support can be built in include:

- Arranging for coaching or consultant input.
- Reporting to someone other than you.
- The agreement of a time scale and steps towards completion.
- Points for 'hurdle-help' when it may be expected that the colleague will need additional support or guidance; i.e. offer to accompany your colleague on the occasion they make a presentation to senior managers' not to interfere but to lend support and boost confidence.

Manage upwards

You will have one or more senior managers with whom you keep contact. Generally such managers are only a concern when there are problems with them. Sometimes it can feel as if the organisation you are part of has a broken link next one up from you. Perhaps your senior manager is a poor communicator; lacks social skills, or is forgetful. Perhaps you are newly appointed and you find your directions unclear. Remember first that your superior is at their position because of their skills and achievements. Every one has flaws and you may think you might progress some matters better than your manager, but if you find their flaws too difficult to work with, then manage them rather than moan about them. It is easy to be resentful or dispirited; instead look upon the problems as a test of your inter-personal skill and a way you may progress your abilities. Managing upwards against difficulties requires assertive ability and interpersonal dexterity.

Managers can get their position because they are good at particular things, and it may be that your manager does not have much understanding of your particular work or is not so good at managing people but is a whiz with accounts. In such situations it may well be possible to gain their trust that all is well with you and you can then carefully work around the senior's flaws but use their expertise so that you can effectively get the support or resources you need to get your job done well. Things to consider include:

- *Ensure common purpose.* Take the initiative if necessary to determine and set out written details of your job and team task objectives. Offer these for approval in order to obtain unambiguous agreement or sufficient allowance for you to operate. Leave a copy for your manager. Use these as the point of reference when you make any later report, if necessary by annotation or additional written comment.
- *Communicate.* Don't be shy about flagging up the achievements of your team or items of personal credit. Your manager may not otherwise recognise these – it will encourage their confidence in you if you are open and positive as well as supply the facts in which there may be some reflected glory for them. Similarly do ask if you can consult or be advised on problems from time to time even if you suspect no insight. You may be pleasantly surprised by comment that comes from a different perspective, and you help your manager to feel valued – it may be they are reluctant to engage as they feel they compare poorly against your standing in the company or your evident operational skills.
- *Accept.* Your manager does have a different job and may have different priorities and different career experiences. Do not get stuck in differences but look first to find agreement and commonalities.
- *Bridge the gap.* Consider how to make good what you see as the shortcomings of your manager. If you need to do so take the initiative to set up routine meetings or other necessary information flows – you may need information from them. Find out how they like to be connected with. You might prefer face-to-face meetings, they might prefer emails. Get to know their work patterns so you know the times you might best interrupt their work on the occasions that it is necessary.

- *Approach with warnings.* Send information memos or a summary of issues ahead of any discussion so that your manager has time to consider them and not feel uninformed. Book times for longer calls or face-to-face meetings.

Critical intervention

Being a manager does mean taking the rough with the smooth and there are often times when all you seem to be doing is chasing up people who are not doing their work properly. Of course you must attend to the greater issues that might lie behind a general malaise: these are usually evident, such as changes to work patterns that put pressure on skills or will cause a team to be underused. Sometimes, being a manager just requires you to be tough and unswerving for clear reasons that have unapparent causes. For example, opposing shifts may do different quality work, and although you change shift membership around it stays like that; you will then know you need to work harder with the one shift leader.

When things are not going well and you have to comment, it will be so much easier and more meaningful to the team or individual concerned when you pin what you say onto a clear task or very evident objectives. The critique is then couched in qualitative terms related to meeting those objectives and used to drive change: this focus is also relevant when acknowledging good work. When making critical comment it is essential to focus on the task.

Tasks are 'impersonal'. Should something be poorly done because someone lacks skills, it is never helpful to point to poor abilities or to imply that one person in some way is one more desirable than another. Apart from the risk of personal hurt and damage to professional confidence, there is always the issue of whether they should have been given the work in the first place, and that will have been someone else's decision. It is always far more effective to focus on what is occurring that needs to improve, and how it may be achieved. This is *solutions focused*; and the outcomes are normally in the form of the support necessary to be successful. Typical support includes additional training or resources, mentoring, or a period of work with a partner.

When deploying people about whom you have reservations, focus on the expected work outcomes and not on personalities; and consider the skills balance before any personal compatibility considerations. Of course some people do work well together, and that is always beneficial. But if you begin to formulate pairings and teams largely because of other people's personal preferences, and it is easier to go along with their wishes, you give up an area of your proper control and responsibility, and deny them the expectation that they can develop proper professional attitudes.

Intervene when necessary to keep everyone on task and working appropriately. When you need to draw attention to poor work there are some advisable ways to best do that.

How to MAKE negative comment

- Make sure that you have all the necessary facts; if there are gaps declare them or ask for them.
- Never put your criticism to a colleague in front of others – keep it private.
- Say what the problem is clearly and simply: say why it is a problem to you or the service.
- If you are feeling upset or angry, say so – but be clear that these are your feelings and that you do not blame the other person for them.
- Focus your criticism on the other person's actions or behaviour – not on their character or personality.
- Ask for a response; listen carefully to any explanation offered.
- Make positive suggestions about what can be done or ask for suggestions.
- If necessary, and possible, ask your colleague what help would assist them.
- Try to reach a mutually acceptable solution.
- Part amicably, and thank the other person for their time and trust.

How to RECEIVE negative comment

- Make sure you accept responsibility for the team and don't pass it on. Keep an open interest in what is happening, good and bad, and always make fair comment, that way colleagues will believe you are approachable.
- Listen to what is being said; make sure you fully understand.
- Regard the comments as a criticism of what you have done for whatever reason, not a criticism of your character.
- Try not to defend, attack, retaliate or justify your actions, although you may wish to explain your thinking.
- If the criticism is not justified, explain why you think that.

- If the criticism is justified, explore what can be done to improve matters by asking and making suggestions.

A problem commonly referred to managers is complaint from colleagues about one individual. Typically this will be an annoyance difficult for them to deal with directly, such as problems of personal hygiene; or the person is too talkative; or spends too much time on the phone or the internet on private rather than work business.

You will need to protect the other colleagues from division so you can't name them as accusers, and subtle comments or hints rarely work. You will need to pass by more often and see for yourself. Once you have two or three examples you can take up the issue as your own observation and make the general point. Keep the discussion private and as brief as possible – it will not normally need long. Be sure to stick to facts, ask the colleague for comment, and end on a positive tone by reference to how you value their skills or contribution to the team. Pass by a day or so later and spend a moment to give the person a nod or coded comment as if to say you see things are well again. If the situation slides, repeat your intervention more formally or take your concerns into their supervision.

Difficult people

The work of managers is to keep the team effective and on task. This means that the different members and their different levels of skill and experience have combined in a coordinated and interdependent manner. As organisations become more complex the ability of individuals to mutually resolve matters becomes more important because, if this does not happen effectively, it will take up a disproportionate amount of manager energy. This is most critically the case in small teams where one difficult person has a correspondingly greater impact.

Example: The 80 per cent team
A small office-bound team in an incorporated organisation had one member, Janet, who never pulled her weight. The team was largely self-directed and the work involved accurate information processing and became increasingly IT dependent. Janet did not seem to benefit much from IT training as she continuously made processing errors. She would also misfile documents and leave

other time-sensitive material unattended in her in-tray. At times it cost the organisation penalty money as well as the time and effort of her colleagues to correct her mistakes and inefficiencies. Despite this she was intelligent and seemingly ambitious; her preferred pastime during office hours was to do personal work concerned with her study for a vocational teaching qualification in an area in which she had real interest and expertise.

Janet's personal manner was confrontational and abrasive to the point of outright rudeness at times: this kept colleagues at a distance. She was also largely unchallenged because of the severe and chronic mental health condition of her husband which brought her sympathy and tolerance from her colleagues. Her colleagues also assumed Janet was medicated at times for depression as this would explain some of the behaviours she displayed.

Over the course of several years the team came under three different managers. Each manager never managed to impact sufficiently upon Janet's practice although team concerns were expressed anew, and the managers made different attempts to resolve the problem. The team became complacent about Janet. They thought Janet had been ignored for too long to be dealt with formally through competency proceedings and although they would moan from time to time among themselves they just put up with her in the hope she would eventually leave.

This malaise reflected the lacklustre of the larger organisation to be functionally rigorous. It was continuously close to inspection failure and twice came close to takeover by a parallel organisation but was rejected after due diligence and scrutiny.

Some people do sap time and energy. In some cases, this is just their personal miserable nature, as nothing ever pleases them. Others may be highly unrealistic, or lack self-awareness and do not see how they are seen. People can have reason to be frustrated or dispirited because they feel they have lost out on promotion, or something powerful in their personal life is carried into work each day.

However, these people hamper developments and usually impact negatively to some degree on the whole team. Leaving matters unattended will drag down team morale and suck away their

energy and focus: it is very rare there is no direct impact to some degree on the quality of the service provided. If they have a persistently disruptive influence they will be difficult to manage, and become more difficult the longer their situation is not properly dealt with. It is very unfair to allow the negative attitude and actions of one person to contaminate and depress the rest of the team. It is essential to intervene early, set consistent expectations, and not let problems escalate.

Unfortunately, social care organisations are known to be reluctant or ineffective at dealing with difficult employees; maybe they just think everyone is honest and reliable, or will become so given time. Too many are just gently encouraged to move on and are given a reference that helps that to happen, and become someone else's problem. Dealing with difficult employees properly is arduous, but generally it only becomes protracted when the problem has been ignored for too long, or the manager has not intervened with sufficient clarity or been rigorous with follow-up.

How you deal with any particular problem will always benefit from some forethought or discussion with a personnel expert or another manager. Maybe you know a manager who has already dealt with similar problems. Managing an employee with problem behaviour requires a clear plan of action within a framework that makes proper use of formal disciplinary steps (also see Chapter 5.4). Here are the advisable steps and procedures.

1. Adopt a sequence for confronting the employee

Seek to deal with issues informally and verbally, and as immediately as feasible, rather than let them grow. That is a lot easier if the incident is fresh, and you are around and about a lot (MBWA) so that staff are used to casual discussion as well as more serious comment outside the formal appraisal or supervision procedures:

- Say exactly what your concern is and what needs to change. Begin to keep a record of your intervention. If informal words on one or two occasions have not made sufficient impact either set aside a time for a formal verbal interview or use supervision – if the individual receives supervision from someone else either relate the matter to them to deal with or ask if you can join the session. Be clear that this is still at an informal level and not yet a disciplinary matter.

- If the problem persists or the behaviour transgresses a core policy try an oblique approach such as words from a more senior manager or there may be a colleague mutually approachable to you both who may be willing to offer friendly advice. Another option may be a form of mediation if you are personally very involved. If your organisation has a personnel officer or a human resources department alert them at this stage and ask for advice.
- Consider the impact of poor behaviour or performance on service delivery and team morale and determine at what point you will begin to use as appropriate either the organisation's formal disciplinary procedures (i.e. unacceptable incidents) or capability procedures (i.e. poor abilities). Sometimes the issues can interweave between both procedures. Apply these normally the moment you have exhausted all other efforts to get improvement, and apply the policy scrupulously as it is set out, or as you are advised. You must ensure the employee has a copy of that procedure. This can be set out in a letter mentioning the matters that have been discussed so far. Make it clear that this is for information and does not constitute a formal written warning or a record of any previous verbal warning, but does warn them of the formal steps that will follow if there is no improvement.

2. Make a record

Keep a log or diary of incidents or things you see or are reported to you. Accurate evidence is almost impossible to refute and an exact recount can help someone who is genuinely unaware of themselves to see how they behave, or otherwise jog their memory into admission. Records are essential if the matter goes onto disciplinary or capability procedures. Keep accurate notes with specific detail. For example, write down what was actually said to a client, not simply 'was rude'. Be circumspect, but whenever possible get your observations independently verified by asking an independent person as well as any complainant or aggrieved person if it was true what was said or done (if very serious get their signature against your entry).

3. Investigate and confront

Ask them about their work to get a viewpoint – very often they will admit there are some problems. Be clear that it is unfair that their problem should impact upon colleagues or service users or even your time. Find out if there is a problem behind the behaviour causing concern. If there is a personal domestic or health issue discuss what temporary support may help. This could include some redeployment or change to working hours or conditions, direction to a counselling service, or other arrangements that the employee agrees with to help them cope better. Be sure to offer whatever reasonable support or help is appropriate. This will be questioned during formal procedures, and you will be slated if the case goes to an industrial tribunal and it is shown that your support has been less than fair, and will also give grounds for compensation. If the problem is work related process that as necessary:

- See below: 'How to make negative comment'.
- If the issue is disillusionment see if the post can be enhanced to make it more interesting or variable or offer some other redeployment.
- If the issue is resentment or anger (maybe they had hoped for your job?) their problems may become resolved once they have been aired and their value to you reasserted.
- If the issue is work overload or too much responsibility that must be reviewed.

4. The disciplinary stage

If all else fails, rigorously apply your organisation's disciplinary or capability procedures to the letter.

Common problems of staff behaviour

Fortunately, if tiresomely, most problems with staff are matters of attitude and minor behaviour. It is similarly so with clients. It can pay to be a bit Machiavellian at times. The lists below outline what to do about some commonly met problems:

1. Staff who emanate negative attitudes

Typically these are people who have been in post a long time and appear to speak from experience when they denounce new ideas. Their seniority or powerful argument can intimidate other staff as well as yourself:

- This person may feel threatened by younger or more enthusiastic colleagues or feel they are better trained or qualified (they may well be so). Ensure that the negative person does not have real skills or abilities that are no longer tapped – if possible play to their strengths by deployment when possible in that direction. Boost their self-esteem by open remarks about their achievements.
- Play on their past experience to defeat current cynicism by valuing their knowledge and give them the responsibility to research, review, or monitor some details (track results?) of the new progress so that they can suggest the best direction because they will 'know why things may have gone wrong before and what will work' (turn 'poacher to gamekeeper').

2. Staff who deny what they have (or not) done

- Leave it there, but remark that if that is the case then that's fine as you won't meet the issue again.
- Explain you have conflicting information and are in the awkward position of having to decide between it – ask what would they advise you to do, and if this is sensible follow it up.

3. Staff who blame or project problems on to others

- With team members use a mediation or reconciliation model that directly confronts the attitude and supports the individuals to process personal change. If the blame is projected onto you ask a peer colleague to do any necessary initial work.

4. Staff who are lazy, hang back, or don't join in with team direction

Although they may always appear busy they are probably over elaborating on one small aspect of the work or concentrating on the bit they enjoy best:

- Ask them to keep a diary for a period (say, a typical week) so that you have an accurate record of their work to review in supervision. Use the 'normative' approach to see in which ways the colleague can develop working practice and gain strengths so that a similar exercise repeated after a given time will produce a second diary record that when compared with the first will show desirable change and development.
- Refer to the job description and use appraisal methods that you have set up openly and in advance of a formal review. Compare your and their assessments and discuss discrepancies. Acknowledge strengths and move towards ways the colleague can develop weaknesses into strengths.

5. Staff who bully or have a confrontational attitude

They may argue that they get good results, or have fixed minds (will blame others) or use derogatory language when describing colleagues or clients (but perhaps not in your hearing):

- Use a mediation or reconciliation model that directly confronts the behaviour and supports the individual to process personal change (go to your reference books on supervision).
- Reflect peer observations.
- Involve in appropriate training to give alternative skills and strategies.
- Bring into the arena for professional appraisal and performance monitoring procedures.

6. Staff who moan

They may moan about other colleagues; blame or pass the buck; or want others to solve their problems:

- If a work issue, hear them out and then ask them to generalise all the specifics into one simple statement that 'nutshells' their problem. If they can do this, this is what you deal with. It also means they have some intellectual ability to focus or summarise the core matter. Thank them for their concern in raising the issue, and as they understand it so well ask them to continue to consider the problem and to forward a suggestion as to how it may be resolved. This releases you from becoming a 'dumping bin' and potentially in a lose-lose situation because whatever you suggest will be rejected. It offers the moaner an opportunity to be valued by encouraging their contribution to the team effort.
- If a personal issue refuse to intervene on behalf of the colleague unless they have repeatedly tried all the socially normal assertive ways to resolve their problem.

- Ask them to set out clearly why it should be your problem (if they are genuinely tiresome to you ask for this to be written down – but if you do that you *must* take some action as you have formalised their complaint for them).
- Use supervision (or you direct them to their supervisor) to review with the colleague how they see working practices and relationships.
- Redeploy for a period with good and assertive practitioners from whom they might learn how to deal with their issues better – and debrief with them what they have learned.

7. Staff who don't do as they should

These may be inconsistent colleagues or colleagues who do not accept or carry out arrangements or agreements:

- Attitudes at meetings and briefings or failure to attend, invariably highlights intransigent colleagues. Ensure they have no valid reasons for not attending. Ensure you do not manoeuvre matters in some way intentionally or otherwise so that they are excluded.
- Ensure they are given every opportunity to share their viewpoint or raise their objections and that these are held up to peers for observation or viewpoint. Any remaining major differences are resolved, out of meetings, by arrangements for support, or as may be appropriate from one of the other responses in this list.
- You must eventually and often sooner rather than later take up on-going and outright non-cooperation as a professional disciplinary issue and give a first formal warning within the procedure as outlined by the policy for such matters. This can be preceded by a verbal warning, if one is not otherwise provided for, but if so make a file note.

8. Know-it-alls

These are people who respond to your every suggestion that they have done that; tried this. You suspect the effort has been tokenistic or done in such a way it was bound to fail. This is a ploy to refute your wisdom and reject their responsibility: don't waste time. Take their response at face value:

- Have no further discussion. Apologise that you have no further ideas, and instruct clearly that

they must think how best to resolve the problem as it is their job to do so. They are the best expert, having been already involved; but they can come back to you if they need further discussion. You only have your advice and experience which has already been shared, but obviously this could be explored more deeply. (If this should happen you tackle at length and frankly how things were done.)
- Feign greater interest. Suggest that if the problem is that exceptional it will need exceptional abilities to resolve it. Tell them they should try again, and if successful with some new or clever way of working they should report this at the next team meeting so everyone can learn from them. Or, if they are unsuccessful, they can return to you after a given time and you will have to ask for a colleague to take on the work, but they also will be asked to report back to the team how exceptional the work was and how exceptionally it was resolved.

9. Time wasters

At a low level of concern, but high on annoyance, are time wasters and the office bore, and the senior manager who sits around wafting indulgence or beer breath:

- Tell very junior colleagues politely to excuse you – you have work – do they not have some also?
- As soon as you have had enough, stand up. This is body language and subconsciously they'll get the message that you need to go. If they're really thick skinned, go through with a charade of needing to visit the toilet – this will usually break the interaction.
- Similarly, open a file and begin to half look at it. Suddenly cut into the conversation with some comment that this must have your immediate attention.
- Arrange a secret signal with your PA or office administrator to ring your extension. Cover the mouthpiece and explain you need to take this important and confidential call.

Common problems of client behaviour

1. Picky clients

There are clients who accept what the service can offer but refuse any other agency support or involvement:

- Some agencies can be accessed directly by clients – appropriate counselling support may result in this as a way forward.
- Review the individual service agreement with the client to see if continued involvement can be made conditional.
- Review the relevant issues of client confidentiality and refer yourself if possible – at least the other agency will know about the client even if their overtures are ignored.

2. *Interfering clients*

These may be clients who interfere, or their friends or relatives

- Politely and consistently refer them to the formal procedures or normal systems that bear on agreements.
- If problems persist refer them first to a junior colleague who is willing to take on a deflection role for you. They may need your support and will need your thanks. Be prepared should new information emerge that must be acted on.

3. *Client complaints about a colleague*

To deal with these, hear them out, and show that you take what you hear seriously:

- As may be appropriate and as they agree: ask them to leave this with you; refer them on to a more senior colleague; or initiate any formal complaint procedure.
- If you are the 'senior manager', apply the most appropriate kind of process outlined in one of the cases above in this list, or seek a more novel resolution according to the particular case and your expertise.
- Always check out some time later with the client if things have improved for them – or if it is now satisfactorily resolved.
- See more on dealing with complaints in Chapter 5.

4. *Aggressive clients*

- Explain calmly that they must understand aggressive behaviour is not tolerated on your premises – refer to company statements or policies on such issues if these are displayed.
- Offer an early alternative time and place when they can return calmer and have their concerns heard.
- Deal with them as an aggressive intruder if their behaviour does not modify, and call for help or the police as appropriate.

- If lower in key but constantly confrontational in manner:
  o Politely and consistently refer them to the formal procedures or normal systems if they have a complaint.
  o Ask if they would prefer you to stop processing their case properly and use the time instead to listen to all their issues.
  o Politely point out they could help you concentrate and deal with the difficult paper work (or whatever) if they would let up.

How to respond to complaints

This applies to any complaint or allegation particularly if you suspect it may be fabricated:

- Don't act as if it is fabricated because it may not be.
- Don't act as if it is fabricated because if it is it will tend to fade away as the formal procedures begin to be applied.
- Always apply the company policy and procedures on such matters, these should include or otherwise ensure that you also:
  o Never compromise client or employee safety and well-being.
  o Inform and invite involvement of any advocacy service or client representation services, or even the police according to what may be relevant, and at the earliest opportunity.
  o Memo the matter immediately to the appropriate senior manager.

4. Demonstrate professionalism

There are things that effective managers do and ways they understand, that set them apart. One of the ways a manager's professionalism can be distinguished is through their repertoire of practical ideas from which they can select the one best suited to any particular situation. It may help to imagine that these managers have a 'Tool Box'. The more experienced (or well read?) the manager is, the more tools he may have in his box. The following are 'Tool Box' ideas.

Traps, trades, and tricks

Managers need to be able to see ahead and recognise the *difficulties* (traps) that they will probably meet, and have some *techniques* to use that will solve them (trades) and have some *skilled techniques* that get things done (tricks).

Traps

- *Inheritances*. Beware you do not get sucked in by expectations others have of you based upon your predecessor. You were selected for your post to take things forward, not to wear an old pair of shoes. When newly appointed it can be an excellent idea to turn your office out, redecorate, and set all out anew; renew timeworn items and bring in possessions to personalise the space. This can help your new colleagues to adjust their thinking, and makes a bold analogous statement that things are now different. It will help to make you feel assertive. In smaller ways, the same is true if you just take on one task that had been the province of another.
- *Comparisons*. A common mistake is thinking it will motivate one person or acknowledge another to openly make comparisons between people. You will make comparisons but keep them to yourself. If there are performance issues you think you should act on do so in more proper ways.
- *Selections*. Beware you do not come to rely on getting things done the easy way by creating cliques or inner circles or favouring individuals. You will enjoy a better rapport with others you find like minded but your personal challenge is to ensure you are even handed in your dealings with all your colleagues.
- *Rejections*. This is discrimination by creating scapegoats or outer circles – the opposite of Selections. It is the nature of groups that many do single out individuals from time to time. Often this person is less sociable, or they do things their own way – and very possibly this is judged as inefficient or poor in some way. It can be the task of a manager to counteract this effect.

Trades

- *Delegation*. When you give someone responsibility be sure to pass on authority as well – pass on clout with the cloth. But if something goes awry that is your responsibility – you chose the person!
- *Shouldering*. Do not prevaricate about what is yours or not or who else may be to blame when things get sticky, but immediately accept responsibility for the team or individuals within it. Do that and others will certainly come to stand beside you.

- *Swapping*. Release another's potential by swapping one of your tasks or responsibilities for a chore they have. (This may be linked to delegation). This gives them valuable experience and can lower your stress or task pressures.
- *Levering*. This is the skill of negotiating to get something you need from senior managers when new expectations are imposed upon you (or your team), and similarly of having something in your back pocket to sweeten putting your additional obligation on to a colleague.

Tricks

- *Ritual knowledge*. This is knowledge from experience about generic matters like data protection or how to deal with a grievance. It shows when it is the manager more than any one else in the team who knows 'the way things are done'. This may be specific or generalised, and can range from routine events to the extraordinary. One example is, the familiarity with how to chair formal civil meetings; another being the only person in the team who understands the procedures of criminal courts.
- *Time management* (see Chapter 5.4). This is the skill that distinguishes good managers from cowboys. It concerns your effectiveness, and ability to prioritise your time and stay focused on the task that must be done. And your ability to look ahead and not put undue time pressure on colleagues. Do not ask for something too close to the day it's wanted – if you must do that, explain why and let them know how much you understand that the short time given is actually an extra demand in itself. Allow time for mind sets to move when change is mooted (sow seeds in season to reap a harvest later).
- *Clarification*. Eloquent words or a passionate manner convey meaning additional to any simple content. No matter who introduced the subject under discussion, if you have some understanding or knowledge about it and you speak eloquently or passionately, people will regard the subject as a personal matter to you. This is the case whether by supportive remarks ownership is implied, or by derogatory remarks rejection is implied; and no matter the discussion forum.

If the subject is the suggested idea of a colleague you must be clear about its provenance, but you will still give the idea additional credibility. The colleague will feel empowered. Managers are expected to help make things clear; when they do so in good oratorical style the impact is much greater. On occasions when a colleague asks you to speak on their behalf this is tacitly understood.

- *Proxy dealing.* Responding to a problem in an off-centre or 'back-door' manner. Examples include choosing to send a poorly committed colleague to represent you or the team to an event where there will be senior managers; sending a stressed colleague on a 'day away' visit or a conference; giving a special responsibility to someone in the team who is otherwise rather disaffected (like asking 'a poacher to become a gamekeeper').

Manage team development

How well you support and promote the training and development of colleagues and yourself is a determinant of the overall effectiveness of the enterprise, as well as it showing how much your enterprise is a 'learning organisation' (the ability to learn and change is characteristic of complex organisations). You should lead by example, which means first know and ensure your own development needs.

If you do feel training and development (T&D) is turgid, stir it up – if learning is not seen as normal to everyone you will have to work on the culture that perpetuates that attitude. One of the easiest ways is to begin by targeting the work-based learning and induction of new staff: ideas can be shifted in this manner without directly challenging the established team. You may be surprised how many 'experienced' staff will think they also want 'in' when word gets around about the training, especially if this is high value, with a decent venue and lunch, and with accredited certification whenever possible. The next step is to link minimum standards to appraisal; competence in most social care environments concerns how the work is done as well as the thoughts and emotions associated with reflective practice. Remember where NVQ awards are relevant they are not centred on learning but actual practice. You may need to soften attitudes by reassuring established personnel that they can easily show they can do the work, and once they can say why they do it in particular ways the accreditation will easily follow.

How to understand the forces and pressures on the 'learning climate' of enterprises, a model is presented, this has three main aspects:

1. The sources of *knowledge and skills* for learning:
   o How well do all the different feedback methods such as appraisal and supervision enable ongoing learning?
   o What access do managers (you) have to a training budget so that T&D can be individually targeted to local needs or persons of merit, or is the system central without any local control?
   o Is T&D 'done in house' or provided through more varied means?
   o How well do any senior managers see a personal role in T&D for junior colleagues through their own knowledge and experience?

2. *Attitudes and emotions* for learning:
   o What is your general attitude as a manager towards T&D?
   o Is there encouragement and good role models down through the organisation so that positive attitudes towards learning are fully supported?
   o Is the emotional or cultural make-up of the enterprise disposed towards the constructive forms of comment that advance learning or is the culture more blame or problem centred?
   o How do you evaluate across your team the individual temperamental differences members have towards T&D?
   o What is the attitude overall of your team towards training? And how does it as a group support the training needs of individuals within it?

3. The *work situation* that supports learning:
   o What are the resources or operational flexibilities that make employee release possible?
   o How well established are the key ingredients of attitude and actual opportunity that are conducive to a 'learning environment', or are there undesirable discrepancies?
   o Is there a model within the organisation, and relevant to its work, that sets out a map for all T&D, and how to access it?
   o How much is the day-to-day work, or current external issues formally deconstructed or evaluated in any manner that focuses on the theories that inform

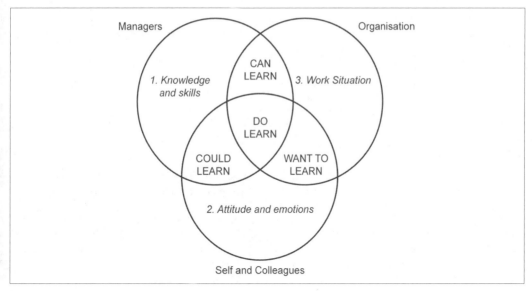

Figure 4.2　Learning climate model diagram

practice so that learning points are routinely fed back to the team, issues discussed, and professional understanding is advanced.

This model supports learning as a proactive process, and not a piecemeal response to events that expose weaknesses.

The learning climate model diagram (Figure 4.2) illustrates the interplay of these aspects.

The model is animated by change to input, for example:

- Consider how sphere 2 'attitudes and emotions' might rise or fall according to the morale of staff, and hence affect their potential for learning. For example, a very common factor in failing enterprises is the loss of belief by personnel in their own potential to change.
- Managers in sphere 1 who have high levels of tacit knowledge and work-based skills, and are active in T&D, can significantly and directly increase the zone of learning potential (move sphere inwards). Conversely, if they can only poorly identify with the work at the front line, or for some reason are not motivated to share their expertise (often fear of losing control), they are likely to be distanced from T&D (move sphere outwards).
- An organisation that places high work demands pulls in that direction (sphere 3 moves up or out). This can significantly reduce the opportunities for T&D, or increase these as

the organisation directs and reduces those employees might want.

Acknowledge your personal position

Most managers find they have some influence or power beyond their prime responsibilities, but some managers have more influence than others and make greater contribution to the development of the enterprise than is generally the case with their peers. When this happens there seems at first to be a high connection with personal charisma or general managerial ability; and certainly managers who are emotionally and intellectually intelligent will stand out, no matter how their organisation is structured. They are likely to impact well with the decision makers within rigid structures as well as carry more influence in fluid or cooperative structures.

Of course, style and methods differ from place to place. Some organisations drive development only downwards though a line of managers, compared with development elsewhere that is facilitated more two-directionally through teams of managers. Some managers enjoy arrangements for empowerment such as regular meetings that provide powerful forums for debate and corporate decision-making: other managers might have only casual opportunities to discuss with their seniors anything other than normal operational matters.

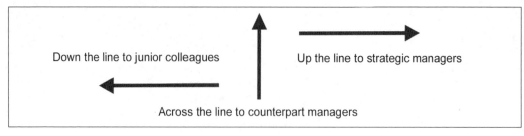

Figure 4.3   Middle management accountability

No matter what their personal situation, the degree managers can 'punch over their weight' largely depends on how well they understand their 'position' and fit within the larger structure, and what the possible opportunities are for being influential. Good 'positional' understanding is critical to how well the manager can then relate their team to purpose and organise the work. Understanding their own position is a prerequisite of a manager for personal authority – it provides the manager with the rationales that make his demands valid, and the confidence to know how strongly his demands can be made. This same authority is then valued in turn by the team, as it provides them with the platform for team assurance and individual confidence about their work.

With high levels of certainty about personal position, any conflicts of action or clashes of belief can be investigated rigorously within and beyond the team, and the common vision and purpose be better resolved. How influential a manager might be depends on how well their ideas contribute to the greater enterprise development as well as directly improve the work they are responsible for. Influential managers think and impact beyond their immediate horizons.

Other than the absolute top or bottom levels of responsibility most situational positions are more complex at all points, and therefore being an effective manager anywhere along the spectrum does require organisational dexterity and alert communication. 'Middle managers' is a relative expression in the context of most organisations depending on their size and degree. Most are hierarchical in structure, and therefore it is middle managers whose position represents the greatest possible complexities, and they are usually active in developments and accountable in at least three directions, as the diagram illustrates (Fig. 4.3).

Middle managers and the responsibilities they carry are mostly associated with the quality of service delivery. How well these managers do depends on the personal support extended to them to progress their own development, in addition to how they understand their personal position. The diagram (Fig. 4.4) illustrates factors that impact upon the potential quality of these managers.

And finally.

Positive Practice Checklist

Do you have?

- A well defined purpose.
- Immediate and longer objectives.
- A plan for what to do next with a set of priorities.
- Good communication so that everyone knows what they need to know.
- Ways to detect and correct problems as they arise.
- Feedback procedures to inform where you might improve.
- Ways to identify and release the potential of individual staff (include yourself) so their professional development can prosper.

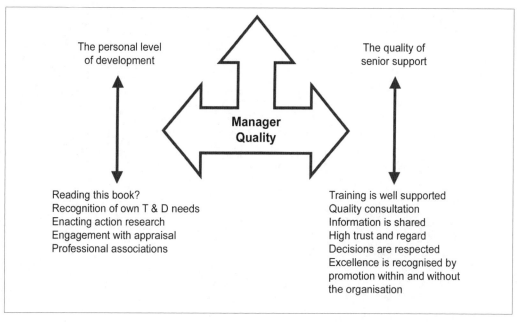

The personal level
of development

The quality of
senior support

**Manager
Quality**

Reading this book?
Recognition of own T & D needs
Enacting action research
Engagement with appraisal
Professional associations

Training is well supported
Quality consultation
Information is shared
High trust and regard
Decisions are respected
Excellence is recognised by
promotion within and without
the organisation

Figure 4.4   The perceived value of the individual manager within the organisation structure

CHAPTER 5

How to Develop your Practical Skills

1. Develop positively

Consult

Once upon a time managers got on unobserved and were never questioned; now managers get on in full view and do the questioning – the best managers a lot. We have to consult and be open to new ideas and suggestions. One good but cynical reason for consultation is that managers can reduce their accountability for a poor decision when they can show they have fully consulted whomever they should have consulted, and have taken the results into consideration. And should the opportunity to comment not be taken up when consultation is offered it makes it easier later to debunk any criticism from that quarter.

Consultation processes do usefully slow up action and give you time to think; and more importantly 'community' or service user groups can be a fund of good advice and expertise and may raise unforeseen issues. So you should do consultation exercises willingly and as best you can. Look for ways to encourage interest, let people know clearly and exactly what they can have a say about and no more, and use methods that really do give people a chance to have their say. Finally tell them the results – that is, summarise to them what they have told you and what you have learned from the consultation – not necessarily what degree of notice you will take or what influence it may have on you. That will depend on the value and sense to you of the outcomes, the trust you have in how well the consultation was done, and perhaps how usefully representative were the consultees. What's left is the final decision – that's yours.

Apply similar considerations to consultants, coaches, and mentors. If these are available to you use them willingly and as best you can. They can be a fund of good advice and expertise and may raise unforeseen issues and provide good sounding boards for your thoughts. Encourage their interest, let them know clearly and exactly what help you need that they can support you with, and no more (not least because fees will be charged). Use methods that support opportunities for open discussion between you and them. Get them to tell you their results and what they have learned or can advise from their contact with you and your organisation. Get specifics and a summary. It will be up to you to decide what degree of notice you take or what influence it may have on your actions. That will depend on the value and sense to you of the advice given and the trust you have in the people who give the advice – perhaps how prestigious or expert the consultants.

Balance risk control with damage limitation

Poor Murphy is accountable for so much, but managers who blame his law duck responsibility for their actions; better to be wise before the event – which is perhaps the value of consultation. Good managers by definition have good foresight. Some events like inspection are certain; others vary in certainty, from high possibility like losing your excellent PA to someone who pays more, to the rarity of major traumatic events such as the murder of a colleague by a client.

The return to normal working is always assisted when there is some kind of plan for the unexpected, either in outline or greater detail as you see fit. Even outline plans are a great help for turning the unexpected around; this is because with some thinking already done you can concentrate on action. Use your time at slack moments to think through potential threats. Exceptional problems are always much better handled when you have done some 'what if' thinking and, at a minimum, jotted a few notes. The following matters are worth considering ahead:

Inspection

This is completely predictable and preparation is actually a full-time job. Unfortunately inspection too often uncovers practice that has slipped or management that has ignored issues. That need not happen to you!

- You should manage as if an inspection could occur at any moment.
- Can you immediately tour what you are responsible for and find everything in place and all practice proper? A short test is go now to wherever records and policies are kept and check all are up to date and in place.
- If there are any routine areas of work that are below par they should be given attention immediately they occur (this what you are paid to do!). If you leave them until a notice of inspection powers your hand it will be felt by you and your colleagues as extra pressure (or embarrassment, if spot checks apply).
- You should know what problems you have and have an action plan in progress in advance of any issues the inspectorate might raise. All kinds of problems are not necessarily a prime concern to inspectors, but a manager who has overlooked an area of responsibility will be!

Physical damage

Such as fire or flood or other cause, and loss of facility or loss of records:

- Where would you go and who would you ask to help?
- What back up systems and equipment do you have?
- How long could you suspend operations in order to get started again (if your service is residential or health with high user dependency you may already have discussed or taken part in scenario planning with other local agencies including the emergency services).

Trauma

This might involve one or more individuals. The main things to consider are:

- It has happened. Focus forward, what you do next can help a lot; wallowing in anguish will not help a jot.
- Know what counselling or trauma support services are available if needs be – if needed get immediate help from them or at least consult with them as they will be more expert than you in the situation.
- Consider a high level of support for yourself foremost because you will need it if you are to

work effectively and sort out the practical matters, as well as absorb the emotional stuff that your colleagues will direct to you.

- Don't look for blame or assume you must know all the answers – let senior managers sort out any changes to strategy or procedure if the trauma has links to work practice.
- Keep all your colleagues well informed.
- Let everyone talk. Encourage anyone who is silent to open up. Make sure no one affected becomes isolated.
- Keep staff together and let them (or direct them) to continue with their work as soon as practically possible.
- Allow that some people may need more rest, or need reassurance from closer contact with their families. Some staff may find some duties more than usually stressful.
- If a death has occurred remember that the stages of bereavement will be worked through by each individual at their own pace. Make full use of ritual afforded by memorial services or dedications.
- Remember that the experience may change the outlook of colleagues or trigger different concerns. Be prepared for the symptoms of post traumatic stress (including self).

Particular threats

Be aware of threats which may slowly develop or suddenly be sprung, and have appropriate contingency plans in place:

- For example, delegated services can lose major contracts; this is much easier to survive if there is already other work in place which may be expanded, or given the slack there are ways the current work can now be grown. There will normally be a couple of months or so before you might otherwise have to look at redundancies.
- Work co-operatively with neighbouring services (get to know your counterpart on a personal basis) so that you are not beaten down by price auctions, and can draw on each other's services and advice at times you might need it.
- Make sure your performance indicators are good – ideally above benchmarks (especially on cost and client satisfaction) and make sure the powers that make bigger decisions than yours are fully informed.
- Legislation can cause major reviews of practice or resources, better by far to know what is

impending and begin any training or review of resources beforehand, and spread the costs and development time.

- Keep service tasks in proportion. Avoid any accusation of poor spending or getting caught up in spending rows by keeping focus on your main service quality. Have only a small handful of manageable other projects, each with a clear client need or cost saving in mind.
- Get appropriate advice as soon as possible whatever the level of need; a clash of personalities can cause you constant and stressful irritation; getting caught up in an allegation of corruption or major client abuse could cost you your career.

Media interest

The tendency is to be wary of the press, but effective use of the press concerns good as well as bad publicity:

- Don't deal with the media yourself unless you have some training or previous experience and your organisation's blessing to do so. If you cannot handle your own public relations find out who does and keep tabs with them.
- If you are free to do so find out who in the local newspaper or radio has an interest in your work. Call them up occasionally. Let them know whenever there is anything of public interest happening or a good story. This can include for example informing them that you are on a recruitment drive or opening a new facility, but particularly if you have an example of excellent work or high achievement by individuals or from a service inspection. Good news does get printed as the local press likes to report 'local does good' – this will be more so if the story links to any national issue.
- If confronted by press over a bad story you can buy time by giving a statement that paraphrases only the facts that are obviously known and adding an appeal rider; i.e. 'I confirm that one of our clients has made a serious allegation, and we have suspended a member of staff while the appropriate authorities make their investigations. Obviously I can't make further comment about the nature of the allegation or the persons involved . . . We are all highly concerned should the wellbeing of that client be proven to be compromised by any actions of our service, as we take pride in . . .'

When unexpected events occur the chances are you will go into 'automatic pilot' and respond sensibly and practically. Stress will arrive later with heightened emotion and the aftermath work that will tax your energy. I once had to deal with a major fire. The following days of limited facilities and distraught people were much more stressful and wearisome than the actual night of the fire.

Also be prepared for the 'what if's' that will haunt your thoughts, as the even worse outcomes that you did escape loom up in your mind.

2. Manage knowledge

Knowledge management (KM) concerns information 'housekeeping'. It is potentially the most wasteful and inefficient part of how organisations work unless intelligent questions are asked about what information is needed and how it will be used and what will be kept. Sometimes organisations do poorly because they do not know what they know – no one has asked the right person the right questions, or because they pass around knowledge without any check to see if it is understood or believed. KM is best when it is a formal and ongoing system of checks, confirmations and innovations designed to improve the business. Its value and ultimate costs start from decisions taken at the top.

Manage information

The sources of useful knowledge that inform the work you do come from that work, from the public body of knowledge and research about the work, and by comparison with other providers. The sources reflect in their different ways how information is sorted and used. Effective enterprises know how to make good use of information and have sleek systems to categorise and store it with ways of quick and easy retrieval.

Knowledge management is becoming more sophisticated as IT is ever more applied to how work is done and services become increasingly reliant on it. Investment in technology is one of the main ways commerce keeps abreast of business rivals and makes sure its employees use their time and effort efficiently. Although the performance pressures in public services are different from commerce, the outcomes of good investment are the same – there is better customer service at lower cost. Public services are always looking for cost savings to allow them to improve the work in some way, and often savings are imposed without much discussion because they reduce the burden on taxes.

It is easy to become seduced by technology as it seems to offer so much. Typically, computers, printers, and shared databases provide efficient support at the work base or office centre, and mobile phones and portable computers allow field personnel to work independently and transmit data and information back to base rapidly and comprehensively. Telecommunication networks allow organisations to be centralised and decentralised at the same time, and offer novel working methods such as video conferencing and three-way calls. Well designed bespoke software can provide decision-support tools to allow decision-making to be a part of everybody's job; expert systems to allow generalists to perform specialist tasks; and high performance computing to give accurate information to assist strategic as well as operational planning.

These new ways of working also offer a better work-life balance as working arrangements can be more flexible; travel is reduced and working from home arrangements increase. The job satisfactions that flexible working provides helps employees stay loyal as well as extending their employability.

In all, technology seems to be wonderful, and so it is, but there are things to be wary of.

The requirement now that employees in services have to be 'techno-savvy' can be challenging to some managers and workers alike, and has associated training costs for the enterprise. Senior managers who lack IT experience and skill will limit enterprise development. Even if they do not themselves input or access much data directly, understanding how the technology might be used is an essential prerequisite to the imagination necessary to be innovative with administration or operational methods.

My advice to managers is to step back. The needs of the enterprise are probably the same as ever, and it is easy to be so impressed by the technology and all the bells and whistles that real needs become obscured. Technology is simply a tool, and by far the most important thing is to know what it is you want it to do.

The skill of managers who deal well with information is that they know who needs what information and they ensure they get it; and they maintain or tweak the procedures so these work

efficiently with all unnecessary 'bumf' screened out. The sheer physicality of paper systems to different degrees protected enterprises from being swamped with information (although apparently during the 1950s when the draft rules for the EEC were drawn up there was an office in Paris where structural engineers evacuated the building because the weight of archive material stored on the loft floor threatened to collapse it).

One of the biggest problems with IT is the great potential for information overload because of the rapid accessibility and apparent 'limitless' storage capacity of electronic filing. However, being purposeful is still the solution. For example, professional journals are a typical 'public body' source of knowledge; what use are they and how might they be dealt with?

It is common that an office base subscribes to one or more professional journals such as *Community Care*. In some offices these might lie about in a common area for a while, some copies will go missing (the manager's desk?) but most copies probably get filed in date order and shelved away. That kind of approach to journals remains quite usual, but it makes the value of them largely hit or miss.

More efficient offices have someone who minds the copy for a while before tidily stripping out the content of value to the enterprise. This is categorised and indexed on a simple data base (a sheet of contents with columns for different types of article) and the article is then placed in a plastic wallet and shelved with similar resources.

Enter the adept manager who will ensure all the above, but before the journal is made generally available they or someone else will give the edition a quick scrutiny to see if any article has strong relevance to the work. If so, attention to it will be made at staff meetings, on an information board, or by circular. Particular individuals may be specifically directed to it. In the days before copyright awareness the article might have been photocopied and distributed. This manager ensures relevant journal articles contribute to team development and maximum advantage is obtained from the subscription.

When IT is involved the same process is applied. The method is different but the perceived value and outcomes are the same; colleagues will be kept informed by a group and individual email, and selected articles will be available online or copied to a PC database.

Managers expert in their field of work know what information is useful, but some specialised knowledge and skill helps to ensure there are efficient 'flow routes' to gather and disseminate material when using IT, even when, as is often the case, setting up the 'flow route' is handed over to IT experts to build and install the necessary software.

Managers must remain in charge – the dog must still wag the tail – except the manager may need certain permissions, as there are legal considerations to knowledge management, and the growing practice of multi-agency work is increasing public and client concern about confidentiality. The information gathered must complement the work. Case records, for example, are kept primarily to provide evidence of the work undertaken for those clients, but these records can be monitored for developments regarding the changing nature of cases by extracting and compiling relevant information.

Manage records

Tablets of Stone?
Make records as tablets of stone
unalterable and set in time;
but what records actually are,
and how they are used,
is not set in tablets of stone!

Records and writing are used to give, get, and retain information and we put energy into keeping records more often than not without considering much why or how we do this. The benefits of occasional review are usually improved recording practice or reduced paperwork. Don't waste time recording unless the purpose is clear; and whenever there is a clear purpose make a record!

What are the reasons *why* you have things written down? Normally it will be for one or more of the following:

1. To create a permanent record..
2. To order or to retain complicated information.
3. Because the matter concerns a number of people.
4. Because the writing down is a tool to getting things done.
5. To prove accountability.

Accountability is the consideration that must underpin and cap all your documentation. It shows:

- what you do
- that you do it
- and all your records prove it?

Next, *how* are things written down? How does your data practice compare with the following considerations?

Data Protection Act 1998

All data should comply with this law: are you confident all is well and can you say with certainty how the data you are responsible for meets the legal requirements and demonstrates good practice? That is:

- Data should be secure, relevant to your service needs and not more than needed:
  - Field worker access to any data at base should be appropriately protected whether accessed via internet or phone.
  - Field workers should keep to the agreed practice to ensure 'mobile' and 'at home' data is protected.
- Records should be accurate and up to date, and the 'whole file' not retained longer than necessary.
- Legal rights of individuals should be protected. Data protection is not a barrier to disclosing personal data without individual consent, but is concerned with the rights and best welfare of the clients involved and to protect the private lives of individuals. There is the infamous example of British Gas who erroneously believed they could not inform Social Services when they cut the gas supply to an elderly couple who subsequently died of cold.
- Protocols and agreed arrangements between agencies to share information should be absolutely transparent and routinely reviewed.
- When sharing confidential data within or across Health and Social Services, the **'Caldicott guidelines'** should be maintained.
- Field workers should understand confidentiality issues well and their training should include trust issues with clients and how to respond to their concerns.
- If appropriate there should be a confidentiality statement available to give to clients to assure them of their rights and how any information they provide will be treated.
- The effect of Article 8 of the European Convention of Human Rights should be understood (to guard the privacy of individuals, families and children).

- Field workers should be absolutely clear when the law allows information to be passed on because of concerns about child or public safety.

Freedom of Information Act 2000

The impact of the Freedom of Information Act 2000 should be understood, principally to mean:

- Disclosure of information can only be refused if exempted within the legislation (23 instances in all, and these are dissapplied if public interest can be shown); if it can be shown to be a nuisance inquiry; or the information will cost more than the given amounts to retrieve.
- Information cannot be withheld to save the service or individual workers from embarrassment.
- Information about a person can be denied or edited by the service when the disclosure of core or detailed information might be thought harmful in some degree to the individual concerned (subjective interpretation only testable in court).
- There is an appeal route: to the service body; the commissioner; tribunal; court.

Copyright restraints

Staff training and development materials should be produced within copyright law and any necessary copyright licences must be obtained for bulk copying (see Copyright Licensing Agency & UK Copyright Service – a division of the Patent Office; or The Newspaper Licensing Agency Ltd for its publications).

Benefit to clients

Record keeping must consistently benefit your clients:

- The purposes of recording should be absolutely clear – all staff must know why any record is kept.
- The test for any information on, or not on records, is 'who would wish to know this and why?'
- Remember you keep many records: the client only has one. Encourage clients to show interest in their file and confirm its accuracy.
- Files are easily accessible, well stored and indexed (paper or electronic) and colour or markers are used to flag client status or the record stage or type of information.
- Electronic files are backed up at least daily and ideally the server is not in the same building (damage protection).
- Proformas should be well designed so that information has an orderly flow; and when IT offers a pre-sized entry box this should extend or compress as needed, and this should be made clear to people entering information (including clients on-line).
- Clear distinctions should be made between types of information and how it is used. There is fact, observation, opinion, the report of others, advice, summary etc. Jon Smith's date of birth is fact; that he appears unkempt and smelly is irrelevant unless this is a clear and adequate reference within the context of the service provided. It is also an opinion whatever the service, and consequently it is contentious.
- Staff should be trained as necessary to help ensure records are:
  o Accurate and complete without being too wordy.
  o Entries (and messages) are signed and dated.
  o Entry information is ascribed if not first hand.
  o Language used is respectful.
  o Accounts are plainly expressed for clarity and to avoid misinterpretation.
  o Paper file components are not separated and if a record is removed there is a system to track who has it and to see it is safely returned.
- With paper records you should ban correction fluid; with electronic records use systems that protect originals with 'read-only' status but allow additional file versions.
- Audits of records should be routinely done as appropriate to:
  o Identify good practice as well as any problem issues.
  o Include a sample of a service user's view (*guidance and training to staff about working in partnership with service users and constructing and sharing written records* SSI: Recording with care).
- Files should be understood to represent quality of care, particularly on occasions when case records have a therapeutic role such as when these assist clients to understand their past and the events they are part of.

Benefit to organisation

Record keeping should consistently benefit your organisation. It should:

- Provide a tangible point of focus for the work undertaken.
- Provide means to determine strategy and evaluate operational efficiency (relevant general information is easily extracted and compiled).
- Assist service continuity and inform new direction (the case record provides testimony to the mission; minutes of meetings are evidence of organisational progress).
- Provide evidence for use in any investigation or inquiry.
- Provide chronologies; i.e. supervision dairy; contract agreements; career development (personnel files); organisational development (BDP and action plans); client development (case studies) etc.

Websites, and the public domain

Web sites and updating should only be undertaken by persons with some competency, as this is 'public domain' – IT jargon for open to scrutiny by everyone; this is easier if you have the backing of a corporate IT department, but is no less important if you are attempting a DIY site for a small enterprise. Make sure your site works and presents well:

- The front page is critical so that site users are impressed from the outset and the menu directs viewers exactly.
- Remember service users will need different information than other agencies.
- Every word should count and every image be informative.
- Your site will lose credibility if information becomes stale.

3. Manage your environment

Although there are practical matters of administration that are less dependent on individuality and emotional intelligence, the overall work environment of any team is very influenced by the manager's personal style and priorities, and his interpersonal skills and sensitivities will contribute massively to staff enjoyment of their work. It is the manager's responsibility to lead in *how* things are done and to orchestrate the relevant matters well and promote excellence at work. There are key different 'environmental areas' that all contribute to job (and client) satisfaction when these are well integrated.

Emotional environment

People need to feel good at work, and the greatest contribution is the quality of interpersonal relationships. Do whatever is necessary to create a positive emotional environment for your team, and that might require whatever effort is necessary to dispel any attitudes or practices that might disparage individual worth or endeavour (not just having an equal opportunities or anti-discriminatory policy); but mostly you will need to lead by your own example how people should relate to each other. The features of desirable emotional support include:

- Learning is foremost. The culture of the enterprise is that learning is the paramount human endeavour whatever the nature of the work done. The belief is that there is always more to know and understand, and how things are done can be improved; this benefits the service, benefits the careers and personal progress of staff, and contributes to the field of work.
- An effective system to deal with personnel development and job satisfaction, with regular progress reviews between individuals and you, or whoever else might be doing this on your behalf.
- Report systems that acknowledge personal achievement by responsibility, pay, or commendation as appropriate and possible.
- A culture that values good inter-colleague relationships above hierarchical ones.
- Access to a confidential counselling service for any personal or work-related stress.
- A collegial or supervisory system that will quickly identify and respond to any personnel whose personal behaviour or work quality causes any concern.

Intellectual environment

People do best when they find work interesting. All work can provide intellectual stimulation when individual aptitudes and interests are encouraged and supported. You can maintain this by attention to the range of training and development, as well as opportunities for discussion and debate. When you know the particular interests of individuals on your team, deployment and options for new tasks can be directed with individuals in mind whenever possible.

Physical environment

People appreciate and respond well when the work place is sufficiently comfortable; and this is obtained by much greater wisdom than the simple application of health and safety requirements. Look to see that the buildings and rooms for staff as well as customers are as attractive and purposeful as possible and try as best as possible to dispel any institutional feel in larger buildings. Some key considerations include:

- Encourage a shared sense of responsibility and ownership for the work environment (provide suggestions box, recycle bins, staff involvement in choosing furniture and fabrics, redecoration, etc; and whatever else might be appropriate for people sharing the same space).
- Comfortable temperature and good levels of oxygen using air conditioning or through-draft as well as adjustable heating.
- Workstations should comply with relevant Health and Safety requirements, especially if using VDUs.
- Notice boards and wall planners are up to date and any display or information that does not look acceptably fresh is renewed, replaced or removed if no longer relevant.
- Décor is kept fresh – paint is comparatively cheap. Colour is chosen with care and applied with some understanding of the psychology of colour.
- Damage and dirt is attended to immediately.
- Soft fabrics and good quality furniture are used, and whenever possible furniture is arranged in non-institutional ways.
- Flooring and other surfaces are chosen or given attention to reduce noise; have the ringer on phones set at the lowest practical level.
- Attention is given to circulation and work zones (typically around the photocopier) to ensure these are safe and efficient.
- There are good systems for maintaining and tracking shared equipment and resources.
- When necessary for their work, personnel are provided with adequate secure personal storage.

- WCs are sufficient and clean (and some work warrants provision to take a shower or wash and dry items of clothing).
- Places to make hot or cold drinks, and heat food, and to take a break away from workstation.

Systems environment

People can do their best when the organisation and its systems support their endeavours and the manner of their administration and deployment is efficient. This efficiency comes from the logical expertise that ensures all the organisational structures or routines are sensible and practical and without awkward arrangements that might frustrate getting things done. There are two key phenomena that managers must watch out for that create difficulties: 'flashpoints' and 'cog-jams'.

Flashpoints

Flashpoints are particular routine occurrences or problems of physical space, typically the moments tempers are tested because of some inadequacy in people or resources. Physical flashpoints are usually easy to identify and can be simple to remedy. They can be strange little matters like an awkwardly placed or too narrow door that annoys every time you use it. Flashpoint difficulties can affect staff and service users. For example, a staff team that is normally dispersed gathers at base in the period before team meetings and everyone tries to catch up on their admin but 'hot desk' arrangements and pressure on resources like the photocopier makes this fraught. The following example concerns service users.

Example: Flashpoint resolved
The dining room in a care home was too small for the numbers of residents on the occasions they were all at home. It was difficult for diners to access their tables from the servery. Those residents first to arrive would take up the tables by the servery even though the later arrivals often had mobility problems. There was always a lot of movement, and chairs had to be shuffled about as people squeezed by, and sometimes food would spill. Mealtimes could be quite tense, and not the relaxed social occasions they should have been.

The problem was resolved by introducing family type serving. A waitress was employed for the main meal. Table serving dishes were bought; and these put out once a table had a full complement of people. Movement was cut dramatically; individuals could choose to sit with companions. Everyone liked the new arrangement.

Flashpoints differ because the tolerance of people differs. A regular problem that everyone has become used to might be raised anew because a new person will not accept or tolerate it. Maybe everyone is glad the issue is raised again as they hope this time something will be done, or if they have to stir themselves to solve it the fuss may be resented. Dealing with people who have become complacent about particular things is a common experience for new managers.

When flashpoints impact on clients, good staff will always try to overcome the problems posed. Good work always reduces anger or distress, as do practices such as advocacy and other preparation work to smooth potential flashpoints, such as planning reviews or placement changes.

Cog-jams

Cog-jams are the organisational ways people do things or use systems that do not work well, and so progress gets stuck or work held up. This might be continually or only at certain times, and typically show as ineffective methods or poor procedures that delay work and take up time. When colleagues or clients experience delay and difficulty they excuse it or get used to it until the day arrives that their frustration boils over into a big upset.

Although ultimately people are behind all inefficiencies, typical 'system' cog-jams are things such as lost mail, mislaid files, running out of copier toner, outstanding equipment repair. Typical 'people' cog-jams include arriving late, cancelling meetings at the last moment, reports not properly circulated, and inadequate minute taking so that an important action point is missed.

Sometimes a cog-jam irritates but continues unchecked because everyone is too busy with their operational load, and no one person can be bothered to raise the issue, or no one has the time or the motivation to initiate (or enforce) more desirable practice. Indirect causes of cog-jams can be decisions or oversights made by colleagues or another manager too remote by time or distance from the people they affect to properly understand what they have caused, or too removed from the consequences to be concerned. Often when these difficulties surface it is junior or less experienced colleagues who must resolve them, not the person responsible for the hold up.

Most systems have some slack that could be pulled in to improve efficiency, and often a tiny redesign can make a welcome difference. For example, if someone cannot take a call, most systems will log or use a duplicate message pad to let the person know they have to make a callback. It can be advisable to introduce a simple tick box or other check that it is done. This will considerably assist quality assurance and consistent practice by informing the office manager about call back rates, and with a delay trigger this kind of system can prompt someone else to ring back and so reduce caller frustration.

Tasks and staff deployment can be most easily prioritised when a case handling system has markers that clearly show the individual case status and progress at a glance as well as the overall flow of cases in hand. Wall planners are best when they do more than just represent a big size diary but are used interactively to flag up and assist the prioritisation of the work, in conjunction with location and time lines to account for the work and whereabouts of staff. Most offices have a 'this week' board. Efficient offices have a 'this-week, next-week' board and a far column for 'coming up' reminders.

Some of the worst 'cog-jammers' can be senior managers!

Example: Cog-jammer
Paul managed a busy delegated service from an office base. The county served is large with several sizable towns, but field workers took pride in arranging their schedules to minimise travel and maximise client time. In order to keep in favour among some service purchaser 'cronies' Paul would at times respond to their enquiries by agreeing to provide sessional support at short notice. This would be passed down without consultation to whoever had a schedule gap and without reference to whereabouts that fieldworker might be. This usually meant the field worker had to cancel some existing arrangements and drive a long unplanned distance to do the work. There was a small incentive not to complain as the extra travel

claim and a pleasant cross-country car journey was seductive.

It is worthwhile occasionally to audit by spot check or a sampling method the work done by a team compared to their job descriptions or how the service is organised, and check that everyone is properly on task for appropriate amounts of time and any gaps or overloads are identified. It is only proper and respectful to everybody in the team that the manager responsible for deployment does make certain that everyone actually does what they are paid to do.

It is very cost effective to avoid cog-jams whenever possible by anticipating problems and making necessary precautions. This saves the financial expense and the damage to morale that can result from poor operational planning or non-completion of work. Often all that is needed is a bit of foresight and wisdom that no one notices except when it is not done. For example, selectively providing or assisting with guaranteed transport for people whose attendance in particular instances is essential (especially to legal hearings): whether such people are individual clients or staff is immaterial, the transport help could well be cost-effective.

Remember the pessimist's rule that 'if it can go wrong it will'. It can be better to over-provide than chance under-provision; 'two pints of milk in the fridge' is always better than none. But that's not true if you are then throwing away a lot of sour milk, which brings us to efficient administration.

4. Make administration matter

Managers supported by personal or administration assistants may not do many actual administration jobs compared to decision making work, but they will control administration – their responsibility is to lead and direct in **how to** get things done.

Efficient administration requires the modes of communication, resources and practical arrangements to be well integrated and to all suit the work. Everything has to be maintained, and the detail reviewed as necessary to keep the cogs working smoothly. The absolute priority is to manage time efficiently as it is the most valuable resource in work, as in life. Other than time management, the ideas below are not prioritised, they are 'mix and match', and some might

contradict each other: it's up to you to be in command, and make your administration matter.

Time and work

No manager ever has enough time, and the commonest difference between a manager and a team colleague is the extra hours the manager will work. Smart managers keep their work SMART as much as they can (see Chapter 1.3). The best way to manage time is to have efficient and consistent routines and stick to them; people will get to know your routines and will fit in with you.

For example, if you are regularly out of the office on a particular afternoon for field or site visits this also provides you with 'protected' time if you wish to disappear for a couple of hours because you have work that must be kept confidential, or spend a half-hour with your old mum between visits, or recoup some hours owed to you by a round on the golf-course – seriously **yes!** If you have a vital piece of work to do that requires some serious concentration – then exit the office with your laptop or notepad and find somewhere you will be undistracted (I knew someone who used a café at a mainline train station).

Your time is also controlled by you when you demonstrate an efficient manner consistently. If people get the idea you are busy and efficient they will be concise if they have something to put to you: conversely, if they think you like to hang around and chat, you will be waylaid for gossip at every corner.

Priorities

Time is managed in the first instance by how you allocate it and prioritise tasks, and how well this is done depends on the usefulness of the tools you use.

Ideally your day plan is checked each Monday or whenever your shift or work week begins, and each morning. Planning is usually a fairly continuous process, but do routinely build in some unallocated time so that you have some flexibility to respond to contingencies. A simple way to prioritise is using *Traffic Lights*:

- Red: stop everything, this must be done immediately or today as prioritised.
- Amber: caution, don't forget – to be done soon, next or tomorrow (last thing at night move from amber to red tray).
- Green: not urgent – to be done when all else is.

The colour code is applied to all work to be done either by you or your PA: then it is not looked at again until dealt with. Mail and documents as they arrive are put into colour coded file trays (with e-files either by 'flag' or 'move to'): everything, phone message, mail, email, request notes or whatever can be dealt with this way.

Other things can also be marked with a colour code; use colour pens or file-dot stickers, and the same colour codes can be used to zone diary pages or wall planners.

Similarly, different highlighters are useful to draw your attention to key words or points on letters, agendas and other documents you handle, particularly when you wish to find things quickly.

Diary

Paper and electronic diaries each have advantages and inconveniences. I can get to any day in my paper dairy or the planner page in a fraction of the time of someone using a PDA; their page is tidy and up to date, mine is full of rubbings out and different scribbles – but it works for me and that's what's important. If you use Outlook, to get the best from it you need to use all the bells and whistles and like the way it organises what you input. This is a one-size-fits-all bit of software and you will either love or hate it, and it will either do what you want well enough or not be specific enough for your work needs. Some people like MS Works which is simple and fresh looking. It's the same if you use a PDA linked to a base PC.

Tasks

Work SMART; think the task through. Work out exactly what you want to do (be specific) know when it's done (measurable difference) know it can be done (achievable) and not a flight of fancy (realistic) and there's a time frame. And then:

- Apply this to routine tasks as well as one-off projects. Even routine tasks benefit from a review to see if the way you do them can be improved; there are often little tricks to work smarter to learn from elsewhere.
- If for some reason any task is not done in your given time, move on to the next in your usual routine. That way you won't allow one task to stop other things getting done. Work out how best to complete the 'hanging' task and arrange

the necessary time during the next day or week or what is appropriate, or maybe if the bulk is done someone else can complete it?
- Once a week (probably Friday afternoons) re-order your tasks and highlight your top three priorities for the following week. By keeping an eye on these, you'll keep focused. Manager and team performance is appraised by proof of achievement – and what better way for you than by ticking off tasks done.

Meetings

Meetings can take forever – because people work hard and not SMART (they are hindered by anxiety and random difficulties). You have to train yourself and others in ways that ensure the meeting of minds results in solutions. It can be worth 'sowing seeds' beforehand to ensure issues are thought through before the meeting (Chapter 2.4). If it's your meeting, make sure you get the most out of it. Know what you want the meeting to achieve:

- Is there a clear purpose and can it only be achieved through a meeting? Do not assume that everybody will have the same regard for the meeting as the person who called it.
- Is there an acceptable *Rate of Return*? Consider the cost of your own time and that of others, both in money and in work not done: will the outcome be worth the investment?
- Some meetings will centre on emotion rather than facts. If you are looking for agreement or change, do some preparatory work with those who will be most affected and so reduce the emotive element in the meeting – make sure that practical issues are kept to the forefront.
- Be sure that people from other agencies do not have their time wasted.
- Train yourself, and your team, to think aloud and share thoughts and ideas beforehand (see Chapter 2.4, *Dialogue in hand*). Thinking becomes enriched when minds merge over time. Tease around problems rather than become anxious about them – it is surprising how often then solutions rise to the surface to be easily netted, but fishing hard produces nothing!

Facilities at the venue

- Ensure the venue and room environment are suitable. Will it be formal (tables to sit behind) or informal (chairs in a circle)? Can everyone get to it (parking, public transport, disabled access)?

- Do not assume everybody will know everybody else. Make new people welcome. Consider whether the meeting will go better with a pre-meeting reception or arrival period somewhere comfortable (a reception area, or a lawn in summer) where people can discuss 'away from the table' and newcomers can become informally acquainted. Offer a brief tour of the facility.
- For the main part of the meeting itself, get material put out at place settings beforehand rather than spend meeting time handing out paper.
- Provide somewhere for people like consultants or finance managers to use their laptops conveniently.
- Latecomers should be welcomed with good accord but make someone else responsible for greeting them, so the meeting flow is not interrupted. Their job may extend to updating the latecomer, outside the meeting room, on the progress so far, as well as helping the newcomer to access the 'pit stop' facilities, like drinks, and cloakrooms.

Having a formal structure for the meeting

- Arrange for an agenda to be distributed or emailed beforehand, attach as bullet memos any ideas or suggestions that are already apparent, and flag any problems or items which you invite others to solve or comment upon (as in the *Writing* example below). Make sure all the attendees know what is expected of them. It is often wise to allot timings to each item on the agenda, so people can see how long is allowed for each topic, whether it is to be discussed or agreed, and when the meeting should end.
- Someone should chair the meeting, and another person take the minutes. The chair need not be you: often you can say more or be seen as unbiased if you are not chair. Chairing a meeting is a trainable skill, a valid experience for junior colleagues; or perhaps you might choose another colleague who can be seen to be independent.
- After the meeting, the minutes should be written up and approved, and distributed to all attendees. Meetings are often about persuasion or getting people to accept responsibilities.

Making sure that everyone knows what was decided, and who should do what has to be done, is crucial.

The chairperson

At the meeting itself, the chairperson's skills are the key to success: a good chair conducts the meeting. They should:

- Sit where they can have eye contact with everyone – this is usually better at a corner of a table than the traditional head or centre of a row.
  Have sufficient personal authority to command events, ensure every view is heard respectfully, even if they are personally not of that view, and should not be so officious that debate and occasional humour is stifled.
- Make sure the meeting starts and ends promptly, and proceeds according to the timescale on the agenda.
- Make introductions; state the purpose of the meeting, its time scale if not already known, and the intended outcomes. If necessary, discussion should be politely but firmly cut short, or summarised. If conclusion cannot be reached, it is better to arrange a further meeting rather than run over the projected time, other than by a very few minutes.
- Respond authoritatively if conflicting views restrict progress, but challenge the issues raised rather than the validity of the views. Obstruction is nearly always because of strong beliefs or impactful personal experience. Sometimes it is difficult to separate opinion from the person making it; if there is a dispute it is better to acknowledge it. Ways to resolve it might include arranging a further meeting, or a majority decision taken at the meeting, or a referral to a senior manager, depending on the circumstances.
- Summarise the outcomes at the conclusion of the meeting, and thank everyone for coming.

And lastly:

- Try to book meetings back to back. It is easier to arrange the next meeting when everyone is there with their diaries.
- Let others at the meeting know that your time is limited: that way they are more likely to keep focused, and your day is less likely to be wasted.

Communication

Quality communication is:

- Effective – it conveys the information well.
- Affective – it causes change or allows others to understand.
- Consistent – methods are established and reliably maintained.

Remember that a key, but not always an explicit, responsibility of managers is to maintain conventions and to ensure the quality of records and communication. Anything you write may:

- Remain as a record long after you have left.
- Represent the organisation to those without direct contact with it.
- Represent **you** to those without direct contact with you.
- **Cause wider judgements to be inferred.**

Writing

Writing is a key tool to getting things done and, like all skills, the more you practice and pay attention to what you are doing the better you will do it. At the outset, know one thing: **Good spelling, punctuation, and grammar are not optional** (SPG). Your letters, email and reports reflect the values and skills of you and your organisation.

The things to be sure about next are:

1. Why are you writing? *I am writing because . . .* (You will be writing for one of these reasons: to inform; to find out; to persuade; to enforce; or to record).
2. Who must read it? *. . . must read it* (Who for determines the format and style).
3. What outcome do you want? *I want to . . .*

   Self-explanatory example:
   When communicating textually utilise commonplace and straightforward terminology in preference than conceivably the vocabulary for which you have preference or twice employing an identical expression eschew jargon in addition circumvent convoluted sentences and be averse to generating more than one key point in any sentence or paragraph through means of review and redraft to obtain concision afforded ideally by access to and familiarity with word processing and punctuate accurately and be averse to blowing your top via correspondence only.

Or, in other words – *Keep It Simple, Stupid (KISS)*:

- Whenever possible use plain English, that is, words that your reader will understand, and only as many words as you need. Use short sentences, between 15 and 20 words in each. Don't write so that your reader needs a dictionary. Make sure that what you write has a beginning, a middle and an end.
- Use specific words, rather than general ones. 'I want to improve turnover by 10 per cent' is much better than 'I want us to do lots more'. Words like 'admirable', 'great', 'lousy' require your reader to work out what you mean, and some expressions like 'remarkable' can be both positive and negative.
- Avoid jargon ('inter-personal dynamic', 'parameters'), slang ('get sorted', 'off her head'), nicknames ('Rambo-man'), and acronyms (SEN, LAC): not everyone will understand them. Very well known abbreviations, such as 'ok' may be okay?
- Avoid clichés, figures of speech, Americanisms: 'at the end of the day', 'Ball Park'.
- Write what you mean, and mean what you say. Say 'people' rather than 'human resources', 'car' rather than 'passenger vehicle', 'get angry' rather than 'blowing your top'.
- Avoid sounding superior or pompous. If you have authority this will come out naturally in what you say. Using 'notwithstanding' or 'in view of this fact' will make the reader suspicious.
- Use active rather than passive language, i.e. 'please let me know if you can attend the meeting' is better than 'it would be helpful to have an indication of your ability to abide with the suggestions made'. It is acceptable to use a personal or informal style, and first name terms, particularly when you know the reader well, or communicate with them regularly.
- Sign your own letters: if you can, write 'Dear John' also by hand.
- Be careful of humour: it can soon become outdated, or more importantly, be misunderstood.
- And lastly, read what you have written out loud to yourself. If you can say it aloud okay, it will read okay.

Letters and memos

Words are joined up letters, letters are joined up words – it's the joining up that matters!

Letters are in danger of becoming underused, but remain a powerful tool because their tradition makes them classical, classy, and concrete. Letters imply importance and dignity and can be sent to anyone. They are private person-to-person communication (even if the same letter is sent to more than one) and can cover the range from formal to informal. They are easily evidenced with record copies and 'proof of posting'. Keep letters as short as possible – not more than one page is preferable, one line is OK.

Memos are internal letters with only an essential salutation. Keep them brief, precise, and single issue. Use them to keep work going smoothly. Typically they are reminders, requests, or a resumé (condensed information). They can be used to reinforce but not introduce significant new instruction and may be sent to one person or many (as identical copies) and can be arranged as one copy for multiple signing.

It can help to structure what you want to say by using post-it notes or scrap paper to jot down points or 'mind map' thoughts. Write out thoughts, e.g.:

> *Annoyed by complaints from clients about appointment delays – More recently – There seems to be different causes – Why is the team not reporting problems? – What's going on? – I want to hear from everyone not just some views. – Such complaints should be exceptional.*

This example becomes:

Memo to all staff (date)
Appointment Cancellations

- *Client complaints to me have suddenly increased. Each one seems to have a different cause (though never staff illness – hurray!) but I need your help to find out what is going on.*
- *Team leaders may not know that cancellations are increasing in all teams.*
- *Everyone please discuss this with your team leader; team leaders to facilitate.*

I am scheduling this top issue for the next whole-service meeting (date).

- *Team leaders, please discuss this matter among yourselves first. I'll be raising the issue in supervision on my two area visits already planned.*
- *At the meeting I will want the total number of appointments which have been cancelled and the number which have been rescheduled since (date). Local info to JJ who will collate this. Share anecdotes and talk before the meeting please.*

- *At the meeting I want to get your views on the core problem and hope to hear your solutions for making cancellations infrequent again. I want us to make decisions then which can be acted on straight away. If that fails I will arrange a further meeting for team leaders.*

Regards . . .

Fax and email

Faxes and email are different from other forms of written communication **only** because you do not send them confidentially in an envelope. With faxes:

- Keep to all conventions as in a letter.
- Head the fax with information that it is a FAX.
- Include to and from information; time as well as date.
- No. of pages (I use 'this page + n.' format).
- A proforma can be useful (especially as a template on a PC).
- Treat an incoming Fax as a letter (ensure A4 hard copy if needs be).

With email, use these rules:

1. Write as if your mum will read it (nothing to confuse or embarrass).
2. Whoever it's for, it is open communication (not secure). Reconsider if information is confidential, sensitive or important.
3. Think Big Picture: preface briefly, anything specific or technical is best as an attachment.
4. Maintain SPG. Use normal business etiquette and avoid text message abbreviations or emoticons.
5. Never sound-off: be composed before composing, or send later. Email is subject to same laws of libel as the written word.
6. Target with consideration. Don't copy or forward messages without good reason – don't jam with spam.
7. Keep good etiquette: use an appropriate salutation and end with 'signature' that includes your email address.
8. Make efficient and full use of Outlook mail tools.

Email is diverting and before you know it you can be working on other people's priorities. There's an idea out there that if you want something done immediately send an email; ergo an email is urgent. Don't fall for it and don't expect others to be so gullible. Check your email routinely, but only when it suits you according to the kind of work you do, and how much you are 'at base' or can connect to the internet or corporation intranet. This may be first thing each half day, or twice a week. Let people you regularly correspond with know your routine.

Some more email advice:

- Use 'request read receipts' selectively and only when it is essential to know your email has arrived.
- Do not deal with your email before you have decided your priorities for the day – anything not 'red-flagged' is just more matter in your in-tray to do, more stuff to decide when best to do it.
- Write your email as you progress work, but send it only at the end of the day after a quick review (think of the times you have later added a post-script or re-written letters done first thing).
- Never email in anger. Emails are queer things. They do not convey tone well and sensitive matters can be misinterpreted, yet if you send an 'angry' email it is never misinterpreted and is invariably regretted – remember that email sent is instant and irretrievable. So don't get emotional and send an email when you are upset or in reply to an email that angers or upsets you. It's too tempting to snap back. Write your response, but don't send it. If a reply is urgently necessary wait at least half an hour, then re-read the original and your response to check it is constructive and considered. Diplomatic actions are admired; emotional actions will either embarrass you, or the other person, or both of you.
- Use the delete button with delight, but do have a 'local folder' to which you select and safely move all email received or sent that you think may be best to 'keep for the record' – best be over-cautious to start with; you will get a nose for this kind of thing after a while.

While emails are in mind, also consider these points:

- Remember **do not** use the internet to send sensitive or confidential material.
- Do not put anything in an email you would not be comfortable saying face-to-face – *should* be said face-to-face or at least on the phone – but email can let you have a 'private conversation' without being overheard and have a period to think between exchanges.
- Consider whether clients or colleagues have assured access to email – don't assume a 'round-robin' message will get to everyone intended.
- If you have a formal communication but wish to use email to speed things up, send a proper letter as an attachment.
- Don't send, copy, or forward email unnecessarily – it is as bad as spam to get a load of stuff irrelevant to you whether this is 'bouncing baby' personal news or another department's case rate.
- Do be light hearted about jokes, pictures, and funny stories. These liven the day and help team bonding. But do watch for any material that may cause offence and take up any issues as immediately as you can. If items are unacceptable they should be met with a disciplinary response rather than wait until a grievance is caused.
- Don't duplicate electronic records with paper copies. Email is supposed to save post and paper.
- Don't send ordinary email at odd times such as the middle of the night – it does not impress and tends to confuse; around late afternoon makes sense to everyone.

Messaging

Email is fine – but the phone is still the premier tool – use it. If the other person is normally available you can phone them if it's essential to connect – speaking is two way in the same moment in time and most likely quicker for you both. If it is difficult to catch someone by phone and you need to talk with them book a discussion call with them via text or email. If you want to concentrate and not take calls use an answering machine or give suitable instructions to your PA. Use text messaging to update a simple fact, confirm a point, or alert colleagues. The most useful text or email is: 'Call me!'

Money

The responsibility to spend the public's money well is down to managers at all levels in public services, whether they are a budget holder or not. Mostly that means using resources wisely, and probably making tough decisions between competing calls on the funds you have. However much your budget it will not be enough. Your budget will reflect decisions made higher up about spending priorities between competing services, and your spending should be likewise planned out between the different areas you must or would like to spend money on.

Make sure every penny spent contributes to your planned outgoings. Managers who focus on minimising cash wastage hold their purses tight. Waste management is not about saving power or paper – although this helps – but about working efficiently and to **never ever forget that people are the most costly resource**. Consider for example the cost of meetings when these waste time by running on ineffectively or are attended by people from your team who could have done something other than attend the whole time.

Most importantly, do you know what you cost for an hour? This is proportionally your salary plus about 20 per cent on-costs (employer contribution to NI and pensions etc.) your share of heat light and power and other office costs, transport and expenses, insurance and other legal cover, your personal training and development costs, the proportion of your work which has to earn money to pay colleagues up the line or contributes to headquarters or civic offices; and then factor out how much of 'the hour' you will actually be unproductive by social talk, moving about, taking breaks, or otherwise 'not earning'. My back-of-envelope calculations suggests middle managers today cost around £60–100 an hour.

Spending is always a complex business as money goes in and out at different rates, some costs are fixed, and others highly variable. Sometimes it is difficult to cost work ahead of actual provision because it is community-based work and there are different funding streams or in instances of multi-agency case-led work it is still in development and the final share is not fully determined.

Knowing exactly how the money in your budget is going out is virtually impossible unless you have cost control software or a good accounts clerk in your office and your organisation is particularly small or is set up as a stand-alone unit. In larger organisations to get information on spending you need to stay on good terms with finance managers or your accountant – and don't be shy to ask for help, explanations or interim figures. Most finance managers welcome budget holders who show early interest in costs, and secretly despise colleagues who ignore issues

only to come complaining at the year end when the pot is empty.

Also, if you have not experienced it, imagine how annoying it is to have money taken from your funds (virement) because someone else has overspent – you not only have a 'public duty' to keep tight control, you probably want to keep friends and influence people.

It is interesting to reflect that a lot of studies have shown that greater funds do not necessarily improve the quality of service to clients. It tends instead to layer the administration, or widen the client base. When more work is to be done it normally requires more workers; and money and energy go into recruitment, training, and monitoring. More work can also result in a debased or a more standardised quality. The best quality services result from expert focus on client needs provided by a mutually bonded team of people who have experience, passion and skill.

One thing you must know is your unit costs for the normal range of routine work when all overheads are factored in (e.g. one hour of home care, or a particular set of client sessions such as a parenting course). This information not only lets you track your outgoings, but when the costs of one particular form of work can be compared with an alternative it considerably aids decision-making.

There will also be occasions when you wish to deal with outsiders, and unless you know what your in-house costs are you cannot be sure what to charge or be charged. For the times when you augment your team with agency or temporary staff or need the additional expertise of a consultant or specialist you must know if the deal you sign up for is affordable. Similarly when selling your service it should be profitable, except perhaps for those times when your team has some spare capacity, and some additional or new work will not only keep things ticking over, but offer your team interesting variation. One caveat: make sure the purchaser understands you are offering a deal because you have spare capacity, and keep the contract time-short: otherwise you risk being automatically dumped when you have to raise prices no matter how well the new work was done, or how much it might become a more permanent feature. Everybody needs to be kept jollied up when managing across your usual borders.

Beyond unit costs, the benefits of good fiscal control are three fold:

- Firstly, regular expenditure reviews allow you to track costs and outgoings so that you can see the financial effect of different actions and decisions – you know the cost of what you do.
- Secondly, performance management and appraisal of employees can only be a fully objective and meaningful evaluation when the costs of this 'resource' are appropriately monitored and well communicated – you and they know the cost of the team and how much they earn.
- Thirdly, you are not solely responsible for outgoings. Everyone can help control costs by working efficiently and reducing waste, but it is up to you to get that message across so that everyone becomes as careful as you to ensure there is no unnecessary waste – the organisation demonstrates cost awareness.

Example: Cost awareness

Not so long ago I was providing consultancy to a child care company that was expanding very successfully but needed urgently to control costs. I began to attend the monthly business progress meetings at which local managers were always being told to reduce costs; they were badgered but not informed. I took some recent figures and composed the graphs shown below and approached the managing and finance directors to illustrate how expenditure could be visualised, and trends and comparisons be made apparent to everyone.

The company took my advice and soon after began producing updated bar charts to present to all managers at their monthly meetings. Nothing very complex, but the outcomes were ground breaking. For the first time area and home managers could see the effect of different decisions and operational changes. The charts were taken back to share with all colleagues, and people who could not read a balance sheet (including some middle managers) could make immediate sense of the charts. Costs became real to everyone; being careful with resources became more understood and accepted, and for the first time the idea of shared responsibility against wastage began to be acted on right through the company.

The Salaries and Wages graph (Fig. 5.1) illustrates the comparative cost of the three types of staff. At the time this company was resisting increasing the number of salaried staff. From November this graph began to show that tweaking the balance to favour waged personnel did not save costs, mainly as I remember, because time sheets meant every extra hour worked was assimilated in various ways for salaried staff but claimed as overtime by waged staff.

The second graph (Fig. 5.2) shows Other Costs. It graphically illustrated the different costs as the company expanded by renting additional houses to use as homes. The very high cost of fleet hire was already a concern but with this graph the true costs could be seen in comparison with other expenditure, and the scale fully grasped (the Nov-Aug line represents some direct vehicle

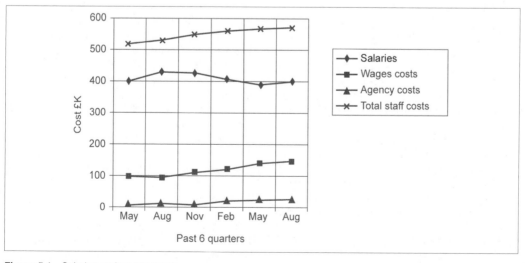

Figure 5.1   Salaries and wages graph

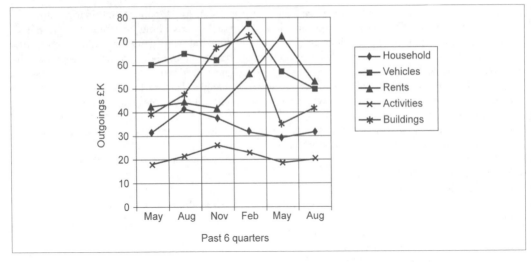

Figure 5.2   Other costs graph

purchases, cutting back on leasing, and reduced travel following changes to accommodation). The building line peaked with a major refurbishment done over the autumn period. The activities (outings for residents) and household (food etc.) both began a costly trend in late summer before they improved.

The checklist provides the critical questions about money that all managers must ask themselves and have answers for:

Money Managing Checklist

- Can I show that existing resources are fully focused on client needs?
- Do my decisions about how money is used show that I try to maintain overall service quality without neglecting specific areas of client need?
- Is every service provided or resource maintained fully needed and utilised?
- Is my budget properly allocated?
- Is money I pass on always spent wisely?
- Can I clearly see the pattern of outgoings over time?
- Can I clearly see and understand well what in the budget is under my control or influence as time progresses, and what money is always already beyond reach as it is accounted for by the core work or standing overheads?
- Have I made contingency for any likely additional, or exceptional, calls on finances?
- What would I do differently or additionally if there was more money?
- Can I show without fear of criticism that I have managed and spent my money wisely and always for the ultimate benefit of clients.

Don't expect to get more money, if you wasted what you had.

5. Make every person count

Selection and retention

People are your main, if not your only, resource. Good people cost money to get in the first place, and money to keep and train up. The section in Chapter 4; *Motivate and inspire* is highly relevant here. If you want to persuade good people to join the team the temptation is to think how best to attract interest and select people wisely. The answer, strangely, is not to worry too much about applicants, but to be concerned with yourself. Interviewing is a social process and you need to know the personality types that are different to you and which might excite or threaten you, and how you may make good choices without unconscious bias. This starts with knowing yourself. Managers dull by comparison with able candidates tend to ask 'clever' prepared questions but then can't process smart answers. Very able managers ask good questions as the discussion flows but can be too eager or probing and can fire them at a rate too fast for otherwise competent persons whose thinking speed is slower.

The matter to concern yourself most with is how you will present the post and the work to be done, and not how exactly you will discover the best candidate. Know your own team, be knowledgeable about the work, and understand how it is done well. Be sure you can say how you are doing exciting or demanding work, what vision drives the work, and how you hope to improve it. Present the enterprise, and yourself, well and honestly and the people who wish to join you and will fit in well will stand out by their questions and comments. The ideal candidate will have already researched your organisation and will stand out from the others with suggestions of what they can do for you.

However, if you are slick on recruitment day, but sloppy normally, the new appointee will not stay. There are some good ways to routinely administer personnel matters that will contribute to your information and help tremendously to keep your team staffed with the people you want. It's good practice to ask people at interview why they applied for the post, and check with them three months later if these reasons remain valid:

- If patterns emerge, it will tell you what people value most.
- If individual reasons are not substantially the same, find out what the let-down is and what has gone wrong (if they are even more positive then there is nothing to worry about except possibly that you are still not presenting strongly enough).

When someone you would prefer to keep is wavering:

- As part of your money management, do you know what it will cost to lose someone and replace them?
- Consider what you can change in their favour in order to retain them for the foreseeable future, or to keep them for a set period and during that time train up or redeploy someone else so that when the waverer does go the impact is lessened.
- Your approach should ideally be part of an overall recruitment strategy, and your retention strategy should be the case you present to the trustees or senior managers when arguing for funds to retain people compared with the costs of recruitment.

If recruitment and retention become a problem it is imperative you find out why. If there is nothing wrong with the enterprise and how you manage, the chances are that the problem is more widespread and external; maybe to do with the public image of the work, problems with low

national pay levels, or the expense of local housing. There may be things you can do about these problems. Some enterprises lease or rent properties or arrange low cost mortgages to give new employees a boost especially at the beginning of their careers.

Use exit interviews – these are two-way discussions to see what is the main reason for leaving, and what the person would like you to know. People leave for good, bad, and indifferent reasons, and for personal or career reasons. If approached sensitively and the right questions are asked, exit interviews will provide data in the following areas, data which can give valuable information about:

- Your recruitment and retention strategies.
- The enterprise's careers structure or development progression.
- Stresses and pressures of the work, and how the enterprise supports personnel.
- Specific colleagues or systems that have been experienced by others as damaging or particularly supportive.
- Rival organisations, offering useful comparison regarding employment attractiveness; including pay, benefits and annual leave as well as matters of job satisfaction and career opportunity.

To summarise: there are things all employees value – and those which they do not; sadly, the latter may drive them away. Although not everything may be under your control most factors can be influenced by your views. The main job satisfaction factors differ in importance according to the situation and the preferences of individuals, but include:

- Fair-to-good basic pay and conditions, and additional perks such as subsidised facilities, and job arrangement attractions like flexible working hours or working from home.
- Job satisfaction – they like the work and believe what they do 'makes a difference'.
- They have a good relationship with you, and you enjoy high mutual trust.
- They have good relationships with colleagues, are well supported by their peers, and feel proud to be part of a 'good team'.
- There are sufficient resources to do the job well, supported by good training.
- The job offers potential for promotion or career advancement.

Legal necessities

There is too much employment law to usefully précis much here; also it can be costly to get matters wrong (see *Discipline and Grievances* below). Ensure you have **all** the necessary and appropriate policies and apply employment conditions and procedures as advised by your senior managers or specialist consultants. Keep everything updated, and when employee behaviour, such as extended sickness absence or competency concern you, consult and take expert guidance at the very earliest opportunity. And absolutely ensure the following:

- Induction period – No matter how skilled or experienced any individual appointee, apply a probationary or formal period of induction, with a specific end date. This can include whatever training or set of experiences is appropriate to the post or person. It allows important points to be secured or taken up without rancour if problematic. It makes it easier for either party to reconsider the appointment, and provides the starting point for ongoing appraisal.
- Induction information – Make sure every new employee has an 'employee' handbook to fully provide all the terms and conditions of employment; and a 'work procedures' handbook setting out any essential key administrative or work procedures that are common to the service (such as how to make visits to client's homes) but which may be additional to the individual job description. In one of these will be copies of the organisation's standard policies, such as those on health and safety or equal opportunities.
- Acknowledgment – When supplying handbooks or policies, and at all times when sections are updated, do not rely on simple distribution methods. Ensure each person signs that they have *received and read and understood* the document, and encourage this to be an accurate affirmation – all too infrequently this is ignored, sometimes with costly outcomes.

Appraisal

Appraisal concerns more than competence and how well someone is working. It must include recognition of a person's unused or potential skills as well as looking to see if the gap is acceptable between what someone actually does

and what else might be possible. This is ground on which job satisfaction and career moves are viewed. Appraisal works well when there is a common method similarly and rigorously applied at all levels. How are you appraised, and does this reflect common practice?

Although it should be a two-way process it is not the same as supervision, because appraisal is usually just once a year and deals with a person's overall situation, compared to the here-and-now issues that characterise supervision. But, as with supervision, appraisals must be undertaken respectfully and viewed seriously. Ensure there is protected time and space, and appropriate effort is made so that both parties benefit from the process. This requires appropriate preparation by both appraisee and appraiser based on an appraisal agenda or some preliminary discussion.

- Appraisal should pick up from induction or the previous appraisal, and remember to base the appraisal on the individual's job description as well as the current work practice. Agendas normally include the following, in the order given:

- Acknowledge strengths and work done well or particularly enjoyed (good to start with positives).
- Review overall performance against a set of personal or team objectives.
- Open discussion to address any other issues. This is best done in a coaching fashion – ask the appraisee what they think they might have done better; once discussion is opened up in a non-critical fashion it is normally easier for individuals to say what they have learnt and what they will do differently next time, or engage in a frank review of their development needs.
- Review outcomes of any training and identify any new needs.
- Review opportunities and career progress. It may be very appropriate to encourage a colleague to go after promotion or work in another service, no matter the loss to your team. Remember this is a process concerned with human potential not just service objectives. One of the most laudable acts of managers that ultimately benefit both individuals and humanity is to ignore their selfish needs when potential is seen and to encourage these people on.
- Agreement on any action for the coming year; whether for the appraisee, you, or the organisation.

- Submit a written-up copy of the record as soon as possible to the appraisee for verification before adding to their personal file.

There are three main appraisal methods and most procedures use a combination of all three:

1. *Self-appraisal*: personal consideration of performance and personal skills, and finding examples to illustrate them (relies on in*tra*-personal skill and knowledge).
2. *360-degree*: a 'round robin' to canvass information and opinion by discreet enquiry or by more blunt instruments, such as questionnaires. Sources consulted may include clients as well as colleague peers. In some teams some aspects are shared openly to provide a forum for debate and self-questioning intended to encourage development and be mutually supportive without 'threat' of senior management appraisal (relies on in*ter*-personal skill and knowledge).
3. *Line manager or senior appraisal*: interview based on the organisation's key performance objectives and standards, acknowledging personal competencies and particular successes, and to resolve any particular problems. Discussion is usually directed towards improving performance and identifying new undertakings (relies on 'benchmarking' skill and knowledge).

Performance management

If any part of appraisal includes a formal evaluation of performance make sure that how it is done is seen as fair, and what is measured can be evaluated usefully and has a distinct focus. The focus should be centred on client needs and the quality of service. Any measured evaluation must be relevant to meeting those needs in a timely and reliable manner that also helps both parties judge the effectiveness of the logistic and other support (such as supervision and training that is provided to the appraisee to obtain his best professional work).

Disciplinary issues

Never think that problems will just go away. It becomes more and more difficult to deal with poor work the longer the situation is allowed to continue un-confronted. Complacent managers deserve complacent staff. The moment something is awry about someone's work or actions deal with it personally and by the usual procedures – supervision or by immediate direct discussion as appropriate. Sometimes this has to be on the spot and can cost time and money. One instance I dealt with concerned an allegation by a child in care that a member of staff had made a sexual assault. Apart from instant suspension and contacting the appropriate authorities, because the staff member lived in close proximity within a residential campus, and to avoid a number of potential problems I arranged with him that he promptly left the site to be accommodated in a local hotel at no cost to him.

Review every employee problem in an even-handed manner and ensure proper support if the work has become unusually stressful, more difficult, or the employee has reasonable personal difficulties that should be considered. For example, if it is a condition of employment to drive and an employee loses his licence because of their own irresponsible behaviour it *may* be grounds for dismissal; if however, an illness means they can no longer drive, the law requires all efforts to have been made to continue employment in a different capacity, before starting any action to cease employment.

Should a situation come to court and it can be shown that a known situation was ignored it considerably weakens the employer case and increases the likelihood of employee compensation for improper dismissal. The law (Employment Rights Act 1996) provides six possible reasons for fair dismissal: conduct, capability, redundancy, legal prohibition or ban, retirement or other substantial reason. Most cases are lost because the employer did not apply fair or proper procedure, and not because the employee did not deserve to be dismissed. There must be clear rules and procedures and these must be applied.

Consult the organisation's disciplinary policy and procedure and your senior manager (or a solicitor versed in employment law) very early in any matter that has you worried or where you think the disciplinary procedure might apply. Better to consult ten times and apply once, than not consult, and on the one occasion you must apply it, you wish ten times over you had consulted earlier. This is because the legislation concerning employment is a pitfall for the unwary, and if you fail to inform properly or otherwise deny a right when disciplining employees (such as union or other representation) you might open your organisation up to claims of unfair, discriminatory, or 'constructive' practice which can be costly and embarrassing.

Make sure you clearly record everything and keep copies of documents and notes of discussions at each step – which is why rather conversely it pays to give employees a formal note when they have been given a verbal warning. Ensure four things at every stage:

- State very clearly what the problem is, and why it is a problem.
- What you expect the employee to do about it.
- How you will support the employee to improve.
- The time scale before review.

If you run a small enterprise without clear procedures pay a company that specialises in such matters to draw some up (the local Chamber of Commerce will help). In large organisations although disciplinary matters will be done in conjunction with personnel officers, do not distance yourself from managing the matter properly by not having face-to-face discussion with them or the employee.

Capability

There are differences between people who are not up to the job, and those who are capable but are not pulling their weight, and this shows differently and should be processed differently. People who have become slack or complacent, once confronted and assisted will often pull themselves up and go on to do good work again. On the other hand if there really is dead wood to cut out you must still apply competency procedures fully and properly or find sound reason for straight dismissal. The effort to do this thoroughly is worth the cost and time to ensure two outcomes:

- A sound position in case the disgruntled employee takes his dismissal to an industrial tribunal.
- The benefit of good internal public relations to show you treat employees with respect but also uphold values regarding how you expect them to work.

There is also a view that occasional dismissal actions to cull dull or tired staff does not substantially damage staff morale but can improve it when losses are not widespread. Valid dismissals can confirm the values held by hard working and conscientious staff, and the appointment of fresh people can re-energise the skills and social mix within the group.

Grievances

Common grievances are claims of racial or sexual harassment or discrimination – for which ensure you respond appropriately as these areas are well covered by law. Other grievances usually concern working conditions or tasks.

As time progresses work patterns and tasks do have to change. This is fine so long as the work is allocated with appropriate consultation and agreement (this is not always achievable). A manager may want changes as part of greater development or to stimulate experience across the team. It is a manager's proper responsibility to deploy people and allocate duties; however this must be done with regard to any greater rights. When responsibilities and duties are clearly stated in a job description there may not be too much manoeuvrability for change unless there is consent or termination (which has to be very evidently for business efficiency); and either the contract is renewed by agreement, or if the action is disputed, by recourse to a conciliation service or an industrial tribunal.

Similar purposeful and reflective responses must be made when an employee raises a grievance as when conducting disciplinary issues. One very useful role of grievances that managers must be knowledgeable about, whichever side of the grievance they might be, is that grievances can be used to address professional worries. This must involve deterioration in the quality of the work done or the service provided that is beyond personal control. It happens that organisations do fail in different ways and in these instances good direction and senior leadership can deteriorate to become anywhere between halting and downright dangerous.

Failing support of any nature is a perfectly reasonable although not a widely recognised cause for grievance. Grievances can be used to protect personal positions as well as raise issues about work quality or make serious allegations. Grievances not to do with pay and conditions or some matter of discrimination must clearly be causing compromise to professional standards. Managers can themselves make personal grievances on such matters and support colleagues with theirs.

All other avenues must be exhausted, and grievance in some instances may be a better action than 'whistle-blowing', but never simply a means to complain just because you disagree with something such as your budget allocation – although this may be at the bottom of your cause. The grievance must clearly show evidence that there is serious compromise to the person's normal professional standards, beliefs, or quality of work; there may also be a risk of legal charges or other damage to career reputation. This must compare with how hitherto there was proper support to enable the work to done to a given (high) professional standard but this is no longer the case because of some deficiency or change to the enterprise system or persons. That or something very similar is a legitimate grievance. This may also be an advisable precautionary move in case it is needed later in any counterclaim for constructive dismissal.

Complaints and client assurance

No one wants complaints – yet they are potentially one of the best sources of information about how well you are doing. Unfortunately, they can also ruin careers and devastate teams when there are serious allegations.

A team that never receives complaints may be one that squashes the occasions when clients can voice concerns. Complaints are well recognised as a way service users can have their issues heard, but they create anxiety and make extra work for staff. Managers dealing with complaints have to balance the expectations that they will support staff, maintain service standards, and resolve the client's concerns. Staff may resent enquiries and feel their experience is seen as less valid than the client's claims. The approach must be to seek information that will benefit future work as well as to resolve the particular conflict, but in the meantime all complaints are emotive as well as often raising other issues such as poor training or procedures. The client may be worried that they are seen as troublesome or testing the relationship they have with the service colleague. Colleagues may fear disciplinary action. Put complaints at the top of your priorities. As always, clear and open methods written up in an active policy are the best way to proceed, together with a personal commitment to keep promises:

- Ideally there should be a named person who receives and manages complaints although these may be passed on to different investigating officers.
- Staff must be confident that the appointed investigating person is competent to evaluate the issues and conversant with the nature of the work and the specific brief staff are given to do it.
- Remember a complaint is about a specific issue and isolated complaints should not be seen as a generalised reflection on one person's work.
- Keep good records and ensure all involved have appropriate access to the file or are given copies. Staff and complainant must be given the opportunity to amend or agree the account and should sign that the record is true (or not, as the case may be). Much of the investigating officer's work can be taken up mediating to obtain agreement of this record; do not resent it as **no complaint will be resolved until there is agreement** and a surprising number dissolve away or are easily resolved once there is this agreement.
- Remember, most complainants simply want three things:
  - To be taken seriously, and heard respectfully.
  - To receive a clear explanation, and an apology.
  - To receive assurance that the problem will not occur again.
- Share and discuss non-active complaints (and compliments) openly with the team.
- Let everyone know what are the outcomes of specific complaints (staff team and user group or representative service as well the individuals concerned).
- Recognise the stress on both parties and involve peer and management or formal care service support for the colleague, and advocacy or representative support for the client.

Complaints policies that include recompense lower the value of the procedure. When recompense is offered it can anger the complainant as it can be seen as an easy 'buy-off'. Remember a client has a whole different level of needs and attachment to the service and should not be seen as another high street consumer; and staff can become complacent if there seems to be a schedule of costed damages. The exception to this is serious harm when the application for damages and a legal process can help everyone to recognise the grievance and can help give back client self-esteem and self-belief and help them move on with their life.

A useful way to ensure service users experience quality treatment is to review the '3Cs' of Culture' as a form of quality assurance. The '3Cs' are:

- Consultation
- Communication
- Confidence

When these are given consistent high regard, the relationship organisations have with service users is protected, and potential difficulties are considerably lessened.

Quality Assurance Checklist

Consultation

- What check, or what information do you have to support any claim that service users or clients feel respected, and are made to feel welcome and their comments invited?
- Are reception personnel trained well to receive clients who phone or call in person – including if they are distressed or angry?
- Are reception areas comfortable, and for example are there playthings to keep any young children amused?
- Is the reception process private when appropriate and always obtained?
- How do you check or ensure that clients do not find assumptions are made about their understanding of service matters (not just information leaflets, but to include initial interview schedules and staff awareness)?
- Are sessions with clients scheduled when possible in ways sensitive to other pressures on them?

Communication

How do you know that staff:

- Consistently consult with clients, as appropriate?
- Invite clients to contribute?
- Inform clients of their rights?
- Offer advocacy to clients?
- Avoid taking action on behalf of a client without it being fully discussed, and certainly not if it is against their wishes? (Even for exceptional matters of legal responsibility, such as Child Protection.)

- Regularly invite clients to raise any issues they may have?
- Involve lay members or service user groups when appropriate and support their interests?
- Give clients clear and appropriate information (brochures and guides, personnel names and responsibilities, contact numbers and times, alterations to arrangements, contact information for external support organisations)?

Confidence

Are you confident that your team is:

- Sufficiently trained and aware of methods for assisting service users?
- Sensitive to clients' diversity (not all will be equally literate, or have English as a first language)?
- Sensitive to clients' history (they have bad recollections or experiences of previous or similar service)?
- Sensitive to clients' difficulties (they intervene before issues develop to a degree of concern)?
- Always well informed about what they may or may not do, and understand their legal obligations?
- Honest in their undertakings?
- Always do what they say they will?

Serious client allegations

Allegations can range from breaches of confidence to claims of assault. There is good evidence that client abuse is under-reported especially among clients such as the elderly, the mentally confused, and young children all of whom share limitations in their ability to understand, communicate and be self-assertive.

The forms of abuse, in the order I think that prevails are:

- emotional
- financial
- physical
- sexual.

Some forms can be perpetuated by collusion or poor central management and are less blamed on one worker so much as a system. A worker who steals from a vulnerable client is fully blameworthy, but if services are extended and charged for beyond proper need there is a manager accountable somewhere. Similarly, emotional abuse can occur when managers make decisions about who does what work without reference to the delicate nature of the relationships necessary for some services.

The best remedy is prevention. This means that clients should know what to expect from the service involvement in their lives; the service is monitored by advocacy services that can sample as well as readily respond to clients; and there is good training and supervision of staff. But no matter how robust is your selection and supervision of personnel, client abuse happens sometimes, and apart from the internal service problems, the abused client may find it difficult to trust similar services again and suffer feelings of confusion or blame. Be aware; include the issue in all relevant training and the agenda for staff discussion from time to time.

CHAPTER 6

How to Apply Psychology

You are in the people business. You must have some insight into how people – including you – think and feel. Intuition is having a sense about a person or a situation that seems unsupported by what can immediately be observed, or substantiated. Intuition stems from some logic or knowledge that is only available on an unconscious level. People who always 'guess right' are usually those who are fully in tune with themselves, and are confident to trust their instincts or intuitions. The more a person feels balanced and confident, the more valuable their intuitions will be. To trust intuition is to trust yourself, and no manager who cannot trust themself will ever manage well. So let your trust grow, at the same time as you gain intellectual understanding.

Ideas that have been most helpful to me are those concerning *emotional intelligence* and how we relate to each other. It has been the psychological ideas about people that have set me thinking or provided an insight, that has served me best in all my dealings as a manager, and although this is the last chapter, maybe this end is a good starting point.

1. Analyse discourse and language

Listen to people and learn

Everyone is familiar to some degree with the idea of body language – at least, as it has been popularised by the anthropologist Desmond Morris, and recognised as one of the ways we communicate whether this is consciously or not (I referred to body language in the section on *Stress* in Chapter 3). The way people speak, and the words they use, can also be deconstructed to discover hidden or additional factors that can be highly informative.

'But "glory" doesn't mean "a nice knock down argument"', Alice objected.
   'When I use a word,' Humpty Dumpty, said in a rather scornful tone, 'it means just what I choose it to mean – neither more nor less'.
   'The question is,' said Alice, 'whether you can make a word mean different things.'

'The question is,' said Humpty Dumpty, 'which is to be master – that's all.'

Listening carefully is a skill that counsellors' use; it's a form of sensitivity to the nuances of speech and the way people communicate because clues can be picked up that point to the power between persons and the structure of relationships. High interpersonal skill and deliberate linguistic dexterity by tone and choice of words can be used for good or bad outcomes; the skills of persuasion when used to manipulate others for hurtful outcomes are much the same as the skills used to influence others for beneficial ends. There are people who are lazy or manipulative and use their talking skill to influence or outmanoeuvre others and get what they want. Instinct and experience has made me cautious, and I note that people who are not sincere become marginalised because others learn not to fully trust them, or they get found out because something practical or obvious shows up their falsehood.

Managers who are aware of discourse analysis will be conscious that all exchanges have an extra message, usually veiled, but at times very overt. Once you begin to listen out, all conversation and comment suddenly seem to have hidden depths! Actually most of this is innocuous and you become attuned without being constantly conscious.

Generally social care work is making increased use of 'discourse analysis' to help understand and gain insights into the relationships between people and how they see themselves – the deals between people. But the approach is not new; it is traceable to Eric Berne and his concept of *Transactional Analysis (TA)* which was expounded in the 1960s and later popularised by Thomas Harris (I'm OK; you're OK). Without doing too much injustice to the detail of Berne's theories, TA categorises exchanges as Adult, Parent, or Child according to the psychic state of the individual and how their language reflects the status and preoccupations associated with the category.

For example, a person may seek to please his boss because of a desire to replay 'the child to parent role'. This person may not resent a domineering attitude in his boss, and will likely be happy to receive patronising remarks when something is done well, although colleagues might think the person ingratiating. A discourse between two professionals who resort to jargon with an associated set of attitudes could in TA terms be seen as communicating in a parent-to-parent mode (knowing all about and being superior to the client) – especially if the client was present.

I have frequently used the terms 'service user' and 'client' in this book. At different times and to different people we all are partners, parents, sons and daughters, etc., and to others we are also undoubtedly colleagues, service users, customers and clients. These terms are meaningful to the persons using them as they distinguish relationships between people. Sometimes we only recognise the degree we fall back on convenient terms when we are confronted by an experience we find difficult to sort out in our minds.

Imagine a nurse who finds her husband in the ward she works in – she will have to make sense of her relationship and find a resolution between 'patient' and 'husband'. Or imagine a mother who is looking after her disabled child; she will likely see herself as mother, not as carer and may resent use of that term. On the other hand, use of a particular term by the general public as well by professionals has increased the recognition and acknowledgement of roles within families. In the instance of care needs the wider use of the label 'carer' has helped those doing this work to see themselves more clearly; it has improved their assertiveness and access to assessment, and improved the levels of intervention and support obtained.

The way people refer to others is always informative.

Example: Inference from language used
During the first minutes of an inspection of a care home for the elderly, it was noted that the manager always spoke of residents as 'they': i.e. 'they don't like . . .' and 'they are usually . . .' Subsequently, the care home was found to be quite regimented. It was not that the quality of care was materially poor, quite the contrary. But there was little to support the individuality of the residents, and provide for personal preferences. Much of the approach and daily routine could be seen as being in place for the benefit of those running the home, rather than the residents.

This regime actually seemed to suit most residents, but one or two others were obviously less satisfied. If someone was being considered to live at that home a factor would be to see if the would-be resident would not feel too much loss of individuality or object to some of the prevailing attitudes and treatment.

Most professionals are aware to some degree of the language they use – they may glibly praise themselves because they do not use jargon except when talking with colleagues. However, both the power and the limitations of language are much more complex (see also the section on *Assertive Language*; Chapter 3).

The Meeting Game Board Activity

An effective way to categorise comment is to use an analytical tool I call *The Meeting Game Board*. The idea is to place comment made during meetings and discussions into a position box; there are variants on this theme, and it can be particularly valuable to apply when involved in negotiation. If you are chairing meetings, taking part in discussions, or progressing any management task the 'game board' is a tool useful to help you analyse others and guide how you might best proceed. The diagram (Fig. 6.1) and terms used are borrowed (Dowling, 1999) from the original application to analyse proponents of Bernstein's Language Codes which concerns other social theory about language.

Put each 'contributor' into the box that applies to them. Do this by deconstructing what they say and if necessary test their meaning by asking them a question or to explain their remark so that you can put the comment confidently onto the diagram (use a coded mark or initials). Remarks will tend to fall into a pattern and reveal the commentator's position. If this is done for each contributor to a discussion it will provide you with additional insight about the beliefs, experiences and motivations of others.

This is how it works:

- *Message*: this is what is said. The message is either produced or reproduced – this concerns the source of what is said. Produced messages are original views, models or ideas that arise independently and originate in the person speaking or writing. By comparison reproduced messages are other people's ideas.
- *Voice*: this is how things are said. Voice is either strong or weak – this is how convincing the person is, not how loud or insistent they are. Strong voices

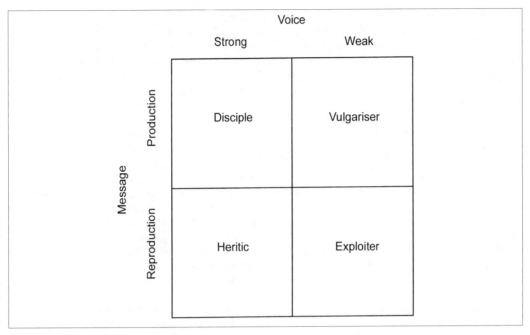

Figure 6.1   The meeting game board

will know what they are talking about. They will have good command of any relevant theory, or lots of experience, useful anecdote or example. Weak voices by comparison will rely on repetition or reiteration; they will not have a strong grasp on their chosen position and may be unseated by argument as there will be inconsistencies in what they say, or they do not have enough command of the issues or sufficient original ideas to close the gaps in their views.

Next, imagine a professional discussion. A person has an original viewpoint or an innovative idea; he speaks passionately and persuasively and substantiates his position with a good argument that draws on your emotions or common sense. Or you may think his ideas completely nuts. He may or may not carry you or others along, but he will stick to his beliefs even if these go against convention. Call that person *heretic*. He may be a natural leader or innovator, or experience has simply given him real wisdom and insight. Hopefully you are heretical when there is need for it. Difficult meetings and halting progress can occur when several heretics have to work together with joint responsibility, or the different responsibility boundaries have not been well demarked. The greatest heretics care for their beliefs more than for themself.

The *exploiter* is the person who seems to have a similar original viewpoint or innovative idea, but as

things progress you see their point is not so well thought out or explained and they are less convincing. They borrow or expand other people's ideas. The idea may be new and sound but it will probably miss the mark or be abandoned later because their grasp of it is weak. Exploiters can have a hidden but quite human motive such as wanting less work or a wish to appear expert. Some senior managers are expert exploiters because their career has benefited from an opportunist gift to appear expert or impassioned but they have borrowed, ducked and weaved, and escaped real testing. Exploiters can be outmanoeuvred by heretics, and may lose an argument to good disciples, but ambitious exploiters do not like to be unmasked or belittled, so tread carefully.

Lucky you if the *disciple* is your right hand person. They are well versed in the necessary issues, and knowledgeable and forthright and can be trusted absolutely to carry out your wishes. Unlike the exploiter they have practised the idea or immersed themselves in its values. Good disciples make excellent managers and may progress to leadership because their work is sound. Good disciples can easily be overlooked and taken for granted. If they are hurt badly they may not show dissatisfaction until they unexpectedly cross the senate floor, or rise to strike Caesar.

The *vulgariser* is the average man or woman. They are part of the team and familiar with the enterprise hymn sheet but can't sing solo. They may be a keen novice, or a fellow professional who is giving voice in an area outside his proper expertise. Politicians or local councillors are often vulgarisers, and similarly governors and trustees can be. Their support is probably valuable, but as a lay person they will only make the right noises when given facts and notions to restate. When associated with your work it is a very important part of management to keep these people well informed and confident about the work. With investment and time you can make vulgarisers into disciples.

Some people may be placed in more than one position or across the lines according to what is being discussed and what they say. For example, if you are negotiating with finance and operations managers, they will probably fit differently according to whether the discussion point is how to meet client needs or how to fund them. The contributions of some people will fit across more than one box depending on the subject matter in hand, or the context of the discussion.

Rise above jargon

Jargon is 'vulgar' language. Jargon is a package of ideas usually concerned with classification wrapped up in a word or phrase that fit within a framework of conventions meaningful to those that use it.

> *Incomprehensible jargon is the hallmark of a profession.*
> Brewster

Language which uses jargon allows a rapid exchange between two co-professionals, and is found in different forms across the whole spectrum of work, and is similar to the use of shorthand forms and specialised meanings that are found in localised or closed groups such as prisons or islands, or where there is a strong ethnic or youth culture. The use of jargon protects precious ideas and restricts access and understanding of people outside the group to the set of ideas, and significantly, it can also limit the understanding or thinking of the select group. It can be a very salutary but difficult experience to be asked to explain in lay terms what is your view and why you hold it.

It is enlightening when professionals seize opportunities to abandon the terms and language they normally use in favour of lay language. To communicate ideas to lay persons they have to find new words; this means they have to review carefully what they seek to convey and consider

the meaning of the common jargon they use and the beliefs and rationales that lie behind particular meanings. The more professionals have to speak simply not only do they become better at doing so, they usually gain stronger insight into the theories that inform their work, and that is very beneficial to loosening up or re-evaluating personal views.

Partnership and multi-agency work can be problematic when dissimilar professionals have to share their different expert views. Transparency is easily lost because different professions use special terms and meaning sets (lexicons), but also use some common words that carry singular meaning. The scenario below concerns the 'safeguarding' of children (as detailed in Chapter 1.2) and illustrates the deliberate use of different terminology and specialised meaning associated with different services.

The operational procedures for safeguarding children are driven by the Common Assessment Framework (CAF). This has five sets of objectives to do with the potential of children in the widest sense, and not just keeping them 'safe' (see DfES *Every Child Matters*). The work of the different contributing services and agencies is managed and co-ordinated locally by managers with trans-service powers who report to the newly created Directors of Children's Services.

The occasion in the case study below is one of the first 'Team around the Child' (TAC) multi-professional children's services meetings to be held.

Although the case is realistic, this scenario is a device to show how professional views can be deconstructed and is not intended to be fully representational, conclusive or concluded. For example, if Jack had been truanting, the Educational Welfare branch would be represented. I have not given Jack a voice; and the representation is wider than is normally achieved – legal representation is unusual unless the child is charged with an offence that may get a custodial sentence. The challenge for the co-ordinating manager is to chair these meetings and to bring different views into a cohesive picture for which discrete service actions can be determined. You may wish to imagine yourself as that manager . . .

Case scenario
    Jack is fourteen. He was raised by his
    grandmother. His parents parted when he

was four. He doesn't remember his father. Most of the time he was in primary school his mother was in prison for benefit fraud and for severely injuring an investigating benefits officer. He spent a period in public care before being returned to his mother at about the time he began secondary school. They live in a council flat. His mother suffers periodic depression and is a binge drinker, and Jack is frequently out of her control. He only has 'fair-weather' friends. He has been caught numerous times trying to shoplift sweets or cigarettes, and has stolen adhesives to supply his habit of substance abuse (jargon example). He was found by neighbours on waste land near his home, torturing a puppy he had found.

Solicitor: *If I may revert to Jack's criminal record it is clear the law has seen his behaviour as* doli capax . . .

(I have looked at his criminal record and it is clear from the sentencing decisions for the charges he has faced in the past that magistrates have thought he knew what he did was wrong when he did it.)

Lawyers love Latin. Although they often seem long winded, lawyers will condense information when opportunity arises, but they always keep to facts.

Teacher: *Jack is a problem; his behaviour in school generally is very disruptive and contagious – he's always fidgety and upsetting other pupils. He is frequently very confrontational, we think he's bright, but he is not accessing the curriculum. He has had a number of fixed term exclusions . . .*

(What Jack does is a big problem to me and my colleagues. He calls out regularly in class when he hasn't been asked to speak. He will shout out the answer, and he questions us all the time; if we don't give him attention he will make rude remarks about our teaching ability or make unpleasant personal remarks. When he is asked to be quiet or keep to the hand up rule he starts to argue and be very verbally abusive. Some pupils like him to do this as it causes a stir they enjoy, other pupils find his interruptions spoil their lessons. Often his confrontations with his teachers

only end because he storms out of class. He misses a lot of school this way and he is behind on what we think he should have learned by now. Also we punish him by expelling him from school for several days at a time).

NB: When teaching breaks down the first blame is always placed on the pupil. Teachers use 'disruptive' to describe all and any pupil behaviour that prevents them teaching. Behaviour in this context means social behaviour and keeping to the school rules. Pupil behaviour is evaluated by teachers in quite subjective ways as good or bad or somewhere in between. Verbal abuse can mean the unchecked comment a teenager might make when there is poor class management, or he is keen and knows answers but is ignored or has to wait a lot for others. The quality and pace of lessons between different teachers and between different schools can be highly variable. And schools differ in the quality of their pastoral practice and the degree they are authoritarian or otherwise manage their dealings with pupils.

Mother: *He's a big worry to me – I do fret so. He's just like his Dad was. You can't trust him. I'm sure he knows when I'm poorly and he can get away with it. He does his worst when I'm not well. I wasn't near so poorly when he was at the foster home . . .*

(I think he has his father's genes and this explains why he is untrustworthy, his father let me down. Jack is the same. He deliberately looks out for the times I am ill to misbehave because at those times he knows I can do less about it, which makes me worse. When I say he's a worry, I mean he makes me ill).

NB: She means none of this is her fault, and she is more self-centred than worried about her son. She thinks: why worry about him, I'm the one who needs care. My depression is a good excuse not to bother. His father didn't want me, I don't want Jack. I need attention.

Psychologist: *Jack's presentation is consistent. His case history suggests his behaviour is learned and has been reinforced by reactions and events that have made him feel significant in the absence of sources for more positive personal constructs . . .*

(How Jack behaves or how he appears to the world does not alter from situation to situation, it is unchanging, and not something he has much awareness about. People have only noticed him when he has done something bad to attract attention; everyone needs to be noticed, but Jack only knows how to by being bad).

NB: Psychologists look for what is different or changing about a person – they call this presentation, and then they try to explain it. The first statement may be presumed a fact if no one contests it; the second statement on behaviour is less obviously a fact, more probably a reasoned 'professional' opinion based on theories about self-esteem. Note also that the meaning of behaviour to a psychologist is very objective, and can include everything a person does – even routine acts like brushing teeth

Psychiatrist: *The behaviour pattern described is highly consistent with the DSM criteria for conduct disorder co-morbid with ADHD . . .*

(The information I have been given about Jack seems to match the diagnosing criteria set out in the main reference book on such matters for a recognised mental health condition known as conduct disorder. This is a pattern of repetitive behaviour where the rights of others and social norms are violated. He probably also has a condition known as Attention Deficit with Hyper-Activity; this means he has problems concentrating and is easily distracted and will switch his attention from one stimulus to another, whichever is strongest or whichever arouses his emotions most and respond accordingly).

NB: Only psychiatrists may make medical diagnoses concerning mental health; and they take this power seriously. The psychiatrist has not made a diagnosis. He has only said there seems to be a

recognisable pattern compared to the Diagnostic and Statistical Manual of Mental Disorders (DSM) the handbook for mental health professionals produced by the American Psychiatric Association and well accepted in the UK.

Adolescent Mental Health Counsellor: *Listening to this, my model is that Jack is still internally very distracted by his Granny's death, possibly to the point of persisting attachment disorder. He was attached to her and became highly bonded with her in his early years when she cared for him during the period when his parents parted, and while his mother was in prison. He was probably already angry with his mother for not being around when his Granny needed care and is now also stuck in the angry stage of bereavement. Anger makes him feel alive, and he is transferring this anger indiscriminately. I think he may well feel guilt and his processing will not be helped by a dependency on solvents which he uses to avoid his emotional pain . . .*

(Jack secretly blames his mother for his Granny's premature death, and has been angry with her for a long time. He is still grieving for the person he loved most and who most loved him, he's very upset she's gone but has had no one he can talk to about this. He desperately wants to be loved but is unsure he is loveable. Actually his actions are communicating his feelings to everybody, but this is not recognised. He feels bad but can't get over it – except his way of dealing with how painful it feels which has been to sniff glue frequently.)

Social Worker: *Our preliminary CAF assessment is that Jack's needs are acute for three of the desired outcomes and vulnerable for the remainder. We are concerned that he is not at all resilient. We have already allocated a family support worker to begin first to address Jack's offending behaviour but have met with limited success mainly because . . .*

This scenario illustrates how professional comment is seldom plain speaking even if ordinary words are used. When one form of work or a particular skill dominates a closed group their communication will develop in ways that suit them. Explaining and sharing experiences using the commonest or most accessible concepts is how mankind has always first tried to make sense of the world. Stylised ideas or models in the forefront of our minds quicken communication. When an issue is raised for our attention we look first to the outlines we have to hand and flesh them out as we see and hear more. For example, think 'domestic violence', and what comes to your mind?

The link between words and emotions

That thinking is influenced by choice of words is illustrated well by emotive words; many of these have polarised meaning whether used in everyday or professional language; for example: victim – bully; abuser – abused; survivor – casualty. All these terms carry value judgements or assumptions, and when bracketed in the mind with the polar opposite views become readily typecast.

Conventional first thoughts usually dominate our concepts, and I might reasonably guess your first thoughts in the instance of 'domestic violence' in the paragraph above. However, we all know instances of domestic violence which differ from the husband-violent-to-wife form that is most commonly found or reported. One particular real case concerns a grown up daughter who remains connected with her home, and in order to extract cash to feed a heroin dependency she will terrorise both her elderly parents by trashing the house and making threats, but has not yet physically hurt them. I also used above a crude bit of *Neuro-Linguistic Programming* (NLP) in the phrase preceding 'domestic violence' to suggest its content: man (mankind) hand; flesh; and raised (suggesting raised arms) and the 'picture form' in which imagination might be realised: outline (body) and seen and heard.

The past decade or so has seen much growth in advocacy services (particularly for children and adults with learning difficulties) and a commensurate growth in complaints procedures and service charters. In no way would I wish these away, but managers do need to be aware how much formal procedures can make more rigid the way enterprises and their people deal with sensitive issues.

As an example, I will deconstruct some uses of 'complaint' in the context of services for children. With the lamentable exception of education, most services for young people are heavily framed with arrangements to ensure they understand their rights in situations and have a voice to put their views and raise issues. The contemporary universality of that framing is most understandable to those of you who remember the 'pin-down' scandal in Staffordshire and other cases of inappropriate controlling power over children in public care. Since that time (and *The Children Act 1989*) there has been a mushrooming of representation services for young people and the development of formal structures to preserve child rights and process their complaints. Unfortunately the perceived need to be quick to respect child rights and the high profile of the formal structures can so dominate the mindsets of child care workers and the children themselves that normal discourse is very often marginalised. The proper and rather painful process of growing up during the teen years particularly can be eclipsed by the adult agenda.

Being a teenager usually means you confront who you are and what you want to be, but in a children's home, although much is normally provided or arranged, it is restricted by risk assessment, policies, and care plan agreements, and boredom can potentially be a big problem to staff and children. On a slow Saturday afternoon on a wet midwinter day, Johnny Awkward becomes dissatisfied. He gets into a mood and is eventually confronted by residential social workers (RSW). The interchange goes like this:

RSW1:   'What's your problem then?'
Johnny: 'Its just f. . .g boring innit?'
RSW1:   'You could have gone to the sports centre with the others?'
Johnny: 'That's f. . .g boring!'
RSW1:   'Well that's your choice! And stop swearing.'
Johnny: 'It's not my choice – you won't let me have my bike here – that's my f. . .g choice!'

RSW1:   'You know you can't. You're not
               licensed or insured.'
Johnny   'You're not licensed or insured.'
(mimicking):
RSW1:   'That's right.'
Johnny   'Its not f. . .g right. There's nowt to
(shouting):   do!'
RSW1:   'This is going nowhere – we can't
               arrange every Saturday to suit you.
               Put up or shut up. Do you want a
               complaint form?'
Johnny: 'Bloody forms – that's all you
               people do!'
RSW1:   'If you don't like it complain.'
Johnny: 'Aaargh!'
RSW2   'Whoa! Johnny ease off. Look, I
(joining):   know you're bored. You're doing so
               well lately, don't let today get you
               down. I'm sorry we can't agree you
               keep your bike, but your review is
               coming up – maybe we should
               think about what you want to say
               about your interests – look, shall we
               make some coffee and have a
               think?'

This discourse illustrates several matters. First,
the formal complaint procedures can be seen (like
a lot of policy and procedure) to offer fixed routes
for staff to the point that they become the first
thought, either because of staff unwillingness to
engage at a deeper level or because it entices
inexperienced staff to believe they are upholding
values and procedures. Secondly, the discourse
illustrates how the complaint procedure when
given as the only route for concerns can become a
barrier to restrict how well the experience of
service users is heard. If you can't imagine
Johnny, image an elderly resident hesitant to
'cause a fuss'.

The discourse also illustrates differences of
professional skill and attitude between the two
staff. RSW1 lacks the emotional intelligence to see
(or is unwilling to admit) that Johnny was almost
certainly complaining in some manner before the
interchange. His suggestion of the formal
complaint route he believes will conveniently
resolve the confrontation because it offers to turn
the control of Johnny more into his hands
through one of three possible outcomes: Johnny
will accept the form; the issue will be shelved, but
the heat of the moment will dissipate. Or, Johnny
will reject the offer, and turn away – very

possibly Johnny dislikes writing and is poor at
expressing himself even with help. Or, Johnny
will become more agitated and the exchange will
deteriorate to the point where Johnny Awkward
has to be restrained.

This RSW focuses his repartee entirely on
Johnny with a series of 'you' messages (your
problem; you could have; your choice, you are
not); and because the associated blame is centred
on Johnny the boy is put in a position where the
only resource is to be defensive, except of course
the lad does not have the language to set out his
case – although he guesses he has a case: it is
probably not right that there is nothing for him. If
TA is used to analyse the discourse, RSW1 rejects
Johnny's problems; he is a *critical* adult
communicating with negative *strokes* known as
cold pricklies. He wants Johnny to be 'adaptive'
(become compliant, perhaps more like the other
children who went out).

Conversely RSW2 has higher emotional
intelligence – or is more kindly disposed to
Johnny. He uses words like 'I' and 'we' and
accepts Johnny's problems. His initial comments
are more responsive to Johnny (*warm fuzzies*). His
exchange begins as 'parent'; but he is positive
and *nurturing*. He quickly moves to a more 'adult
to adult' level of communication by restating a
truth and the suggestion of discussion both as a
solution to the here and now problem, and as a
way to try to resolve better how well Johnny's
interests are met. The opportunity for discussion
and how best to represent his interests imagines
change as possible for Johnny; whereas the
outcomes from what RSW1 says confirms Johnny
as an un-cooperative and difficult person (his
potential *life script*).

While 'complaints' are in mind consider these
two statements:

- 'Service users should be told of their right to
  complain in writing.'
- 'Service users should be told in writing of their
  right to complain.'

The same analytical approach can be applied to
the dominant expressions used by groups of
people; these give insights into the ways they
think (their *philosophical models*) and help to
explain why they go about things they way they
do – the usual practice in the case of a work
group.

Analysing Expressions Activity

Look at the paired expressions in the list below. Tick any expressions that resonate with you or you hear used among your colleagues (or perhaps one or two in particular):

Something should be done . . .	I'm concerned that . . .
That man is impossible . . .	I find him difficult . . .
We don't do . . .	We've never tried . . .
We are stopped by . . .	We find we have difficulty with . . .
We shouldn't be expected to . . .	We will find it difficult to . . .
I'm always telling her that . . .	She needs reminding that . . .
You are useless . . .	I was let down by . . . when . . .
XX is unmanageable . . .	We find XX extremely difficult to manage . . .
You're on your own here	I'm feeling isolated
I'll have to . . .	I'd prefer to . . .
Pigs will fly before . . .	I keep hoping that . . .
You must know that . . .	You could consider if . . .
I don't expect . . .	How might I . . .?
They won't let us . . .	We have yet to convince . . .
No one cares . . .	I feel unnoticed . . .
They should meet and sort . . .	Would a meeting help to . . .?
I warned you that . . .	I see that . . .
I can't . . .	I don't easily see how . . .
You don't understand . . .	I'm not sure I made myself clear . . .
You are a lousy manager . . .	I need more clarity from you about . . .
They should . . .	We could . . .
I wish you would . . .	I like it when . . .
Don't ask . . .	I'm sorry . . .

Very probably your ticks will span both sets of expression, but be predominantly on one side. Analyse the results: embedded in the list are examples that represent the two extremes of a continuum. Given what you know already about discourse analysis, review the lists and determine what they represent, and then perhaps add some expressions of your own that you hear. Or you may decide to begin to collect expressions you hear among colleagues or that you use yourself; you will be informed.

Other than by direct action, for which the rationales can be debatable, groups of people do give their attitude away with the language they use and the manner in which they discuss issues.

Continuums Activity

One way of looking at people and their organisations is to see where they might fit on *continuums* that represent ranges of beliefs, attitudes, and actions, and the given points exemplify the ethos that informs or influences how things are done. The continuums given below each illustrate possible variants of ethos that could describe an enterprise. You may wish to think which point in each continuum the ethos of the enterprise or team you work with is typified, or include other points along any continuum, or create others of your own.

open	guarded	closed
optimistic	realistic	pessimistic
proactive	responsive	reactive
give	earn	take
exceptional	variable	ordinary
believe	hope	know
modest	equal	superior
led	independent	driven
erratic	variable	fixed
evolving	static	devolving

The same continuums can be applied to individual persons; and we must recognise our own part in interpersonal exchanges as well as seek the real motive or feelings of others if we are to understand or analyse the discourse between people. Our own dealings with others will trigger reactions that lead to conflict or conversely are soothing and empathetic.

Professional skill shows in the choice of language used; for example, consider permission seeking approaches such as 'May I ask a question about . . .' and 'Would it be alright for . . .?' At first sight this does not seem assertive or 'proper' manager language; but permission-seeking language is the way to approach sensitive or difficult issues. It allows a moment of time for the other person to adjust by signalling that a sensitive issue is coming up. This is much less confrontational than a direct launch into a sensitive matter and not so likely to provoke a defensive or angry response. Similarly there are subtle differences between 'would you' and 'could you' when making requests, and differences between 'will do' and 'can do' answers. The former form is positive and implies agreement; whereas the latter is requesting and tentative and implies a different power balance between the parties. Imagine the circumstances that would make each form appropriate when used between worker and client, or when used between colleagues.

Managers need to give exact instructions and get good information, and sometimes they are not sure how to give or receive the information they have in mind. There are two simple different ways to speak that deal with this.

Firstly, managers who are precise with their words and use assertive language (Chapter 3.5) firmly underpin their expectation or intent whether they are giving instructions or asking specific or 'closed' questions. Conversely, imprecision implies the speaker is not clear themselves about what they want, and their lack of clarity or hesitation causes their wishes to lose transparency. There is also a thread through 'English' culture that masquerades as politeness, but causes poor communication as it produces waffle and half-hearted phrases. Consider the following phrases, how they will be understood (bracketed), and the to-be-prefered expression that follows:

'I hope I . . .'	(uncertain about self: I don't believe in me)	'I intend to . . .'
'It might be better if . . .'	(unassertive suggestion)	'I want you to . . .'
'I'm not sure, but . . .'	(unassertive question)	'I think that . . .'
'Do you think you could . . .?'	(two steps away from 'you do it!')	'I want you to . . .'
'If this goes on I think I . . .'	(two steps away from 'I will')	'I will . . . if . . .'

Secondly, to receive open information ask open questions. Be very aware of the difference between open and closed questions. Closed questions usually contain a presumption of the sort characterised by 'when did you stop beating your wife?' For example:

'So who was to blame for last Thursday?' is a closed question that does not invite dissent from the assumption it contains.
'Tell me what you think about last Thursday?' is an open question that invites all information.

One of the difficulties of closed questions is that even when the other person recognises that the question is not properly relevant to their view or they have other information that they may wish

to give, it may not be forthcoming. This is because of the effect of neuro-linguistic programming (NLP: see above) and the tendency of people to 'automatically' answer or follow a question put to them rather than question its validity. When this is compounded by a power imbalance it is even more likely that the line given is the one responded to and the interrogative validity not questioned. This is why people who have had to address a series of questions when they have given evidence in enquiries can feel tricked or outmanoeuvred, and feel they have not said what they meant to say.

To manage well, ask more open-ended than closed questions, say what you mean, and mean what you say, and recognise circumstances when communication may become confused–transference events.

2. Understand transference

Transference is a phenomenon where one person subconsciously associates another with the feelings and emotions rightly belonging to someone else. This can be emotion loosely or immediately carried over as a mood that properly belongs in the past (e.g. we argued last time we spoke) and properly directed to those people concerned; or be a buried 'prejudice' – subconscious and unaware attitudes that are directed improperly towards people not responsible for how we feel. Apparently cats experience the effect of their owners' transference a lot.

Transference is commonplace within the caring professions because the work often causes emotions to be heightened, subconsciously or otherwise, and often a strong feeling will sneak up unexpectedly and emerge when not expected. Common transferences include the range of emotions associated with the stages of bereavement, such as denial, anger, and depression. The transference can be internal and cause us to feel differently than we might expect about an event, or be externalised and cause us to regard others inappropriately.

We have an expression about 'carrying emotional baggage' which is used to describe feelings that spill over inappropriately; transference is such an event. It can have positive or negative effect – for example, the immediate way it is possible to like or dislike another person without knowing exactly why. This is the phenomenon interviewers experience when within minutes of meeting a candidate they favour them, or otherwise.

Almost any association can trigger the transference effect, and they happen unbeknown to us quite regularly as we go about our lives. Typical triggers include physical resemblance, manner, style of dress, some aspect of discussion by use of a phrase or accent; in fact any manner or feature that evokes an emotional or feeling memory. A personal example of internal transference was the occasion I experienced loss when a consultancy contract finished. I had completed a period of successful training and staff support work with a team of people. I should have felt satisfied and pleased. I immediately thought I had become over-identified and over-associated. This was true, as I do find it difficult to keep emotional distance from people I become involved with, but it was only later that I realised that the parting had caused to surface emotions more properly connected with a recent bereavement.

Counter-transference

This is a phenomenon that is very useful when recognised. Anyone who has had counselling training and experience will have met, understood, and used its effect. It means you recognise the way you feel is actually the other person's emotional state. A subliminal exchange has happened between you. The counsellor's feelings are supposed not to be acted upon, but focused back.

This is a form of self-awareness, as the feelings developing in oneself are one's own real emotions. When counter-transference happens and you are not aware of the effect the clue is that the feelings (if you stop to consider them) are a bit puzzling; probably not how you normally feel in that kind of situation. The other person's true emotional state will appear on the surface to be different or well disguised – for example, a slightly heated exchange happens between you and a colleague or client. They appear angry or sulking, but you feel frustration (they don't seem to understand, or will not agree to something); remember counter-transference and consider that they were the first to feel frustrated. If you can declare how you feel and ask if that is the problem, the chances are high that the real truth will be revealed, followed by some sensitive discussion. Consider two people in a negotiation

that is getting stuck. The one with high emotional intelligence might remark:

We seem to be at loggerheads here, and it's not helpful to either of us. Actually I've begun to feel quite frustrated. I guess you feel the same. This is very important to you, isn't it?

Here are some highly typical ways that people behave, in instances where there is a disguised emotion behind their attitude or actions. It can be useful for managers to have an insight into these.

Stubbornness

They refute logic, argue that black is white. The issue is clear to you, so you are confused by them; the chances are that they are confused because the issue is *not* clear to them.

Rudeness

The other person takes on a supercilious attitude, or more directly uses sarcasm, or makes disparaging or personal remarks, uses innuendo, or otherwise tries to 'put you down'. You may feel insulted, so they may also feel slighted, disrespected or insulted by what you have asked. If you feel you need to hit back or be defensive, the chances are that some differences between you have been highlighted. This causes them to feel inferior to you, and they are hurt.

Domination

They try to tell you what to do (there may be a sexual element here). If you feel that they are trying to control you, they are themselves controlled by something or another person that they cannot challenge, so they feel powerless. Be particularly alert if the other person's gender (or ethnicity) is very much in the minority in the workplace or team. It may be they feel put upon a lot, even if you, and others around you, think that is untrue.

Frustration

They deny that you can help, or they knock down your suggestions: you are puzzled about this. They feel stupid about something; frequently this will be a silly error that they can't now put right, and they are already kicking themselves about it. The more you try to help, the worse they will feel – change tack immediately.

Obstruction

They will find reasons not to agree, or other things must be done. They are generally difficult to negotiate with, and you cannot progress your idea or instruction, and you begin to feel angry. This is similar to frustration, but in this case there is fear behind obstruction, sometimes something that cannot be owned up to. Anger is a survival response to fear. You might have (very reasonably you think) asked the other person to do something that should be within their expertise, or job routine, but they won't admit it because they may lose out. Their loss may be material (a benefit or perk) or less tangible (loss of face, perhaps they exaggerated their prowess at interview). If they try to change the subject or avoid your attempts to get details, or make a counter-complaint they may be worried you will expose something about them. I once dealt with someone reluctant to take up training, and later found this was because they had falsified their credentials.

Guilt

They (indirectly) complain about their work allocation, or they suggest some difficulties were caused by you or the work systems. They give you a list of their troubles. This is all done indirectly and not assertively. If you are usually supportive and effective, but this time you have let them down, they seem to home in on it too much. They are conscientious and are genuinely overburdened, but not sufficiently assertive to deal with matters more directly with you. There is something they did not manage, or are not managing, and because they are conscientious, they feel very bad about it. They need your support but can't ask.

3. Use professional supervision

Professional supervision is found in a variety of forms and how it is regarded varies in importance from place to place. It can be provided in-house or independently, and the session frequency can vary from monthly, as is most frequently practised, to more or less frequent, or be on demand. Good supervision is essential for most persons working in care and interpersonal services of all kinds and whatever the level of work, but absolutely essential for first line staff. For many services supervision is a requirement set out in legislation or guidance. For example, *The Children Act 1989* requires all other personnel in children's homes that may come into routine contact with children to have individual supervision as well as the residential social workers.

Supervision, where it occurs, is a general management responsibility linked to the quality of communication within organisations, and is how personnel are encouraged and monitored and their career development supported. It is not just for people who need 'supervision' because they are trainees or new to the organisation, but is the healthy way to evaluate practice and deal with work pressures and stresses. Not all supervision need be formal, but although many matters can be dealt with in the normal course of work discussions no amount of passing chat will provide the space and opportunity for the deeper reflection intended by proper methods of supervision. The most widespread model for supervision is described by the *Four Functions model*:

1. Administration

- Deals with *quantities* or how the overall work *load* is managed.
- Encourages or reconciles the quality of the work done, and the time and resources necessary to do it. For example, in the instance of case work these are discussed together with the through put and rate of referral and how the individual is managing the different aspects of the work, such as report writing and administration as well as developing skills and knowledge.
- Ensures all policies and procedures (such as record keeping) are understood and carried out.
- Reviews how much of the work assigned is being satisfactorily carried out, and how any other responsibilities (such as budget keeping) are being met.
- Gathers information from individuals on a variety of issues some of which will be generalised and passed up to senior managers by the supervisor to help with strategic development.

2. Support

- Deals with *qualities*, or how well individual tasks and specific work is managed or carried out, and any associated tension and frustration.

- Offers direct practical guidance concerning supervisee welfare and acknowledges the emotional demands of the work. Assists in identifying and expressing feelings about the work and deals with the joys and satisfactions, as well as tensions, and frustrations. Checks that the manner in which the work is viewed and carried out is appropriate.
- Intervention when necessary will usually attend to task or attitudes to task. This may include some change to deployment or operational re-direction resulting in responsibilities becoming greater or smaller or otherwise altered in some way; or by additional support (may well be from someone else) such as mentoring, coaching or counselling.

3. Training and development

- Deals with all issues of personal progress.
- Provides direct and ongoing instruction or discussion related to task in order to pass on skills, techniques, knowledge, and information.
- Reviews professional progress needs and the indirect support available through mentoring, training or other arrangements that progress careers and skill development.

4. Mediation

- The two-way process of listening to the colleague and relating their experience to organisational direction and expectation; determining when issues need action, and determining or negotiating the issues that relate to concerns – the 'who, when, where and what'.

There are also many people whose work or level of engagement with clients is such that they would benefit from supervision, but the practice is non-existent, or poor and not well established by their employer.

> Example: Assistance through supervision
> A care agency looking after an 'out of county' child agreed to pay for a Teaching Assistant (TA) to accompany that child to her mainstream primary school each day. This was part of the overall package of support thought necessary because the child exhibited a high degree of sexualised and difficult-to-manage behaviour.
> A TA was advertised for and duly appointed but she soon found the work a

very great strain because of the child's behaviour. The TA was not directly part of the school establishment, and her line management was unclear. Mostly she needed help in understanding, dealing with, and processing the child's behaviour and this was beyond the expertise of school staff to assist with. She also found herself bridging relationships daily between the care home and the school. Unfortunately none of these issues had been foreseen.

I was indirectly involved as a consultant to the school on another matter, and became aware of the stress the TA was suffering. I brokered an arrangement whereby the care agency area manager would provide the TA with regular supervision during her paid time and the child would go home early those afternoons. This stabilised the situation by providing the training, support, and clarity of accountability the TA needed. The TA's bolstered confidence resulted in the child being better managed by her at school and the risk of exclusion was considerably lowered.

A key determinant that supervision is essential is when service users can be seen as primary clients whose demands or needs are likely to exhaust or challenge the emotional strength and practice skill of front line staff. This is particularly the case with childcare and mental health care workers who, without proper support, can quickly become worn out, or will close down their empathetic receptivity in order to survive the onslaught of difficult client behaviours and the associated emotional strain.

It is helpful in such situations to regard front line workers as secondary clients who also need support from the enterprise. Staff needs are understood in the context of enabling or supporting them in whatever ways are necessary so that their direct care and support of the primary client is enhanced. The need for care of staff is greater the more the emotional or skill pressures they experience. The more staff might feel intimidated, humiliated, and much challenged by the behaviour of the clients they work with the greater is the need for good supervision.

When supervision is absent or poor some unfortunate phenomena can occur with damaging results. Workers who feel strongly that their needs are ignored compared with the needs of clients (following specific events or accumulated experience) can begin to react in dysfunctional ways. Usually they seek to redress their feelings by exercising power over the client in whichever ways they can. Their behaviour may become bullying or neglectful, or in some other way show jealousy or anger with clients who they may feel are given more consideration than they. Often this is compounded by guilt and staff rapidly lose self-regard and become depressed, or they may self-protect by developing a 'them versus us' culture. Historically over the past two decades a large handful of institutions have been damaged or have not survived because this phenomenon has been central within a downturn of fortunes.

Whenever a job description or performance appraisal concerns how a worker relates with service users it will help to look at the supervision model that is already well established in the health and social care professions. Here, supervision is seen as the prime means to progress personal, service, and organisational development, and will be understood as a two-way process within agreed contracts, with confidentiality assured.

Whatever the supervision model and the method practised, there are appropriate approaches and core functions of supervision common to all best practice.

Appropriate approaches

- If supervision is practised you should normally make it available to all staff.
- When it is not routinely practised be particularly vigilant for staff who may benefit from a period of supervision (and they know they can request it) because you see signs of stress, or the particular work demands they face are exceptional in some way.
- Provide a protected environment that is quiet, private, and without interruption.
- Ensure that the time set aside is mutually convenient and that the time is used as planned. If either party has to cancel do not accept that that session is lost – reschedule it.
- Set the session time as appropriate. Perhaps two hours for a field worker with quarterly supervision; but 30 or 45 minutes for a fortnightly schedule. Experienced workers will hopefully need less time than a trainee, but not always – old hands can 'burn out' unless well supported, or need high levels of support

because some issues only emerge from experience and high identity with service quality.

- Have an agreed contract that sets out the schedule for supervision and how it will be dealt with, including a normal agenda. Agree on the normal balance of issues in any sessions with reference to the supervision norms within the service or by reference to a model such as the *Four Functions model*. Ensure there is discussion that allows any concerns about professional boundaries and confidentiality to be resolved. Agree sessions in advance. Review this contract at least annually.
- Keep notes and share an agreed summary record of each session that can go on file. Keep a record of sessions done.
- Ensure that the issues are as agreed agenda; usually action or discussion points from the previous session are picked up. This is helped when both participants do some preparation or think ahead.
- Ensure that the discussion and any action points are initiated with an appropriate balance – particularly that the session is not dominated by the supervisor's concerns. It is good to start and end on a positive note.
- Be prepared to suspend a supervision session if an issue is raised that you feel you, or the supervisee, need a bit more time to think about; or you wish (or should) discuss first with a senior colleague.
- If you provide supervision ensure that you receive it in turn from a senior manager or peer-colleague. Know what are your practice limitations (about the work and the experience of providing supervision) as well as your areas of expertise, and refer on when necessary.
- Supervision has a legitimate and highly important role in maintaining consistent service quality and through-put of work, but resist unhealthy ethos or time pressures to provide limited forms of supervision with particular slants, typically towards only issues of accountability or performance.
- Supervision is time consuming and doing too much can also affect how well you do it. Make use of other models such as peer or co-supervision. Additional supervisors or periodic changes to arrangements will relieve schedules. This can be a legitimate extension of responsibilities for colleagues with skills or extend the skill base with appropriate training support for people new to the role. These

arrangements can be illustrated by a 'supervision tree' diagram.

- A conflict that can arise in supervision is that workers want emotional support, but feel their supervision is being used to ensure individual performance achieves corporate targets. Once this polarisation begins it tends to become confirmed as a result of the stances that the people involved impose on each other. The answer is to discuss that issue, and to remember that supervision is a shared responsibility.

Supervision is seldom perfect. Supervisors may not have the appropriate experience or training, and sessions can become relegated because of other work pressures, or essential trust has not been established. Your support for supervision is a sure way you can stop resentments building up, and avoid difficulties from being ignored.

Supervision and self-monitoring are mutually supportive practices. Supervision based on personal observation of developments and an honest approach to one-self will help to resolve the conflicts, inner and external, that inevitably arise in all forms of managing services for people. You also have a legitimate need to 'feel good'. Do not be so modest or self-disparaging that you deny or make light of the things you have done well. Keep your seniors informed through your supervision, or otherwise let them and co-managers and colleagues know when you are particularly self-satisfied – this is easier to do if there is a learning or development point that may relate more widely than just to yourself. Analyse how you made an achievement and raise it as a staff development or service issue at a staff meeting or during training.

If you let colleagues know when they have done well they will be more likely to do the same to you – but maybe at the outset you will have to ask or make it clear that even although you have greater responsibility you still welcome such comment. But there will be plenty of times when no-one will notice you; when you are pleased with yourself, give yourself a pat on the back and organise yourself a treat – you will have earned it.

4. Look after yourself

Managers will have experience of providing supervision or keeping a formal eye on the general well being of others be they clients or junior colleagues. To manage others does mean the first person to be managed is yourself. It is not simply important that this process is also maintained for yourself – it is essential.

Keeping a watchful eye on yourself, self-supervision in effect, will benefit you and those you manage. There is an important correlation to maintain. To work well on behalf of others – to manage them with wisdom and sensitivity – requires the same attributes as those the best managers will be keen to promote in their team. The essential attributes include emotional stability, self-assurance and self-esteem, reasonable physical health, a positive personality, a reliable and a consistent attitude to tasks and honesty and trustworthiness.

The different problems that all managers most commonly face centre on people rather than things; and the insight and understanding about others always begins with the knowledge of the person we think we know best – our self. If we cannot understand our self, or we loose our self-empathy, we lose the ability to be wise about others. Everyone who works with others must keep their interpersonal sensitivities healthy and developing well; that requires that you maintain an awareness of the effect of your work and life upon yourself, and this is what is meant by self-monitoring. There are a number of important areas to self-monitor.

Tolerance thresholds

A self-monitoring check that is always useful is: are your words and actions considered, and not reactive? When your response to problems becomes reactive and with less consideration than normal for you, it shows that you are under stress, and seeking to deal with things quickly to get them out of the way. You will make snappy, poor decisions. Remaining within your tolerance threshold is indicated by the degree to which you can still prioritise well or contend with problems such as interruption.

Your tolerance thresholds will be different from those of other managers and different from your colleagues, and will vary, dependant upon other factors such as your degree of experience or expertise, and how tired you are at that particular period.

Personal thresholds become breached when demand or pressures increase. The pressures, whether a special project or routine work, become too much and too many hours are worked. It is important to know what your normal tolerance threshold is for any one set of circumstances; this is your *personal base line*. Accept it for where it is and do not allow yourself or your critics to make unsupportive comparisons, especially if this threshold drops away because you are stressed. Try to see what is the true cause of any tolerance shortfall and do something about it. Typically this will mean delegation, deferring deadlines, or asking for more resources.

Other pressures occur from time to time that have personal origins; we should all have a life. It can help everyone to let junior colleagues or your line manager know when you have personal difficulties. This should preferably be done without asking for confidences to be kept; it is seldom necessary and usually inappropriate to share too much personal detail in order to get some leeway.

Personality

Check that you remain 'in character'. Anxiety is a common cause of altered behaviour. It has links with your tolerance threshold in feeling unable to cope with the amount of work, or unable to cope with specific parts. For example, meetings begin to seem more difficult, or now make you nervous. Certain events may precipitate physical symptoms like palpitations.

The main objective of self-monitoring is to reduce your incidences of anxiety. This is because of the links between anxiety and aggression, anxiety and depression. Your temperament should not change. Changes to watch for include uncharacteristic short temper, having a bullish attitude, or a tendency to be very critical or blaming others. You may feel mild paranoia about the demands made upon you by service pressures.

Conversely, you may become foolhardy and impetuous with lost sensitivity. Not putting things off might appear to be a positive approach to a task, but might also mean the hasty decision produces greater problems. Your junior colleagues may view the increased pace and bustle you see as necessary to get through work as aggressive and demanding. Beware you do not become too intent or lose your usual humour.

Unfortunately, it is the most conscientious managers who are the least willing to divert or off-load their commitments when these become burdensome; the managers most at risk of some breakdown are those most anxious to maintain

good service. It is important you monitor your temperament and seek help, or otherwise respond to your needs when necessary, and reduce the risk of handling matters awkwardly, getting into a conflict, or becoming depressed.

Health

Your health is linked to the demands that work and life place on your psychological and physical energy. Watch out for the physiological signs of stress and tension that will reduce the strength of the immune system, when you will be more prone to colds and infections. You will take longer to get better. Stress will show in things like a tense jaw or shoulders, or the bunching of fists, and loss of self-awareness about physical needs. Carrying such strains for long will lead to physiological outcomes such as back and muscle pain, headaches or poor digestion, and the psychological co-morbidity of depression or cardiovascular problems (see in detail, Chapter 3.3).

> Example: Ignoring own needs
> I once had a crisis to contend with, and I'd been away for several days renegotiating ontracts. I was driving and nearly home when the traffic slowed outside a cafe; it was three-thirty in the afternoon. The smell of food made me suddenly aware how hungry I was – I had not eaten since five o'clock the previous evening.

It is well worth knowing how you can relieve tension and avoid fatigue at work and by means of a healthier option than sinking a few pints at lunch time or coping by drinking strong coffee all day. I was discussing this at a conference recently when someone who described themselves as a Buddhist claimed that they could relax and re-centre within a minute as they had trained themselves to meditate using a mantra that they would chant silently to themself. Proper breathing – slow and deep – is advocated by complementary health practice and relaxation therapies, and is at the core of many Eastern approaches to healthcare, including meditation.

When our day is busy with lots of low-level stress our breathing can gradually become shallower. This shallow breathing is known as chest breathing, and causes less oxygen in the blood as the finer alveoli in our lungs become congested with carbon dioxide and cease to absorb oxygen well. The lack of oxygen increases muscle tension and fatigue. Deep breathing initiates the *Relaxation Response* – a physiological mechanism which counteracts the effects of stress and puts the body and mind into a state of relaxation. Being aware of one's breathing, and readjusting to ensure proper breathing will help lower blood pressure and levels of stress hormones, improve lung function and digestion, decrease blood sugar and cholesterol, and generally improve your immune system as well as your emotional stability. All slow breathing exercises will help to regain mental clarity, and inner calm and self-awareness. Here are two good ones.

Quickie relax; guaranteed to reduce blood pressure

- Place your index and second fingers on forehead.
- Put your thumb and ring finger lightly each over a nostril. Let the little pinkie hang free.
- Press to close one nostril and breathe slowly deeply in. Hold.
- Close that nostril with finger pressure and breathe slowly out through the opposite nostril, letting shoulders drop, and then back in through the same nostril.
- Swap nostrils and breathe out and in through the opposite nostril – and so on, for as many breaths as you feel comfortable with.

Big relax

- Stand and slowly stretch fully out once in a X shape.
- Lie flat with your back on the floor, feet flat and knees bent. Be comfortable; a pad (very thin only – a folded scarf or similar) under your head might help.
- Place one hand on your chest and one on your abdomen (to monitor your breathing). If for some reason this position is not practical for you (perhaps you are at a desk or in a car – not driving!) relax back, ideally with a head rest, and lace hands across your tummy – maybe put a 'do not disturb' sign on your desk?
- Be aware of your body and consciously relax it, starting with your head (forehead and face, mouth slightly open, jaw slack), neck, shoulders, arms and so on down to toes.
- Take deep and slow breaths in through your nose. Let your stomach swell and not your

chest. Exhale through your mouth without forcing the breath out. (Your abdomen should rise further than your chest, and you should take about 4–5 breaths a minute).
- Continue for a count of 30–60 breaths – count and think of nothing else. Or if you have time, breathe for 15–20 minutes but also use an aid to keep your mind idle (mood music, natural sounds, or a chant).
- Once done, roll slowly on to your knees and front, and stand up.

Some other stress busters

These can also work as aids to thinking and include:

- Putting on the answer phone or getting your PA to field calls for two or three periods of 20–30 minutes during the day, especially when starting a new task, or at lunch time if you are at your desk (not advisable but exceptionally unavoidable).
- When driving, sing – accompany a tape or the radio if you wish; try different tones or keys, or use silly voices – have silly fun. You know its working when you stop singing because you are laughing to yourself (but generally not when stopped with windows open). Sing nursery rhymes, or Sunday school ditties. These all help voice power and control as well as release tension.
- Have a supply of A3 paper (it needs to be big but you can fold it in half to file). Get into the habit of letting your mind idle and wander. Doodle and mind map what arises, whether drawings, or words and phrases. Don't try to consciously control what is coming to mind. After a while and you feel relaxed stop; examine what you have, or keep the paper and add to it if you sense that will be preferable. It will tell you something sooner or later.
- Similar to this is going to bed confidently without letting a problem worry you because you know you will dream about it and wake up with fresh thoughts. If you think this will happen it will; and the more it occurs the more you can rely on the phenomenon happening as you need it. If you have never experienced this, try it.
- Play music that you like quietly – best is highly regularised music such as Gregorian, baroque, classical, spiritual or mood music, but not the radio with its distracting chatter and news.

Work-life balance

A good work-life balance is essential to employee wellbeing and effectiveness. This is equally true for managers; except that the nature of work for most managers is that at times of need they may put in many excess hours. However, not so many will agree to easing up or recouping time during settled periods. They may feel guilty slipping home at 1.30 and think that they should now begin that pet project waiting at the bottom of the in tray.

It is a well-observed phenomenon that many people in the caring professions themselves had a past, which included difficulty, trauma or deprivation. This is an experience which has been overcome, but remains as a touchstone for the way the person is empathetic, or expert in meeting or understanding the particular needs of others. People whose work is in any way therapeutic or caring will meet issues relevant to themselves. They will find themselves in process to some degree. It is important to allow for this. It may mean you will at times be uncertain about work or personal decisions.

Highly conscientious managers can also become over concerned with their clients or colleagues and expect too much of themselves. Managers who do well, acknowledge that reality, and act on it. They recognise the times they need additional support for themselves and ask for it. There should be no false modesty or heroics. Having a clear sense of your own professional as well as personal needs is important, because if a manager cannot see and admit their own needs what surety is there that they can see the needs of others? Of course, the long hours and stresses of managerial work are best supported when there is some tolerance and understanding at home from friends and relatives, and this does mean letting others at home know about your difficulties as well as you seeking ways to reduce or manage them well. And knocking off early occasionally, to enjoy the afternoon; balance is everything.

Employers increasingly offer flexitime or home working options so that staff can feel in better control of their lives. A number of social care organisations make a point of flexible arrangements when recruiting because they know that staff will do best for clients when they can have working arrangements that suit them and their families. When these matters are so well understood, please ensure you apply the principles to yourself. A professional who values themselves will behave in ways that ensure they remain productive and satisfied with what they do. They will:

- Know they are not indispensable and will delegate work or make new promotional appointments when necessary to manage their work load.
- Look out for any signs of stress showing in themselves (Chapter 3).
- Realise that relaxation and leisure are not treats and they do not have to 'earn them'.
- Prioritise their work well and understand the difference between 'important' and 'urgent'.
- Know when to refuse tasks, and put off developments, until they are ready to do them well.
- Take a career break or negotiate an occasional extended holiday in order to travel, or study, or do whatever they feel will fully refresh them.
- Seek periods of secondment, or relief from duties, from time to time so that some major change or development can be researched and implemented (a project management).
- Know how to look after themselves in body and mind with regard to lifestyle and diet, intoxicants, exercise, and leisure interests; and understand how exercise and fresh environments are good for them in regular doses because they release the 'feel-good' endorphins.

Also, if you are in deep dodo for whatever reason:

- Declare it before someone else points it out and holds their nose.
- Do not deflect blame or trash colleagues or your senior managers.
- Do not defend the indefensible. Admit mistakes and suggest how you can put things right. Show determination to address underlying causes whether these are to do with your personal management or the system.
- Rely on your high employable value because you know other people who are influential in their help to you; you keep abreast of issues and ideas; or you have a local reputation for able service; or because you have contributed articles to professional journals.

At any one time, as well as the work in hand, it is a good idea to have other training or experience goals, or ways you can enrich your life as a way of sustaining freshness and interest, and of finding new viewpoints. Wide study, other experience, and different perspectives will enable you to manage with improved confidence and ability, and give you useful connections and analogies to relate to your work. These are also the things that can make a significant difference if you wish to progress your career and link to the fact that the managers most valued have high self-esteem. This correlates with a resilient and positive outlook necessary to cope with work pressures and to resist the thought processes that can result in depression or negativity.

All people who enjoy good personal significance never need to resort to dealing with others aggressively or arrogantly as they do not need to seek dysfunctional rewards. Managers who positively impact and transform the lives of others, colleagues and clients, end up feeling positive about themselves. A great deal of psychological research has had very clear results on this one point. Professionals who have high self-esteem do good work. This congruency should never be overlooked.

The manager whose ideas and wishes are in line with their organisation's objectives and how it works will prosper, which in turn will feed into a cycle of personal significance. Look to see if you are valued and given the encouragement to be yourself. Anything less than this means some amount of compromise, the reality for most managers, but the important personal check is that you look for this congruency between yourself and your organisation. The evaluation you make is about any compromise, and if there is one, can you live with it, can you change it, or must you leave it behind?

Finally, an interesting view on how to manage the burdens of life is the vignette that with unexpected synchronicity was doing the rounds on the internet while I was writing this book. You may wish to think how the advice connects with my mentoring for you.

A lecturer asked, 'How heavy is this glass of water?' Answers called out ranged over different weights. The lecturer replied: 'The absolute weight doesn't matter. It depends on how long you try to hold it. If I hold it for a minute, that's not a problem. If I hold it for an hour, I'll have an ache in my right arm. If I hold it for a day, you'll have to call an ambulance. In each case, it's the same weight, but the longer I hold it, the heavier it becomes.'

He continued: 'And that's the way it is with life. If we carry our burdens all the time, sooner or later, as the burden becomes increasingly heavy, we won't be able to carry on. As with the glass of water, you have to put it down for a while and rest before holding it again. When we're refreshed, we can carry on with the burden. So, before you return home tonight, put the burden of work down. Don't carry it home. You can pick it up tomorrow. Whatever burdens you're carrying now, let them down for a moment if you can. Relax; pick them up later after you've rested. Life is short. Enjoy it!'

And then he shared some ways of dealing with the burdens of life:

- *Accept that some days you're the pigeon, and some days you're the statue.*
- *Always keep your words soft and sweet, just in case you have to eat them.*
- *Always read stuff that will make you look good if you die in the middle of it.*
- *Drive carefully. It's not only cars that can be recalled by their maker.*
- *If you can't be kind, at least have the decency to be vague.*
- *If you lend someone £10 and never see that person again, it was probably worth it.*
- *It may be that your sole purpose in life is simply to serve as a warning to others.*
- *Never buy a car you can't push.*
- *Never put both feet in your mouth at the same time, because then you won't have a leg to stand on.*
- *Nobody cares if you can't dance well. Just get up and dance.*
- *Since it's the early worm that gets eaten by the bird, sleep late.*
- *The second mouse gets the cheese.*
- *When everything's coming your way, you're in the wrong lane.*
- *Birthdays are good for you. The more you have, the longer you live.*
- *Some mistakes are too much fun to only make once.*
- *We could learn a lot from crayons. Some are sharp, some are pretty and some are dull. Some have weird names, and all are different colours. But they all have to live in the same box.*
- *A truly happy person is one who can enjoy the scenery on a detour.*
- *You may be only one person in the world, but you may also be the world to one person.*

Have a great life and know that someone has thought about you today . . .

Bibliography and References

Some information for Chapter 1

An overall rating of 45–60 is the target score. Any differential between self-score and an independent score approaching 20 or more means either you are too modest – or too vain – to be an effective leader!

Bibliography

I explained in the *Introduction* that this is a book that distils my experience and understanding. It is about ideas and what to do rather than a source of academic reference. If it has made sense it has done its work and you trust me. I did not feel the need to shore up my words with borrowed credit.

The other trouble with a bibliography is when they are used by a reader to follow an interest or learning track, the way suggested is one trod before. It would be mine. It may or may not suit you. For example, if you need to develop your supervision skills you may start with what has become a pretty standard work *Supervision in the Helping Professions* by Hawkins and Shohet, but there are other work and models. If you need to get skilled with budgets and the business side of what you manage one of the best and most accessible ways is to borrow (expensive to buy) *Business Knowledge Units 24–28* of a set of text books for the Foundation Stage (NVQ2) qualifications of the Association of Accounting Technicians (AAT).

I cannot know your interests and needs. It is better by far that you take the subject and see what is available than you are unduly influenced by any reference I offer. Or ask what has helped inform and develop other managers within your enterprise. Follow whatever winding path and little offshoots that meet your desires or intrigue you. One decision you will face at times will be – do you need generic manager skills (explicit knowledge) or something that will focus on the particular service you work in (tacit knowledge)? I'm sure you understand that I'm not being rude when I suggest 'go Google'.

One book that I fully concur with, for its pointers for releasing the potential of people, and not otherwise mentioned is *The One Minute Manager* by Ken Blanchard and Spencer Johnson (Harper Collins).

Having said all that, below are the details of some published sources referred to in this book.

References

Berne, E. (1973) *Games People Play: The Psychology of Human Relationships*. London: Penguin.

Bernstein, B. (1971) *Class, Control and Codes*. London: Paladin.

Blanchard, K. and Johnson, S. (1983) *The One Minute Manager*. New York/London: HarperCollins.

Brewster, K. American Ambassador to London, 1977–81.

DCSF (2007) *Common Assessment Framework: Best Value*. London: HMSO.

DETR (1999) *Local Government Act 1999: Best Value, Circular 10*. London: DETR.

DfES (2003) *Every Child Matters*. London: HMSO.

Dowling, P.C. (1999) Basil Bernstein in Frame: *Oh Dear, Is This a Structuralist Analysis*. Presented to the School of Education, Kings College, University of London. 10 December 1999. Available at: http://homepage.mac.com/paulcdowling/ioe/publications/kings1999/index.html

Follett, N.P. (1941) *Dynamic Administration: The Collected Papers of Mary Follett*. London: Pitman.

Harris, T. (1976) *I'm OK – You're OK*. New York: Avon Books.

Hawkins, P. and Shohet, R. (2007) (3rd Edn.) *Supervision in the Helping Professions*. Milton Keynes: OAP.

Mabey, G., Salaman, C. and Storey, J. (1995) *Strategic Human Resource Management*. Oxford: Blackwell.

Russell House Publishing Ltd

We publish a wide range of professional, reference and educational books including:

Averting aggression
Safe work in services for adolescents and young adults
By Owen Booker   Second Edition   2004   ISBN 978-1-903855-44-7

Managing social care
A guide for new managers
By Paul Harrison   2006   ISBN 978-1-905541-00-3

An elephant in the room
An equality and diversity training manual
By Blair McPherson   2007   ISBN 978-1-905541-16-4

Managing uncertainty and change in social work and social care
By Ken Johnson and Isabel Williams   2007   ISBN 978-1-905541-07-2

Leadership
Being effective and remaining human
By Peter Gilbert   2005   ISBN 978-1-903855-76-8

Get it right first time
A self help and training guide to project management
By Peter James   2004   ISBN 978-1-903855-12-6

Partnership made painless
A joined-up guide to working together
By Ros Harrison, Geoffrey Mann, Michael Murphy,
Alan Taylor and Neil Thompson   2003   ISBN 978-1-898924-88-3

Team development programme
A training manual
By Joan Walton   2002   ISBN 978-1-903855-05-8

Performance appraisal
A handbook for managers in public and voluntary organisations
By Philip Hope and Tim Pickles   1995   ISBN 978-1-898924-45-

The write stuff
A guide to effective writing in social care and related services
By Graham Hopkins   1998   ISBN 978-1-898924-41-

For more details on specific books, please visit our website:

www.russellhouse.co.uk

Or we can send you our catalogue if you contact us at:

Russell House Publishing Ltd,
4 St George's House,
Uplyme Road Business Park,
Lyme Regis DT7 3LS,
England.

Tel: (UK) 01297 443948
Fax: (UK) 01297 442722
Email: help@russellhouse.co.uk